W9-BCV-169

First
Nations
in the
Twenty-First
Century

James S. Frideres

OXFORD
UNIVERSITY PRESS

Toronto, ON M6V

OXFORD
UNIVERSITY PRESS

8 Sampson Mews, Suite 204, Don Mills, Ontario M3C 0H5
www.oupcanada.com

Oxford University Press is a department of the University of Oxford.
It furthers the University's objective of excellence in research, scholarship,
and education by publishing worldwide in

Oxford New York
Auckland Cape Town Dar es Salaam Hong Kong Karachi Kuala Lumpur Madrid
Melbourne Mexico City Nairobi New Delhi Shanghai Taipei Toronto

With offices in
Argentina Austria Brazil Chile Czech Republic France Greece
Guatemala Hungary Italy Japan Poland Portugal Singapore
South Korea Switzerland Thailand Turkey Ukraine Vietnam

Oxford is a trade mark of Oxford University Press
in the UK and in certain other countries

Published in Canada by Oxford University Press

Library and Archives Canada Cataloguing in Publication

Frideres, James S., 1943–
First Nations in the twenty-first century / James S. Frideres.

(Themes in Canadian sociology)
Includes bibliographical references and index.
ISBN 978-0-19-544143-7

1. Indians of North America—
Canada—Textbooks.
I. Title. II. Series: Themes in Canadian sociology

E78.C2F72 2011   971.004'97   C2010-907720-2

Cover image: Doug Plummer/Gettyimages

Oxford University Press is committed to our environment. This book is printed on
paper that contains a minimum of 50% post-consumer waste.

Printed and bound in the United States of America.

3 4 5 6 - 15 14 13 12

Contents

Preface

This is a book about First Nations people, otherwise known in Canada's legal language as Indians. Although references are made to other Canadian Aboriginal peoples—the Inuit and Métis, as well as non-status Indians—the focus here is on First Nations, those who have been under the direct control of the Indian Act since it was first cobbled together in 1876 out of earlier colonial statutes. Our singular focus is a result of the enormous amount of information currently available about the First Nations and the pivotal role they have played in the development of Canadian society. To include other groups would require another book for each. Chapter 2 will give more detail to the various terms used in this book, such as 'Aboriginal', 'status Indians', 'treaty Indians', and 'Métis'. In addition, the topics to be discussed have been limited to those of importance for First Nations people and those misunderstood by non–First Nations people, and I seek to demonstrate how the federal government and First Nations are trying to resolve a number of significant issues. Moreover, the topics covered in this book are central to the evolution of Canadian society, and resolutions to today's problems (whatever forms such resolution takes) will have major impacts on the future of Canadian society.

Colonial thought during the 1800s reconstructed First Nations people as homogeneous, unchanging, and limited to a state of 'uncivilized' nature (Brownlie, 2005). As such, at the time of Confederation, as well as before and after that seminal date, Euro-Canadians generally placed First Nations people outside of history and merely identified them as background as the settlers evolved into a more civilized and technological society. Others took an easier route and simply wrote them out of history. One way of doing this was simply to write about the history of settlers in Canada as they came into the new land.

More recently Aboriginal leaders and scholars have taken on the task of writing their own history. However, prior to the 1950s there was an unreceptive climate with regard to writing about First Nations people, unless it was in the journalistic vein and catered more to fiction than to fact. However, the works of George Copway and Peter Jones (neither of whom are widely recognizable names and remained outside the scope of academic historians until recently) were the first Aboriginal scholars to write about their history. Today their works are considered invaluable contributions to understanding

Canadian history and the role First Nations people played in the development of Canadian society. Nevertheless, publications written by Aboriginal people were scarce until the 1970s (Timpson, 2009). Edward Ahenakew's (1929) brief tales about First Nations life, outlined in a scholarly journal, were one of the exceptions during this time. Joseph Dion (1979) and Michael Mountain Horse (1979) were among the earlier First Nation historians who provided insights about First Nation peoples' history. While their books were published in the last quarter of the twentieth century, they had initiated their work many years before; trying to bring First Nations history to the foreground and inform Canadians of the role that First Nations played in the social, economic, and political development of Canada. The works of Harold Cardinal (1969) and Howard Adams (1975) also are relatively recent accounts of First Nations life, although they are as much political statements as they are historical. Nevertheless, these scholars championed Aboriginal history and created the groundwork for those who have now followed, perhaps most notably the Métis scholar, Olive Patricia Dickason, whose *Canada's First Nations* (1992, 1997, 2002, 2009) remains the authoritative history of Aboriginal peoples in Canada from the earliest times.

In order to understand today's situation, we need to have an understanding of history. How First Nations people find themselves today is a result of government and First Nation peoples' actions and inactions over a long period of time. The general theme of this book is that European colonization and colonialism have had a long-term impact on the lives of First Nations people and have transformed them into a marginal people within Canadian society. Moreover, it has been an insidious process, encroaching upon First Nations communities without a face—government just acts and consequences follow. But colonization also has impacted non–First Nations people. It provided non–First Nations people with the standards by which they evaluate the performance of others; it allowed them to build stereotypes about First Nations people; and it provided Canadians with the normative support to engage in individual and systemic discrimination against them. Colonialization has been a pervasive force, yet only recently has the Canadian government issued an official apology to First Nations people, recognizing that policies and programs enacted in the past were inappropriate, devastating, and long-lasting.

The issues discussed in this book are major and far-reaching issues, and will transform the nature of Canada when they are addressed. We have an opportunity in the twenty-first century to deal with the architecture of Canadian society and our relationship with First Nations people. The formal apology made by Prime Minister Stephen Harper in 2008 and the creation of the Truth and Reconciliation Commission are a good beginning, and perhaps that bodes well for how relations between First Nations and other Canadians will unfold. In the end, we must fully appreciate that no matter what actions are taken to restore relations, it will take time. The impact of colonization took many years and so we can't look for the magic 'solution' that will restore the identity, integrity, and trust that many First Nations people had when they first encountered the settlers. It will take years to make the social change, and then, only if we, as Canadians, insist that our politicians must make special efforts to deal with the legacy of colonialism.

Organization of the Book

Each of the chapters in this book is a 'stand-alone' discussion of a specific topic. The references and websites will take you further into the details of the issues under consideration. In some cases, issues such as gender are interwoven into the chapters. Any discussion about the uniqueness of different First Nation peoples will be nuanced, and some topics, such as inter-Aboriginal conflicts, are not covered. These are certainly important, but they are not the focus of the work at hand. Recent books by Suzack et al. (2010) and Sunseri (2010) focusing on Indigenous women and feminism explore how Indigenous women are addressing issues confronting them.

Chapter 1 provides a brief historical outline of settler–First Nations relations and of the introduction of colonialism and its initial impacts, and discusses who writes history—and why. Chapter 2 focuses on who are the members of a category of people called 'First Nations'. This question seems innocent enough when first asked, but usually by the time you get the answer your eyes are glazed over and you are lost in a quagmire of legal and legislative doublespeak. You also will see the disjuncture between real life and the abstract realities of social policy. But in the end, the intent is to show why First Nations people see the issue as important.

Chapter 3 outlines Western ways of knowing and Indigenous ways of knowing. It provides the reader with some basic understanding of how the world is viewed by the two groups and looks at points of congruence and difference. The residential school issue is documented in Chapter 4, showing that Canadians were able to deny or conceal the impact of this policy for nearly a century. This chapter also examines how the issue—once it reached the policy agenda—was resolved in less than 10 years and in a manner that has circumvented the wishes of First Nations people. Chapter 5 deals with the impact of colonialization and specifically with the impact of the residential schools. It provides an understanding of what trauma is, how it is transmitted from one generation to another, and how it impacts individuals and communities. The importance and role of language in culture is the focus of Chapter 6. Here we see that Aboriginal languages are stressed and at a 'tipping point'. Depending on the changes taking place in the next decade, many Aboriginal languages could be strengthened or swept to extinction.

Chapter 7 examines the well-being and health of First Nations people, how they access health, and how different they are from non–First Nations people. Chapter 8 explains the duty of government in its relation to First Nations and reveals how the courts have determined the fiduciary responsibility for First Nations. The issue of self-government and Aboriginal rights is covered in Chapter 9. This chapter demonstrates how the rule of law has taken over Canadian society and how political decisions are now dominated by the courts—with some interesting results. Chapter 10 looks at the political economy of First Nations and why they have been relegated to the socio-economic fringe of mainstream society.

No book on First Nations in Canada would be complete without a discussion of the bureaucracy that deals with them. Chapter 11 looks at the mammoth organization of Indian and Northern Affairs Canada, which is so pervasive that it regulates First Nation peoples' behaviour from boardroom to bedroom, from birth to death. In every waking moment of life, a First Nations person is constrained by the policies and legislation administered by Indian and Northern Affairs Canada. The activities of the Assembly of First Nations, Canada's national status Indian organization, are also discussed, and provide an insight into how it has dealt with Indian Affairs bureaucracy as well as with other federal agencies.

Finally, Chapter 12 looks at the social and demographic aspects of First Nations. Beginning with a historical profile, it shows the changes that have taken place over the past 100 years. Although the Aboriginal population of Canada, including First Nations, came to the brink of extinction early in the twentieth century, this population rebounded and is now the fastest-growing group in Canada. The chapter also considers the future, in which there will continue to be a major disjuncture between the needs and aspirations of First Nations people and those of the rest of Canada.

Acknowledgements

I would like to thank Lorne Tepperman, Susan McDaniel, and Monica Boyd for first contacting me to take up this task. They have been exemplary role models during their careers as both teachers and scholars. Their encouragement led me to accept the challenge of trying to address thorny and controversial topics in the area of First Nation studies.

I also would like to thank my students and colleagues at the University of Calgary and elsewhere, who have given their support and advice as I struggled with each of the topics examined in the text. Specific thanks to Cash Rowe, Jim Webb, Monique Passalec-Ross, Marc Stevenson, Jennifer Kelly, Shawna Cunningham, Marie Delorme, Jerry White, Martin Cooke, Mike Lickers, Beverly Jacobs, Ryan Heavy Head, Lori Villibrun, Dr Reg Crowshoe, and Vivian Ayoungman. Each of these individuals has made a unique contribution to this work and they have provided me with information, advice, and criticism when I needed it. While they have supported me in this project, they are not to be held responsible for the contents of the book.

I am grateful for the support by those working with Oxford University Press, especially Phyllis Wilson, the managing editor, who has seen that the production of this book went smoothly, and Mark Thompson, who oversaw the development of the text. I am particularly grateful to the copy editor, Richard Tallman, for providing a keen eye, critical commentary, and additional commentary during the editorial process.

1 Knowing Your History

Learning Objectives

- To understand that history is a key to understanding current events.
- To be able to appreciate why it is important to know the author of history.
- To learn to critically evaluate the histories of First Nations people currently available.
- To discover how colonialism has impacted the traditional way of life for First Nations people.
- To learn how First Nations–government relations changed over time.

Introduction

Every group of people has a history, whether oral or written or both. The contents of written history reflect the points of view of those who have written it, just as the oral history of a people will reflect the world view of those who keep it and transmit it from one generation to the next, in countless tellings of tales, myths, legends, and genealogies. In the case of Canada's First Nations people, their written history for much of the past 400 years can hardly be called 'theirs', for it was produced by non–First Nations people. Is it an accurate history? Does it capture the essence of what First Nations life was like? The answer is both 'yes' and 'no'. Some elements of the existing history of First Nations are fairly accurate. On the other hand, many elements of that history reflect a non–First Nations perspective and distort the lived experience of this country's first human inhabitants. What kind of information about First Nations people do we have? Lomawaima (2004) claims that between 1850 and 1950, over 90 per cent of all objects ever made by an Indian person ended up in a museum collection. Even if this is a bit of an exaggeration, with that amount of information, we should know a lot! However, much of that information has been ignored or viewed from a specific perspective. For example, policy-makers in the dominant settler society homogenized the many different First Nations peoples in Canada, as it was easier to ignore cultural and linguistic differences among groups such as the Cree, Algonquin, and Mohawk and categorize all under the term 'Indian'.

Who Writes History?

The writing of any people's history reflects the cultural ethos and perspective of the writer. If you were asked to write the history of a group of people, how would you go about it? In all probability, you would go to the library, search the Internet, and listen to people who have some knowledge about the group. If you had the time and money, you might even go to the area where the people live, talk to some of them, and study their architectural contributions, their social organizations, and their culture. The question is, would this give you an accurate description and explanation about a people's history? As you would probably agree, the answer is no. Certainly it would provide some insights, but it would take many years of study, examining evidence from many different perspectives and sifting through a considerable amount of information, to reconstruct the history of a people. And you would need to obtain information and evidence from descendants of the people to fully provide the reader with an accurate history. But even then, how accurate could your history be without your being 'in their skin', without being one of them and having the lived experience and knowledge of generations that comes with being part of a historical-cultural group? For example, you would need to become an expert in the language so that you could communicate and understand the people.

Does this mean that only Aboriginal people can write Aboriginal history? As J.R. Miller (2009) points out, this suggestion is unjustified because what is being considered is not something that only Aboriginal people have experienced or can comment on; rather, Aboriginal history is part of Canadian history and, equally important, Canadian history is part of Aboriginal history. On the other hand, if we are talking about secret societies, traditional homelands, or traditional ecological knowledge, then certainly Aboriginal people have a proprietary right and you, as an outsider, might not be privy to such information. For example, if a song is owned by a family, then using such information without the approval of the owner would not be right and you would not be given information on this song. In the end, such restrictions will bear heavily on your reconstructed history.

First Nations History

The view that First Nations played no significant part in Canada's history was first set in place when non-Aboriginals began to write the history of Canada. Today we find that the majority of written historical sources, from which First Nations history is constructed, are from elites who had an interest in representing First Nations social life in negative terms (Francis, 1992). For example, the historian G.F.G. Stanley (*The Birth of Western Canada*, 1936) clearly established that 'primitive' people (First Nations) had little to offer and only the 'civilized' peoples could contribute to the history of Canada. He also set in motion a belief that First Nations widely supported the Riel Rebellion of 1885, although later researchers, such as Stonechild and Waiser (1997), have shown that this claim is false. Nevertheless, for much of the twentieth century and earlier, a pervasive belief held that First Nations societies had contributed little to the development of Canadian society, had lost their cultural vibrancy, and were a people headed for extinction. These views helped perpetuate the view of First Nations irrelevance reflected in much of the historical and literary writings by Euro-Canadians. The history of First Nations people has been, by and large, written by non-Aboriginal people using non-Aboriginal sources. This is not bad per se, but it does point out the limitations of writing history from one perspective—that of the dominant settler group. To more fully establish the history of First Nations people, the historian must incorporate the perspectives of the people themselves.

Over the past centuries, the dynamic of concealment (consciously and unconsciously) has ultimately served the settler population in covering up the violence—physical and, especially, cultural and psychological—that has been visited upon First Nations people. 'Colour', too, has had an impact on the conceptions of Canada as shown in historians' portrayal of Canada as a Northern European outpost, although today, for statistical purposes, First Nations people are not considered a visible minority. The implementation, cover-up, and resistance for nearly a century to address the residential school atrocities also reflect a kind of sanitized, revisionist history on the run, as presented by the dominant majority. These concealments have been embedded in the political, social, and economic history of Canada (Reid, 2008). As such, these factors make it difficult to accept much of what has been written as an accurate history of First Nations–settler relations.

First Nations people argue that Canada's history is based on several false assumptions dating back over a millennium and that these assumptions present a biased view of what 'really happened'. For example, early European explorers and settlers are seen as particularly clever in their adaptation to and settlement of a 'New World', not to mention their 'discovery' of that world, and this cleverness is related to their superior technology. Often forgotten is the extent to which Aboriginal technologies, means of social organization, ecological knowledge, and direct assistance made that adaptation and settlement possible. First, these false assumptions of inherent European superiority build on the belief that First Nations people are incapable of self-government. Second, there is a belief that the treaties between First Nations and the settlers are not really binding covenants of trust and obligation but rather are simple negotiated contracts from the past that have long outlived their usefulness and legal basis. Third, for over a century the belief—and the policy that followed from it—was that the relationship between First Nations and the government was one of **wardship**, meaning that when social changes had to be made, First Nations people were incapable of making decisions and did not need to be consulted. Aspects of this 'infantilization' continue today. And finally, the development of First Nation communities, it is widely believed, must take place on the basis of the dominant society's neo-liberal philosophy and not on terms desired by First Nations (Nobles, 2008).

However, over the past four decades, dating from the 1966–7 **Hawthorn Report**, which recommended a 'citizens plus' approach to the government's treatment of its Indian citizens, and the infamous 1969 White Paper on Indian Policy, which failed to heed anthropologist Harry Hawthorn's recommendations, more and more materials have been produced by First Nations people with regard to their culture and history, and it is this information and perspective that we will weave into this book (Dickason, 2002). For example, John Burrows (2002), a Chippewa, has skillfully integrated evidence from both Western and Indigenous ways of knowing in his work with a result of producing new insights into Canadian law. Aboriginal historians have shown that contact between the two cultures brought both negative and positive consequences to both sides. As Miller (2009) points out, to study the treaty-making process, one must go beyond the Euro-Canadian perspective but also take into account the contributions of First Nations people to the process. Only by incorporating a history that accounts for both settler and First Nations narratives can our understanding of the past become fuller and more comprehensive.

Pre-Contact

An estimated 500,000 First Nations people occupied what is now Canada during the thirteenth and fourteenth centuries. These people were spread across the country in small 'bands', many of which were semi-nomadic, although eastern First Nations, such as those in the present-day Maritimes and in southern Ontario, were more sedentary than nomadic, and the peoples of the Northwest Coast, because of the riches of the sea, notably salmon and shellfish, lived a sedentary and hierarchically ordered life in villages along the coast. Although many political institutions were developed by First Nations people, families were the basic social unit in pre-contact time and these were supported by tight kinship units such as the extended family and clans. This was reiterated in the *Report* of the Royal Commission on Aboriginal Peoples (1996), which notes that the family is the foundation of culture, society, and economy. Moreover, the social and political structure of First Nations life was not separated into the different dimensions we find in Western culture, although among many groups different leaders were chosen for different activities, so that there would be leaders or chiefs of the hunt, of warfare, and for peace. Generally, however, there was little separation of the political, social, economic, and spiritual dimensions of people's lives. As Helin (2006) points out, many First Nations people had a more holistic world view that placed social concerns at the centre of everything.

Prior to European contact, First Nation families were organized communally and non-hierarchically, without coercive authority (Leigh, 2009). Moreover, some First Nation societies were, to varying degrees, women-centred, matrilineal, and inclusive of women in the political aspects of the society (Mihesuah, 2003). In many societies women were considered sacred and respected as wise advisers. As Emberley (2001) points out, Cree women were considered to be at the centre of the circle of life. Moreover, in a hunting society, the distinction between work and home was not important. Only with the introduction of a wage economy did the roles people play become linked to economics, making the role of the 'breadwinner' the more powerful role (Dick, 2006). Women tended crops in agricultural societies, gathered roots and berries, and prepared the products of the hunt for food, clothing, and various household needs. Much of this would change when European colonialism and settlement began. The resulting impacts on the family, kinship, and social structure of First Nations groups would be significant.

Before the Europeans arrived there was considerable contact and trade, as well as warfare, among First Nations. Through trade networks and established trade routes, goods travelled considerable distances: for example, archaeologists have found coastal seashells well into the interior of Canada. Conflict between some of the tribes was ongoing. We know that by the early seventeenth century, the Algonquins had been driven from their homeland by the Mohawks and Mi'kmaq; conflict between the Mi'kmaq and the Abenaki continued for nearly the first seven decades of the seventeenth century before it subsided. These conflicts focused on obtaining slaves, controlling trade routes, and obtaining loot from the villages captured. Although First Nations did not fight explicitly to acquire land or, as a rule, to slaughter the enemy, these were secondary consequences of conflict. Larger units, called 'tribes', were political arrangements that allowed smaller groupings to have some linguistic or cultural affinity with others. In other cases, they formed alliances among themselves, such as the Abenaki and Huron confederacies and the League of Ho-de'-no-sau-nee (the Five Nations of the Iroquois), which allowed greater political organization and control, as well as expanded trade, and ensured that enough food was available for survival (Harris, 1987).

Across Canada, prior to contact, there were seven major culture areas and over 50 languages that linguists have divided into about 12 language groups (Morrison and Wilson, 2004: 4–5, 14–18); the peoples in each culture area developed their own political, economic, and social structure that allowed them to fit into their ecological niche. For well over 10,000 years, these units were self-sustaining and prospered (Helin, 2006). There were times of famine and times of war, but these were episodic in nature and each of the tribes developed strategies to deal with the exigencies. No evidence appears to indicate that many tribes were decimated due to ecological disasters or wars. But all of this would change when the Europeans came to colonize. As Helin points out, a way of living involving co-operation that had worked well for First Nations people prior to contact would be a major weakness once contact occurred. It would become the basis for a strategy that the newcomers would use consistently with devastating impacts on First Nations life.

While many First Nations people were hunters and gatherers, their lives were ruled by a high degree of co-operation, not only within bands but also between them and sometimes inter-tribally. Traditional First Nation communities were one of two types: highly structured or egalitarian. The highly structured societies were found in areas with large, mostly sedentary communities and had distinct political structures based on rank, status, and hierarchy such as the Tsimshian of the Northwest Coast. The second type had less structure and is associated with small populations residing over extensive territories, such as found on the prairies. Thus, there were various forms of political structure, with differing degrees of formality, in the many tribes occupying Canada. Moreover, there is considerable agreement between First Nations and non–First Nations people that most tribes were self-governing nations, and this view was recognized by the American Supreme Court in the famous Marshall decision of 1831 in *Cherokee Nation v. Georgia*, when the Court determined that the Cherokee Indians were a 'domestic dependent nation'. Although there is no equivalent court decision in Canada, the **Royal Proclamation of 1763** suggests that First Nations people did control their lives, and the Proclamation set conditions by which land could be taken from First Nations people living in the unsettled lands beyond Quebec and the Appalachian Mountains.

Contact and European Settlement

The earliest time of contact is unknown but archaeological and literary evidence suggests that it took place around 1000 when the Vikings sailed the North Atlantic from Greenland to the northern tip of Newfoundland, where they established a settlement that lasted for several years. However, ongoing contact can be said to have begun in 1534 when Jacques Cartier made his first voyage and was in contact with the Iroquoian village of Stadacona, near present-day Quebec City. Cartier returned to France with two sons of the chief, and the following year returned and wintered over, this time kidnapping the two sons, their father, Donnacona, and other villagers. The Indians all died in France, but Cartier would return again in 1541 to establish a colony at what is now Montreal. Later, other early explorers, notably Samuel de Champlain, came in contact with Native peoples. On his first voyage in 1603 Champlain encountered Innu, Mohawks, and other Aboriginal groups, and he founded a permanent settlement at Quebec City in 1608. When settlers entered the country, they brought with them the notion of a **patriarchal** family as the most important component of settlement. In order to civilize First Nations (the **white man's burden,** in the later phrasing of the English author, Rudyard Kipling), the Europeans subjected them to reorganization along patriarchal lines, aligning the interests of First Nation families and the social organization of the communities with the interests of the colonial power (Leigh, 2009). This brought about the displacement of First Nations women from the positions of government and power they had traditionally held within some groups, such as the Iroquois. Leigh argues that First Nations men were brought into line with the patrilineal system of the settlers by the use of punitive strategies for those who resisted and rewards for those who accepted this new role and reorganization of the family.

Finally, the introduction of the 1876 Indian Act cemented the new social organization for First Nations people when it defined Indian women through their relation to men (an arrangement that would continue until the passing of Bill C-31 in 1985). As Leigh (2009) points out, as a result of the new Indian Act, First Nations men gained recognition under European law in exchange for dispossessing Indigenous women of their power. As Christianity was introduced, from a very early time in New France, it added to the shaping of First Nation families so that they met the settlers' conception of 'family'. Thus began the transition of First Nations cultures to better align with the settler society. The Indian Act also began to create the gender tensions in First Nations communities that continue to this day. The result of colonialism has been the forced acceptance of settler family structures, values, and behaviours by First Nations people, a process that has permeated First Nations cultures. The consequences of the settler project of assimilation have been dramatic for First Nations peoples, perhaps most especially in regard to the residential school system, which we shall examine in Chapter 4.

Canada's relationship with First Nations can be described as a series of phases in which interests and policy changed substantially. Generally, five phases have characterized the relationship with First Nations people, although it might be argued that in recent decades we have moved into a sixth phase, which has politicians and courts jousting for predominance in determining how First Nations people are to be treated.

Phase 1 (1610–1680). By the early seventeenth century both the French and English had made inroads into the northern half of North America. Small French settler communities were established, trade routes were formed, and a thriving barter system had developed with the First Nations population. Of course, considerable conflict between the two powers vying for control of the continent continued, and each side sought Native allies in their ongoing dispute. By 1610 the French had re-established their control in present day Nova Scotia, although 100 years later, in 1713, the Treaty of Utrecht would cede Acadia to the British.

First Nation peoples were essential to the survival of the early colonial settlements in Canada. This early contact between First Nation populations and the settlers could be best described as symbiotic in that each group was able to benefit and learn from the other. First Nations people taught European settlers about the land and about survival in a harsh northern climate—about the wild foods and game to eat, the clothing to wear, the physical geography and routes of travel. In return, Europeans provided metal, firearms, and other materials and foodstuffs that, it appeared, would enhance the quality of life of First Nations (Patterson, 1972). As such, the initial contact brought an influx of material objects (technology) that led to significant changes in the lifestyle and culture of the Indigenous population.

Phase 2 (1680–1800). The second phase of contact saw First Nations drawn deeper into the economy of the settlers through the fur trade as they became more dependent on the trade goods brought by the Europeans. During this phase, too, the devastation of First Nations populations by European diseases such as smallpox began to have a huge impact, so that the pre-contact estimated Aboriginal population of half a million was reduced to barely 100,000 by the end of the nineteenth century. The French had established various posts in which they could carry out trade with the First Nations in the region. At the same time, Jesuit missionaries were sent to the interior of Canada to convert the First Nations people. The French fur trade in its infancy was linked to the European hat trade and was controlled by the Ministry of Marine, responsible for colonial affairs. It created a company called *compagne des occidentals*, which controlled the fur and moosehide trade in Canada. While it was made to look like a private enterprise, it was in fact a French Crown corporation. All permanent residents of the French colony were compelled to deal with the Crown company while others could trade with other companies. The intent of the company was to begin with the fur and moosehide trade but then to develop timber, minerals, and other foodstuffs for the West Indies plantations. As such, the French sent thousands of single young men to the new colony to begin development of the new land. By the early eighteenth century, there was a glut of furs and hides on the market, but in 1715 it was discovered that rodents and other pests had destroyed the hides and furs in French warehouses. This immediately revived the fur and moosehide trade. Until the 1750s the fur trade expanded, and it served both economic and political purposes for the French. The fur trade was profitable, and it also allowed the Crown to control the settler population. Such trade also influenced the way of life of First Nations people: in some instances, local animal populations were decimated, and the pursuit of furs drew the men away from their traditional activity of hunting to provide for families and communities.

In 1670, the English Hudson's Bay Company (HBC) was chartered and given control over a large area of present-day Canada. The Company was given wide powers, including exclusive trading rights within the area called Rupert's Land, which consisted of all the territory in the Hudson Bay drainage basin. In establishing the fur trade, the HBC began to develop trade relations with First Nations people. Initially, it did not push inland but rather established posts on the coast and expected the First Nations trappers to come to them to trade. By the late eighteenth century, however, the North West Company (NWC), a Scottish and French-Canadian trading company based in Montreal, and the Hudson's Bay Company, based in London, England, were in strong competition that forced the HBC to push inland and to the north in an attempt to increase its haul. As considerable competition for furs from First Nations trappers increased between the NWC and the HBC, by 1821 the two companies merged and the new HBC gained a monopoly with regard to the trade with First Nation peoples. The fur trade—primarily in beaver pelts—resulted in a relatively peaceful pattern of social contact between the settlers and First Nations, but it also drew the Native peoples into the European market economy and away from their traditional way of life. This in turn weakened their political, social, and economic autonomy and increased their reliance on settler goods, politics, and technology (Patterson, 1972). In short, they became involved in a status of **dependency** rather than that of independence.

Nevertheless, the Royal Proclamation of 1763 recognized the principle of First Nations' rightful interest in and common use of their ancestral lands, and stipulated that no First Nations land could be purchased or infringed upon without the negotiation of a treaty or consent of the people within the land area. Moreover, the negotiation of the treaty would have to involve the British government and the First Nation population. The subsequent British North America Act (1867), while recognizing the primacy of French and English, nevertheless also acknowledged the existence of First Nations peoples who had a unique relationship with the British Crown (Carter, 2004). This relationship created the foundation for the recognition of First Nations' special status within Confederation. Under the British North America Act (now known as the Constitution Act, 1867), 'Indians, and Lands reserved for the Indians' were made the responsibility of the federal government. Subsequent governments and changes to the Indian Act have divided this 'Indian' community into many different 'castes' and groups, such as status Indians, treaty Indians, non-treaty Indians, and Métis. By the late twentieth century, the success of this strategy is easily recognizable in that two-thirds of the Aboriginal population have no legal status as Aboriginal (Reid, 2008).

Throughout the seventeenth and eighteenth centuries, conflict among European powers enlisted the support of First Nations people in their attempts to win various wars. In other cases, First Nations were simply caught in the middle of conflict between the French and English. The end result was that First Nations were forced (voluntarily or involuntarily) to choose sides with regard to increasing hostilities among the nations that claimed parts of North America. Each European nation offered enticements to their First Nations allies, and thus many Indigenous people fought for the imperial powers with the promise of land, goods, and services if they were on the 'winning side'. During this period a number of **friendship treaties** were signed between the colonial powers and various First Nations. The First Nations were considered 'assets' that could be co-opted or convinced to fight for one side or the other. Consequently, considerable 'cultivation' of First Nations through gift exchanges sought to ensure they would remain allies. At the same time, there were extended conflicts between the European powers and First Nations, e.g., Iroquois War (1609–1701), Fox War (1710–38), and Mi'kmaq War (1613–1761), as the French and English attempted to take control of what is now Canada and limit the resistance of First Nations (Dickason, 2002).

Following the British defeat of the French at Quebec City in 1759 and the taking of Montreal the following year, the 1763 Treaty of Paris formally brought to an end the conflict between the French and English for control of the northern half of North America. During the War of 1812–14, which pitted the British army and navy against the United States, most of the fighting was along the Canadian border and First Nations allies played a significant role for both sides. Such figures as Tecumseh and Major John Norton were trusted Indian leaders and fierce fighters on the British side, and some battles chiefly pitted Indians against Indians. With the end of this conflict, however, and with no territory gained by either side, those First Nations people who remained alive—following centuries of fighting and decimation by disease—were no longer considered useful allies and battle-field equals. Promises of land, technology, and other goods made in prior times to Indian allies were ignored, rejected, or qualified, and First Nations now were viewed as impediments to expansion and development. The long period of wardship was about to begin.

Phase 3 (1800–1830). As the wars ended and Europeans began to settle in what is now Canada, the third phase of contact between First Nations and the settlers emerged. The relationship with First Nations people was no longer symbiotic or based on alliances. Moreover, First Nations were seriously impacted by the settlers after 1820 as colonization began to have an impact on the land, the way of life of First Nations people, and their position in Canadian society. First, by this time there was considerable European settlement across eastern Canada, and second, disease and colonization had catastrophic impacts on First Nations people. It was clear to Canadians at this time that First Nations people were 'doomed' and would soon be extinct. In fact, the Beothuk of Newfoundland did become extinct, with the last known survivor of this cultural group dying in 1829. Epidemics decimated First Nations populations because they did not have immunity against such European diseases as measles, typhoid, smallpox, and a variety of common European maladies against which Europeans had built up natural resistance over many years.

As Canada moved into its third stage of dealing with First Nations, it began to move jurisdiction of First Nations from the military to civil society. Throughout this period, Canadians attempted to gain the allegiance of their Indian subjects by providing some degree of self-government with limited power. The beginning was the creation of reserves and the establishment of the Indian Act. At the same time, the Canadian government denied First Nations rights, such as individual citizenship, including the right to vote. The philosophical assumption was that First Nations people were incapable of making an adult decision and thus must be placed in a position of 'guardianship' with the federal government. As immature, uncivilized people, they required special protection from the Crown.

Phase 4 (1830–1920). The creation of reserves was a major undertaking by the federal government in the fourth period of relations with the First Nations. The need to open lands for colonial expansion, develop transportation routes across the country, gain control over a people that might pose a potential threat, and thwart the possible annexation efforts of the Americans soon led the federal government to impose treaties. The Riel Resistance in 1869–70 and the Northwest Rebellion of 1885 gave further evidence that Aboriginal people posed a potential threat and thus needed to be dealt with in such a way that they would be extinguished or forever be subservient and dependent. By 1867, more than 100 treaties and land surrenders had already been negotiated by the colonial powers. Today that number has exceeded 500. However, the most important period of treaties was between 1850 and 1923, when 66 major treaties were signed and the government took control over most of the land area of Canada.

These treaties were overt actions to extinguish First Nation land rights and to legislate control over First Nations people. Their chief purpose, however, was to free title to the land for European settlement and for the westward expansion of the railway. The government of the day had not thought through a number of issues with regard to the impacts and conditions of the treaties, in part because political leaders in Ottawa and their administrators were convinced that First Nations would soon be extinct or, if not, would have assimilated to such an extent that special consideration of this group would not be needed. Once the first formal treaties—the Robinson Superior and Robinson Huron treaties of 1850—were signed in Ontario, these became the template used by subsequent treaty commissions as they travelled through the prairies, northwestern Ontario, and into the Northwest Territories to achieve the so-called numbered treaties over the course of a half-century from 1871 to 1921. When requested by First Nations to customize a treaty to their special needs, government officials claimed they could not change the template, and evidence shows that changes were very few. Only when the government could extract more concessions for less land set aside for Indians were the treaties changed from the standard template. Moreover, evidence has shown that when expedient, the federal treaty commissioners would make oral promises to the First Nation groups assembled to 'negotiate' a treaty, but these promises were never put on paper—a fact that has been used by the federal government to reject First Nations' claims. Since Canada has cultivated a written 'evidence-based' society, any claims about the oral agreements have been largely ignored and rejected.

Once the initial Robinson treaties were signed, it was clear that the government could coerce and intimidate the First Nations, and misrepresent the nature of the signed written agreements such that First Nations found themselves signing treaties that they only partially understood or, in some cases, misunderstood. A comparison of the 11 numbered treaties, which opened up the West and Northwest for settlement and development, reveals a striking similarity and the rejection, in most instances, of any special conditions or grants to First Nations people. (The concession of a 'medicine chest' in Treaty 6 is a notable exception, for it established a federal responsibility to provide health-care for its Aboriginal 'wards', although this responsibility often was not met.) In short, the treaties were imposed rather than negotiated, and when that posed a problem, the community was threatened, ignored, forgotten, or defined as not First Nations people and thus omitted from the treaty process. The end result was the takeover by Ottawa of most of the land in Canada in less than a century.

Widespread Settlement

As the initial European colonial powers left Canada, the non-Native settlers took over power and continued to dominate the Indigenous population. The white settler population looked at the evidence at hand—the superiority of their technology, their military developments, the truth of their god, and the fact that there were more and more settlers residing in Canada—as clear evidence that they were a superior race. The nineteenth-century American concept of **manifest destiny** simply added to the belief that European settlers were superior, and dominant colonial societies began to confer upon themselves a set of privileges they did not earn (Episkenew, 2009).

As Jo-Ann Episkenew notes, this myth of superiority allowed the European settlers to develop a stratified society in Canada with First Nations at the bottom. The sense of superiority became a powerful tool in the development of a scientific, capitalistic, Judeo-Christian world (King, 2003). This world assumed by the majority population became the foundational basis for dealing with First Nations people and allowed for the establishment of laws that still remain to the detriment of First Nations people (Wright, 2004). For the majority of white society, change meant having to surrender some of their power and influence, something they were loath to do. It is never easy to change or for political leadership to seek radical change—conservative social and political forces work against it.

The establishment of reserves through the terms of treaty settlements was an integral part of the process of subjugating the First Nations. Through the treaties, land was set aside for First Nations, but under the wardship of the federal government. This arrangement coincided with the belief system of the British—and then Canadian—majority, and represented a continued belief in the inferiority of First Nations people and in their inability to make appropriate or acceptable decisions. Land set aside for reserves generally did not involve First Nations input as to where and how much. Surveyors were sent to establish reserve lands in remote locales on marginal lands that did not encompass existing known natural resources. By and large, this process created isolated enclaves in areas that were not desired by settlers. When First Nations leaders selected the land they wanted to be reserved for them, officials frequently rejected their selection and forced them to make alternative selections. The quantity of the land set aside followed a template created by the federal government and did not, in many cases, take into consideration the type of land or the number of people, in the present or future, who would live on the reserve land. In the end, small areas were set aside for First Nations in return for their agreement to give up all rights to other lands, waters, and their resources and to maintain the peace. In some cases, if a First Nations community disapproved of the land set aside by the government, they were denied rations until they were forced to capitulate and move to land that the colonial officials preferred. In 1927 the federal government decided that one way to stop First Nations people from expressing their disagreement with the government over land issues was to make it illegal for First Nation tribes to hire a lawyer (or any other third party) to initiate legal claims against the government. This law was not revoked until the 1950s. Moreover, over time, many parcels of land initially allocated to First Nation communities were alienated through various legal procedures initiated by private interests and enacted by the federal government. For example, thousands of hectares of land in British Columbia were taken away from First Nations—'cut-off lands'—on the claim that these communities did not need that much land or that they were not using the land in an 'effective and efficient' manner. In other cases, the land was simply removed from the inventory held by Indian Affairs and sold to settlers or other non–First Nation people with or without Native agreement.

Government Action and Inaction

Once reserves were established, the well-being of the First Nations was largely ignored by the Canadian government, except for the presence of local Indian agents whose principal task was to see that federal rules and regulations were followed. The promised provision of animals, agricultural equipment, and seed, in numerous instances, was not forthcoming for the prairie First Nations so that they could enter the agricultural sector. Carter (1990) documents how these First Nation communities, eager to enter the agricultural economy, were systematically denied the provisions that would have allowed them to develop their land. And when some First Nation communities were able to successfully circumvent those barriers, white neighbouring farmers objected to First Nations people placing their goods on the market, citing unfair advantage. Consequently, revisions to the Indian Act made it illegal for First Nation farmers to sell their produce on the open market. The deputy superintendent-general of the Department of Indian Affairs at the time concluded that Indians could not make an 'unnatural' leap from 'barbarism' to a nineteenth-century agricultural environment. First, they would have to become 'peasant' farmers, with Indian Affairs as their feudal lord. While Indians might want to emulate the whites, federal officials felt that this could not take place too quickly or too soon. Indian agents were instructed to discourage the Indians from engaging in potentially lucrative grain farming and, instead, encouraged them to cultivate small vegetable gardens without the help (or cost) of plows and draft animals. In short, First Nations people and communities who had become successful and competitive were defined as 'unnatural' because they had achieved success in only a few years rather than through the slow process of evolution that the whites had experienced. As a result, oppression of First Nation economic/agricultural development continued. In addition, social barriers were created when the **pass system** was put in place. This meant that individuals could not leave their own reserve to market their goods (or for any other reason) unless they had a valid 'pass' from the Indian agent, a procedure of control that was later used by the white South African government during the apartheid era to limit the movement and possible organization of blacks in the townships. This system, though never enacted into Canadian law, continued for some prairie reserves into the 1940s. Even when First Nation communities were starving, government officials moved slowly in providing for the people.

Phase 5 (1920–1970). By the 1950s, the 'democratic phase' began when government shifted its philosophy of assimilation, which was centred on the residential schools, and changed to a policy based on integration. Major revisions were made to the Indian Act in 1951, repealing existing laws against such ceremonies as the potlatches and sun dances and allowing First Nations people to begin to exercise some control over their lives. Nearly two decades later, the introduction of the White Paper of 1969 proposed a new government policy concerning First Nations. The White Paper outlined a plan by which First Nations would be legally eliminated through the repeal of their special status and the end of their unique relationship with the federal government, and the treaties would cease to be living documents. The responsibilities for First Nations education and health and welfare would be turned over to provincial governments (Reid, 2008). In short, the government proposed to do away with the concept of a legal 'Indian'. The protest that started with the National Indian Brotherhood found support in a number of other social, political, and religious organizations, which eventually brought the withdrawal of the policy by the federal government. It would not be until the twenty-first century, when the government introduced the First Nations Governance Act, that First Nations once again rebelled and successfully fought off the proposed policy.

Current State of Affairs

Since the 1970s, a steady stream of court decisions has given both legal and moral status to the claims that First Nations have rights and that these have been systematically rejected or ignored. Beginning with a 1970 Supreme Court decision that acknowledged that First Nations people could drink alcohol, legal decisions have given support to First Nations people who have argued they have 'Aboriginal rights'. The Constitution Act, 1982, gave constitutional status to these rights. Following a short-lived Indian Claims Commission in the mid-1970s, the present Indian Claims Commission was formed in 1991 to expedite outstanding land claims. In short, over the past four decades politicians and government officials have had to change their view of Aboriginal rights and how they deal with them, and have accepted 'the honour of the Crown' and its **fiduciary** duties with regard to First Nations people. This has been a difficult journey for governments (both provincial and federal), which for so long claimed that their definition of reality and their way of doing things were correct, only to be told by the courts that they were not. The federal government in the 1970s embarked on a policy of devolution of political and economic control to local bands, and yet nearly a half-century later not much has been devolved. First Nation communities have been allowed to manage their affairs but they have not been allowed to control their lives. They were successful in achieving the enshrinement of Aboriginal rights in the 1982 Constitution Act, but only in some instances have they been successful in enacting the principle of self-government.

Nevertheless, the changes in the Constitution have allowed them to use the courts to advance their interests in an unprecedented fashion (Reid, 2008). A good example is the *Guerin* case (see Box 1.1), which was based on a land transaction in 1956. It reveals the mentality of the government as well as the strategy it often has employed in dealing with First Nations.

Box 1.1 ❖ THE MUSQUEAM: GOLF VERSUS ABORIGINAL RIGHTS

In 1956, the Shaughnessy Heights Golf Club in Vancouver wanted to lease 160 acres of land from the Musqueam Reserve (in the city of Vancouver). The Musqueam band, lacking legal expertise and just emerging from the era when it was illegal for First Nations to hire lawyers to represent them, asked the Department of Indian Affairs to represent their interests in the land transaction. They instructed the department regarding what conditions they wanted in the lease and waited. Within a few months, a contract was signed and the Musqueam people were informed that an agreement was in place and the golf club would now have a lease on the land. When the First Nation community asked Indian Affairs for a copy of the lease, it took 12 years for this to be provided. At first the department couldn't find the lease, then it claimed that the Musqueam leadership did not warrant the right to see the confidential lease, and finally it said the band would have to get a court order to release the lease. Eventually the band obtained a copy of the lease, and on the basis of that disclosure the Musqueam, led by Chief Daniel Guerin, sued the federal government in 1975. The court ruled in favour of the band and awarded it an additional $10 million. The government appealed the decision and the ruling was overturned. However, the Musqueam people appealed to the Supreme Court of Canada, which overturned the lower court ruling on the basis that the Crown breached the fiduciary obligation it owed the community and had to make good the loss suffered by the Musqueam band.

The Musqueam experience reveals the lack of concern for the welfare of First Nations people and reflects an ethos of 'we are right' on the part of governments. Notably, it took until 1984 (nearly 30 years) for this dispute to find its way through the courts and result in action against the government. In the meantime, the golf club had unfettered use of the land at a value well below its commercial value had it been put to some other use. In short, golf club members were advantaged for this period of time and the only 'cost' to the federal government was the legal costs of the court proceedings as well as the 'fine' that was eventually imposed—all paid for by taxpayers.

Many other cases over the years parallel this one, demonstrating the common strategy employed by the federal government when dealing with

First Nation communities. There are few circumstances when the issue of 'principle' is at stake and almost always the reason for continuing the litigation is based on cost and claims that the government's view of reality is correct. The strategy of forcing First Nations to engage in litigation and expend large amounts of money and time often results in First Nations dropping their claims or having to negotiate with the federal government for less compensation than they might otherwise could have gained (Leslie, 2004).

Recent history has seen attempts by First Nations to participate in political processes such as the repatriation of the Canadian Constitution. However, there was active resistance from the provinces, and even though various Aboriginal groups petitioned the British government for recognition of the legitimacy of their claim to inclusion, they were not included in the discussions in an official capacity. When the initial draft of the amended Constitution was made public, Aboriginal rights had been omitted from the document. Through active lobbying by Aboriginal organizations over the next year, the redraft did include Aboriginal rights: 'The existing aboriginal and treaty rights of the aboriginal peoples of Canada are hereby recognized and affirmed' (section 35), and, in section 25, the Royal Proclamation and past and future land claims agreements were recognized as bases of Aboriginal rights and freedoms.

In continuing to engage in constitutional reform and in an attempt to persuade Quebec to support the new Constitution, the provincial first ministers and Prime Minister Brian Mulroney in 1987 drafted the **Meech Lake Accord** to address the concerns expressed by Quebec. Once again, Aboriginal leaders were excluded from the discussions. To pass this amendment to the Constitution, the legislatures in all of the provinces first had to ratify the agreement. Ironically, Elijah Harper, a Cree chief and NDP member of the Manitoba legislative assembly, steadfastly withheld his vote on procedural grounds, thus stopping Manitoba from ratifying the agreement and derailing the necessary unanimous consent of the provinces within the stipulated three-year period for ratification. Two years later, in 1992, the Charlottetown talks focusing on constitutional change were brought to a national referendum. Among other aspects of the **Charlottetown Accord**, which largely involved a devolution of powers from Ottawa to the provinces, was an agreement by the provincial and federal governments and Aboriginal groups that the Aboriginal groups would be recognized as a third order of government and would have an inherent right to self-government that would be negotiated on a case-by-case basis. However, the Canadian electorate—including a wide majority of on-reserve First Nations people—emphatically rejected the Charlottetown Accord (Jedwab, 2007). A year earlier, to address—or to put off—the growing demands of Canada's Aboriginal population for social, political, and economic justice, the federal government established the Royal Commission on Aboriginal Peoples (RCAP in 1991).

The RCAP spent five years carrying out research and consulting with Canadians (both Aboriginal and non-Aboriginal), and its findings and recommendations were presented in five volumes. The Commission made many recommendations as to how the federal government might change its relationship with First Nations people. In the end, as with the Hawthorn Report of 30 years earlier, nearly all the recommendations were rejected or ignored. Ten years after the final report of the RCAP was presented, the provincial first ministers, federal government, and Aboriginal leaders agreed to a new policy in late 2005 referred to as the Kelowna Accord, which would see substantial changes in government–Aboriginal relations. The $5 billion budget included in the Accord was to improve the life of First Nations people by funding health-care, education, and housing, and would seek to close the socio-economic gap between First Nations and non–First Nations people. However, when the Liberal government was defeated in February 2006, the new minority Conservative government rejected the Accord and said it would seek to implement a new plan—which has yet to be implemented.

The Indian Act has not seen major changes for years, and when there have been changes, because of the fractured nature of politics within individual First Nations, between non-traditionalists and those who adhere to a traditionalist view, these revisions in some instances have been divisive. In 1985, for example, Bill C-31 reinstated the status and band membership of Native women who married non-Indians, and extended this status to their children as well. For Native and non-Native women's groups this was a long-overdue and just change; for traditionalists and leaders within many bands, it was an imposition of non–First Nations values that they were reluctantly forced to accept. In general, however, government policy towards First Nations developed early in the history of Canada continues to be employed. There is no disagreement that the policy is shortsighted in its planning, repressive in its application, and largely negative in its results (Buckley, 1992). Yet, apart from a couple of constitutional conferences involving Aboriginal leaders that were mandated by the Constitution Act, 1982, which accomplished nothing, successive governments have not seen it as important to sit down and work with First Nations people to remove/revise the Indian Act or to create an overarching alternative relationship.

Why First Nations people have not made a lasting impression on Canadian interpretations of the history of Canada is an important question. There has been an assumption that since First Nations people didn't contribute to the technological expertise of the settler society (although in many instances they did) and lived on isolated reserves for which there was limited movement on and off or interaction with the larger society, these First Nation communities had little direct or indirect impact on the development of Canadian society. Miller (1990) notes that for many non-Aboriginal Canadians, First Nations people have existed in a kind of 'limbo of irrelevance' even though their participation in local economies and environments has had a major impact. For example, Nobles (2008) points out that in a study of Canadian political party platforms from 1867 to 1960, one reference was made to Aboriginal peoples in 1887 and then the next one occurred in 1958. This rather clearly suggests a lack of impact on the larger society.

Keith Regular (2009) emphasizes that First Nations were not irrelevant to the processes of Canadian social and economic development. There were no 'empty spaces' that the Canadian settlers moved into. Rather, as settlement into the occupied spaces occurred, a melding of peoples and cultures resulted. Calvin Helin (2006) argues that the Iroquois Confederacy developed an Iroquois Constitution that formed the basis of the governing body of the Iroquois League. Moreover, he notes that this system of government influenced the drafting of the American Constitution. Arthur J. Ray (1974) clearly shows how First Nations people were pivotal players in the development of the early economy of Canada. Regional studies such as those by Sarah Carter (1990) and Hana Samek (1987) reveal that the development of Canadian society has been heavily influenced by First Nations people. Indeed, much about First Nations life and mythology permeates our cultural and literary heritage.

Throughout the history of Canada, the government developed its policies and programs with regard to First Nations people based on a philosophy of displacement and assimilation. These policies assumed that First Nations peoples were inferior to Europeans and incapable of governing themselves, and were designed to destroy First Nation institutions and to undermine their cultural values and identity. An essential tenet in all societies has been that the majority group, the conquerors, has the right to determine history and to dictate what rights the conquered will have, and this view has played out in Canada since the time of first contacts.

Non-Aboriginal peoples have continued to define 'civilization' as social organization that has reached a level of complexity reflecting intensive industrialization, large permanent settlements, technological advances in metallurgy and to create more lethal weaponry, and state political systems. In short, the argument is that more 'complex' societies are an indication of 'progress', which in turn makes them more civilized (Flanagan, 2000). At the same time, this view refuses to acknowledge that many of the attributes considered emblematic of a civilized culture were actually attributes held by First Nations people. For example, Warry (2007) points out that there is nothing simple about potlatches or sun dances or Anishnabe ecological practices. The ceremonies, cosmological systems, and political systems of First Nations are no less complex than European forms.

The fact that Europeans were able to subjugate First Nations people is not taken as evidence by Euro-Canadian historians that such action is a sign of barbarism rather than of civilization. In their view, history is a natural process whereby hunters and gatherers are displaced by more 'advanced' cultures, which precipitates a shift from a 'stateless' society to an organized and bureaucratic one (Warry, 2007). This perspective is built upon eighteenth-century Enlightenment philosophy, which argued it was inevitable that nations would plunder and conquer other nations as part of a natural law. This, of course, means that First Nations people, by European definition, were inferior because they were not using land for agricultural purposes—although, in fact, many were—and since that is defined as an attribute of a 'civilized' state, it confirms that First Nations people were not civilized.

Aboriginal people have used many different forms of resistance, whether overt, implicit, or symbolic. These actions have been less about opposing the state than about claiming a continued right to exist as separate socio-political entities with their own autonomy and the right to preserve their culture (Hall and Fenelon, 2009). Over many years, however, the First Nations of Canada have been unable to resist the encroaching European civilization. As such, they have had to accept some of the new rules, e.g., European law, capitalism, institutionalized education. Nevertheless, they have resisted assimilation and integration and continue to exhibit cultures that remain apart from the majority society in significant ways.

Conclusion

First Nation cultures have changed considerably over the past four centuries. Yet, many elements of traditional culture continue as a powerful influence on the lives of First Nations people and within the larger society. Until the last 30–40 years, federal and provincial governments have not considered First Nations as having special rights that they have to deal with, and even when they have accepted this fact it has been with considerable reluctance and equivocation. Historical and contemporary government strategies for dealing with First Nation communities have insisted that Aboriginal peoples have no special rights. Then, if a First Nation community challenges this claim, legal steps are taken to deal with it: passing special legislation to keep First Nations people from proceeding with litigation; revising existing laws so that previous legal rights are considered inappropriate; or imposing legal machinery to intimidate the First Nation claim. There have been few instances when a federal or provincial government has voluntarily agreed that its previous actions placed First Nations in a disadvantaged position. The courts, in recent years, have had to carry this burden even though they have repeatedly suggested that various claims by First Nations would be best resolved through a political process.

The history of settler–Indigenous contact shows that the settlers initially held a bifurcated view of Indigenous people. There is still a belief that North

America was *terra nullius*—uninhabited territory—when Europeans arrived to 'discover' it. Although the settlers would admit that a few First Nations people were living in what is now Canada, they still would argue that the substance of the concept was correct. That is, there were no 'real' or 'civilized' people living in Canada who had some control over the land. They were more like the animals of the forest. And, as the settlers began to control Canada, this view determined legal and moral thought. At the same time, there was a belief that First Nations were sovereign. Why else would the French and English 'take treaty' with the various First Nation groups? What would have been the reason for signing treaties with non-sovereign nations—ones that the US Supreme Court in the early nineteenth century had said were 'nations within nations'. It is sometimes argued that the treaties were simple 'contracts', yet contracts are different from treaties, and the French and English knew the difference between the two. Once the treaties were signed and land sold and settled, their concern over the power of First Nations people dissipated. From that time on, there was no need to 'take treaty', and one can see this in much of mainland British Columbia and the North, where the historical treaty process was never pursued. Were these First Nations less 'nations' than their counterparts on the prairies or in central and eastern Canada? The answer seems to lie in the fact that once the settlers had achieved power and First Nations were no longer viewed as a threat, they were ignored and relegated to the margins of society.

At the same time, treaties signed were then subject to revisionist history in that they were redefined to not be treaties in the legal sense but rather a kind of 'agreement' that would only be considered legal or binding for a limited period and then jettisoned. In other words, treaties were signed when it was in the interest of the imperial powers/settlers, and once those interests were met there was no incentive to meet the conditions of the treaties. Redefinitions of First Nations people by revisionists began to conclude that there were no substantive differences between First Nation groups such as the Ojibwa, Cree, and Dene, and a mythically homogeneous group of people called 'Indians' was created. Actual cultural differences were ignored and a singular definition emerged, one that has been enshrined in settler law and society. Ample evidence, such as the 1969 White Paper and the proposed 2001 First Nations Governance Act, indicates that governments have tried to 'wish' the treaties away and to relegate them to history.

First Nations did not accept these revisionist views. They accepted the settler society as an independent sovereign nation, just as they were, and objected and continued to object to being told that they were not and are not independent sovereign nations. First Nations people have consistently maintained their definition of their own nationhood, which existed long before the settlers arrived. They also have not viewed the treaties as 'giving away' or 'surrendering' their rights.

By the middle of the nineteenth century, the precipitous population decline among First Nations suggests that between three-quarters and 90 per cent of the population had disappeared since the time of first contact (Ubelaker, 1988). While scholars may argue about the specific percentage of loss, all agree that mortality losses were immense, that impacts on cultures were substantial, and that the entire continent of Indigenous people was traumatized. Moreover, as Wesley-Esquimaux and Smolewski (2004) point out, First Nations people never had enough time between the various impacts of epidemics, genocide, trauma, and forced assimilation to develop resiliency sufficient for dealing with the periodic social and cultural disintegration of their nations. Under colonialism, First Nation cultures were and continue to be devalued, and symbols of the culture, e.g., sacred sites, are destroyed and usurped for the purposes of the majority society. In the past, religious, health, and legal systems have been denigrated and criminalized by the colonial powers, and the cultural productions of First Nations, such as art, music, and spiritual ceremonies, have been exploited for private profit.

Canadian governments have not been innocent bystanders trying to deal with demands from First Nation communities. They have played a central role in creating the very identities that governments now want to reject. Markers such as cultural practices, skin colour, political access, legal status, formal education, and property ownership were used to create the boundaries of inclusion and exclusion. Today the government is trying to argue that dealing with the claims of First Nations threatens modernity, weakens the state, and reduces the social cohesion of the country. On those bases alone, the new strategy blames the victim in an attempt to escape responsibility for what it has created.

Questions for Critical Thought

1. How could the history of First Nations be written so as to acknowledge their contributions to the development of Canadian society? How might this have affected our views about First Nations people today?

2. How have First Nations people influenced how we think about Canada and being Canadian? Provide some specific examples.

3. Why did the federal government decide to treat First Nations people as it did? What were some of the structural reasons for such a choice—over 140 years ago and today?

Suggested Readings

Adams, Howard. 1975. *Prison of Grass: Canada from the Native Point of View.* Toronto: New Press. A history of Aboriginal people from the perspective of a Native.

Cairns, Alan. 2001. *Citizens Plus: Aboriginal People and the Canadian State.* Vancouver: University of British Columbia Press. The author, a political scientist and one of Canada's leading scholars in the area of Aboriginal studies, seeks a vision of Canadian citizenship that reflects both pluralism and a need for common symbols of shared identity. He presents a statement on the global movement for decolonization.

Dickason, Olive Patricia. 2002. *Canada's First Nations: A History of Founding Peoples from Earliest Times*, 3rd edn. Toronto: Oxford University Press. Canada's premier Aboriginal historian provides a detailed account of Aboriginal–settler relations from the time of first contact and also examines the pre-contact arrival and history of Aboriginal peoples in North America. A fourth edition (2009), with Métis historian David T. McNab, includes some useful revisions and a new final chapter bringing the story of Canada's First Nations up to the present.

Ray, Arthur J. 1974. *Indians in the Fur Trade.* Toronto: University of Toronto Press. The author presents a thorough account of Aboriginal participation in the fur trade that characterized the economy of Canada for so many years. He outlines the relationship and how Aboriginal people influenced the development of Canadian society.

Suggested Websites

Early Canadiana Online
www.canadiana.org
Early documents, periodicals, and books are available at this site, and many of them relate to Indian–Euro-Canadian relations directly or indirectly.

Jesuit Relations and Allied Documents
http://puffin.creighton.edu/jesuit/relations
Creighton University, a Jesuit school in Omaha, Nebraska, provides the complete English translation of the 73-volume *Jesuit Relations*, dating from 1610 to 1791, in facsimile from the classic 1896–1901 edition by Reuben Gold Thwaites. The *Jesuit Relations*, first published in Paris on an annual basis to raise money for the Jesuit missions, are accounts written by the missionaries to New France. The *Relations* provide a wealth of contemporary data and European observation on the First Nation peoples of eastern and central Canada that the missionaries sought to convert to Christianity.

2

Who Are You?

Learning Objectives

- ⊛ To recognize the implications for defining a person in a certain way.
- ⊛ To understand the concept of identity and its importance to First Nations people.
- ⊛ To see that the definition of 'Indian' has changed over time.
- ⊛ To see how identity is manufactured by state institutions.
- ⊛ To understand how First Nations people have responded to the government's definition of 'Indian'.
- ⊛ To learn how First Nations have changed their own identity.

Introduction

When someone asks, 'Who are you?', it would seem to be a pretty simple question to answer. If someone were more specific and asked, 'What is your ethnic background?', once again many of us would not have a problem in answering the question. However, suppose that your ethnicity was 'legally' defined, not by you but by a government agency. Such is the case for First Nations people.

From a cultural perspective, most societies have the right and ability to define who its members are and are not. Boundaries are set and criteria are presented that define who falls within a particular social group. The criteria might include language, phenotypical traits, various cultural traits, and geographical location. As a member of the society, individuals then determine whether or not they are part of the group or not. All of this was circumvented for First Nations by the Canadian government when it introduced the Indian Act in 1876 (Dempsey, 2005), and this has led Guimond (2003) to refer to 'fuzzy definitions' and changing identities in regard to First Nations people. Box 2.1 lists and defines some of the various terms that are central to understanding Canada's First Nations. How did this all come about, and why is the question of simple identity problematic for First Nations people?

Box 2.1 ❖ TERMINOLOGY

Aboriginal peoples: The Constitution Act, 1982, recognizes three groups of Aboriginal people—Indians, Métis, and Inuit.

Aboriginal rights: Rights that First Nations people have as a result of their ancestors' long-standing use and occupancy of the land.

Aboriginal self-government: Any government system that has been designed, established, and administered by First Nations people under the Canadian Constitution. This definition is contested by some First Nations people.

Band: A group of Indians for whose collective use and benefit lands have been set apart or money is held by the federal Crown.

First Nations: A term that has come to replace 'Indian bands', which many people found offensive. No legal definition of this term exists. It generally refers to Indian peoples in Canada.

Indian: A person who is registered as an Indian under the Indian Act.

Reserve: Tract of land, the legal title to which is held by the federal Crown, set apart for the use and benefit of an Indian band.

Tribal Council: A regional group of First Nations members that delivers common service to a group of First Nations people.

Source: Indian and Northern Affairs Canada, *Words First: An Evolving Terminology Relating to Aboriginal Peoples in Canada*, 2002, at: dsp-psd.pwgsc.gc.ca/Collection/R2-236-2002E.pdf.

History of Who Is Indian

Two centuries ago, the question of who an Indian is would not have been complex, nor would it have been problematic for an individual to answer the question. When settlers came to Canada and met the Indigenous population, they referred to them generically as 'Indians'. They did not understand the complexities of tribal affiliation and thus settlers simply lumped all Indigenous people into one category—Indians. It didn't really make any difference to the settlers if an individual was Ojibwa, Cree, or Dene. Since the Indigenous people spoke a different language, dressed differently, had different **phenotypical traits,** and had a set of cultural attributes and a way of life that were distinct from those of the settlers, it was easy at that time to distinguish between Indigenous and non-Indigenous peoples. However, after a generation or two, there was some mixture between Indigenous and non-Indigenous peoples, especially in regard to the fur trade as European traders and trappers mated with Native women. Thus, a new group of Aboriginal people—the **Métis**—emerged. Moreover, legal pronouncements by the settlers began to make some people 'non-Indians' who initially had been defined as 'Indian'. Now it became more problematic for everyone to make a distinction between Indians, Métis, and non-Indians. Many of these 'non-Indians' had some of the phenotypical traits of Indians, they usually spoke both an Aboriginal language and English/French, their dress was similar to both non-Indians and Indians, and their way of life had elements of both groups.

By the 1850s there was enough European settlement that the colonies began to implement legislation dealing with Indigenous peoples and the land they occupied. Thus, at this time, Canada began to create a legal definition of who was an Indigenous person and subject to legislation. The initial definitions generally focused on cultural attributes, although sometimes **blood quantum** factors were introduced as indicators of who was a First Nations person. But inheritance rules had to be established to ensure that individuals from the next generation were properly identified. The first rule was that inheritance and heritage would take place through the male line, despite the fact that many First Nations people traced their inheritance and heritage through the female line. Section 12(1)(b) of the Indian Act ensured that the patriarchal system would be enshrined in law.

If a person wanted to opt out of being identified as an Indian, the government introduced a process (enfranchisement) by which an individual could be relieved of his/her Indian ethnicity. This could be voluntary or involuntary. In the former case, an individual could ask to be redefined as a non-Indian and she/he thereby lost legal status and any rights and responsibilities that went along with it. In return the person could vote and perhaps make claim to a piece of land as a single property-owner. Alternatively, the government could unilaterally decide that an individual was no longer an Indian through the process of enfranchisement. For example, if an individual Indian had obtained a certain education level, spoke English/French fluently, served in the war, or was integrated into the economic system, he/she would automatically be declassified as an Indian. Although it was enforced until the 1950s, this involuntary process was particularly active in the early 1920s when First Nations soldiers who fought for Canada returned from World War I. Moreover, during this period, the superintendent-general was given power to declare any Indian over the age of 21 fit for enfranchisement (Taylor, 1983).

As we shall see, there has not been any single continuous definition of an Indian over time. Even today different definitions exist, depending on who is asking the question. Cultural definitions were initially used, but by 1871, with the initiation of the first Canadian census, the federal government enumerated Indians by means of a question on **ethnic ancestry**, that is, the

ethnic or cultural group to which one's ancestors belonged. With the patriarchal system of the settler society, this applied to one's father's lineage. As
Guimond (2003) points out, since very few persons actually have knowledge
of their ethnocultural genealogy, only a fraction of the actual descendants
of pre-colonial Indigenous peoples self-declare an Indigenous origin on the
census. These 'objective' indicators turn out not to be objective and have a
built-in bias, although this is not always recognized. Moreover, in 1986 the
census dropped the 'objective' criterion for determining who was an Indian
and introduced the concept of 'self-identification' for all ethnic group affiliation. This 'subjective' indicator of a person's affiliation with an ethnic group
is maintained today.

Making the Definition

At the same time, Indian and Northern Affairs Canada has chosen to use the
Indian Act as the sole basis for determining who is and isn't an Indian and
has rejected the subjective definition. This, of course, means that different
Aboriginal population figures are provided by different branches of the
federal government. Long ago this department created an 'Indian register',
which identifies all those people who are legal Indians, and it has become
the basis for determining who in the current generation is and who in the
next generation will be considered a legal Indian. Once struck from the
roll, an individual and any offspring are permanently removed from being
considered an Indian in the view of Indian Affairs. This Indian 'roll' was
established in 1876 and is part of the Indian Act, which explicitly defines a
specific subset of people called 'registered Indians'.

Through its initial colonization policies the government shaped First
Nations identity by using it as a marker of collective exclusion. Thus, the
Canadian state, historically, played a central role in creating 'Indian' as a
legal category. First Nations people argue their 'claims on the federal and
provincial governments are legitimate because these levels of government
have used a variety of techniques such as racial, cultural and linguistic
markers to establish and maintain the boundaries of ethnicity in ways that
did not include the indigenous population' (Jung, 2009: 4). Such claims
arise from their experience of being marginalized and oppressed over the
past two centuries (Thompson, 2001). In short, the Canadian government,
through its actions, has created a strong political and cultural identity that
has now come back to haunt it.

In addition, this definition empowered Indian men to control the definition of who is an Indian. This, in turn, created a giant chasm between the
two sexes. Unfortunately, the government has not known how it might deal
with the three categories of claims for reparations for historical injustices that
First Nations people are making: claims by individuals who were victims;

claims by members of communities for injustices done to the community; and claims for compensation for individuals who are descendants of victims of injustice (Thompson, 2001). The recent residential schools settlement deals with the first set of claims; the creation of the Aboriginal Healing Foundation and the establishment of the Truth and Reconciliation Commission deal with the second type of claim; and the third type—descendants of victims—has not yet been dealt with.

Record-keeping and Related Issues

Until the 1950s, officials keeping records as to who was on the Indian register and who was included/excluded from various treaties were sloppy and unsystematic in their recordings. In other cases, individuals were not placed on (or cut from) the roll because of cost-cutting measures by the Department of Indian Affairs. Consequently, over the years thousands of individuals have been deleted from or never placed on the register. In other cases, entire First Nation communities were missed (deliberately or by accident) in the registration process and were never recognized as legal 'Indians'. The Labrador Innu are one example.

The Indian Act

Today, numerous groups consider themselves Aboriginal but are not necessarily First Nations (Indians). The concept of 'Aboriginal' is now enshrined in the Canadian Constitution and refers to individuals who are Indian, Métis, or **Inuit**. Viewed somewhat differently, there are still three major groupings (see citoyen.onf.ca). First are those individuals who claim to have Aboriginal ancestry/origin. These are people who report some Indigenous origin (North American Indian, Métis, or Inuit) on the ethnic origin question in the census. Second are those who report Aboriginal identity. This refers to people who report identifying with at least one Aboriginal group, such as Indian, Métis, or Inuit. Third are the registered, status, or treaty Indians (now referred to as First Nations people). This category refers to those who are registered under the Indian Act. Treaty Indians are persons who may or may not be registered under the Indian Act and who can prove descent from a band that signed a treaty. Hence, it is important to remember that 'Indian' is a legal term in Canada and reflects certain rights and responsibilities for the Indigenous population as well as for provincial and federal governments. In the end, 'Indians' can be either registered treaty or registered non-treaty. However, from the perspective of government, only registered Indians are considered as part of their legal responsibility.

Now, to make things just a bit more complex, consider some historical context that will show how the definition of an 'Indian' has gone through changes over the years. As we noted earlier, the concept of an Indian is embedded in the Indian Act and thus has a legal definition. However, one would have to look at different versions of the Indian Act over history to identify exactly what that definition was. This is because the Indian Act has been amended over time and the definition has changed. Until the introduction of Bill C-31 in 1985, the definition of an Indian followed a **patrilineal** system. This meant that the heritage of an individual would follow the male line, so that if an Indian woman married a non-Indian male, both she and her children would lose Indian status. Conversely, if a non-Indian woman married an Indian male, she and her children would automatically become Indians (section 12[1][b] of the Indian Act). In addition, if an Indian woman gave birth and did not identify the name of the father to officials, the assumption was that the father was non-Indian and thus the child would not be included on, or would be struck from, the Indian roll. The Native Women's Association of Canada and Indian Rights for Indian Women supported a number of court challenges by Indian women who had lost their Indian status. All of the cases were rejected by the formal court system. However, the international courts did not support the Canadian decisions and thus international pressure was brought on the Canadian government to change this section in the Indian Act. This action by First Nations women was rejected by the National Indian Brotherhood (primarily run by First Nations men), which argued that the patrilineal system was preferred.

Bill C-31

In 1985, the government, despite considerable First Nations opposition, passed Bill C-31, which was designed to bring the Indian Act into accord with the provisions of the Charter of Rights and Freedoms. Bill C-31 introduced a new definition of who was or wasn't an Indian (Fiske and George, 2006). It ostensibly removed the sex discrimination that First Nations women had been arguing against for decades. The Native Women's Association of Canada (1986) pointed out that the major effects of the new status provisions of this bill resulted in the following: (1) no one will gain or lose status through marriage; (2) people who previously lost status through the provisions of the Indian Act and enfranchisement would be entitled to regain status; (3) children whose parents lost their status are now able to regain their status; (4) no one will have status unless at least one parent has or would have had status; and (5) the concept of enfranchisement is abolished (see the Association's 'Guide to Bill C-31' for a full statement: action.web.ca/home/narcc/attach/GuidetoBillC31-%20 amendment%20to20%).

In short, Bill C-31 allowed for the children of women who had been stripped of their Indian status to be recognized as Indians. The end result of this new bill meant that people who had lost or were denied status because of the earlier discriminatory sections of the Indian Act would be reinstated on the Indian registry and, perhaps, reinstated on their respective band list (Canada, 1987). By 2009, over 200,000 people had applied for reinstatement and approximately 123,000 individuals were placed back on the Indian register—a startling fact is that more than 75,000 people (close to 40 per cent) who felt they were 'Indian' were denied that identification by government officials.

Now the question is, who is an Indian and how is Indian status transmitted from one generation to the next? The new bill (C-31) created different ways for a person to become a registered Indian in Canada. At the same time, not all people of Indian ancestry are entitled to become registered Indians and not all Indians who lost their status previously are entitled to be reinstatement (Daniel, 1998). The Minister of Indian Affairs at the time of the implementation of Bill C-31 noted that he may be able to register these people but it was not certain that he would. Given the figures above, it is clear that many applications were denied.

Bill C-31 was touted as resolving all the problems related to sex discrimination. However, two types of Indians—section 6(1) and section 6(2) Indians—were created. At the outset both of these types are considered legal Indians, but if the marriage patterns deviate from the ideal, the second-generation offspring and subsequent generations may lose their Indian status. For example, if a parent falls under the conditions listed under section 6(1) and marries another person who falls under the conditions of section 6(1), their children will be Indians and considered section 6(1) Indians. If the marriage pattern continues in this fashion, then all subsequent offspring will be defined as Indians. However, if one of the marriage partners is a section 6(1) Indian but marries a non-Indian, then any children from this union will be section 6(2) Indians (still on the registry). Then, if that section 6(2) Indian marries a non-Indian person, the children of that marriage will no longer be Indians. In short, the new bill imposes a new rule for women regarding all second-generation descendants. In order for a child to have Indian status, both parents must be status under section 6(1) or 6(2) or at least one parent must be under section 6(1). If this ideal situation is breached, the offspring will no longer be considered Indians. One can quickly see that there will be more variations in which one can lose his/her Indian status than in which can maintain it. It also means that siblings who are Indian, depending on their marriage pattern, will produce offspring that may or may not be Indians. Consequently, among second-generation children from the same family, some may be defined as Indians and others not (see Table 2.1).

TABLE 2.1 **Implications of Descent Rules under Bill C-31**

Parental Combination			
Father	Mother	Status of Child	Implications
6(1) Indian	6(1) Indian	6(1) Indian	Both mother and child on register
6(1) Indian	6(2) Indian	6(1) Indian	Both mother and child on register
6(2) Indian	6(1) Indian	6(1) Indian	Both mother and child on register
6(2) Indian	6(2) Indian	6(1) Indian	Both mother and child on register
Non-Indian	6(1) Indian	6(2) Indian	Both mother and child on register
6(1) Indian	Non-Indian	6(2) Indian	Child on register, mother is not
Non-Indian	6(2) Indian	Non-Indian	Mother on register, child is not
6(2) Indian	Non-Indian	Non-Indian	Neither mother or child on register

Challenges to the Indian Act

During the 1970s, First Nations women challenged the Indian Act as discriminatory against women. Jeanette Lavell, Sandra Lovelace, and Yvonne Bedard claimed that they were discriminated with regard to their Indian status and their ability to pass on Indian identity through marriage. These cases were eventually rejected by the courts on different grounds but began to set the stage for government to address this issue, especially since Canada had signed the UN Human Rights Covenant in 1976. From the government's perspective, Bill C-31 was enacted as a way of addressing this issue. However, the thinking behind it was still sexist and a recent court case involving an Indian woman (*McIvor v. Canada*, 2007) argued that certain sections of Bill C-31 still discriminate against women in that, if a woman marries a non-Indian, her children are not accorded Indian status (see Box 2.2).

Since the Court of Appeal decision, Indian and Northern Affairs officials have travelled throughout Canada to hold 'discussion sessions' with the Assembly of First Nations, First Nation women's groups, and regional First Nation organizations. Again, while First Nation groups can give 'input', they do not have the final say in terms of what the amendments will be. Thus far it would seem that the government has developed and proposed legislative amendments that respond specifically to the Court of Appeal ruling. There is little interest in taking a broader view of the Indian Act. In March 2010 the federal government's Bill C-3 proposed amendments to the Indian Registration Act:

Indian registration under s. 6(2) of the Indian Act to any grandchild of a woman:
   a. who lost status due to marrying a non-Indian, and
   b. whose children born of that marriage parented the grandchild with a non-Indian after September 4, 1951 (when the 'double mother' rule was first included in the Indian Act), as well as any sibling of that grandchild born before September 4, 1951. (www.ainc-inac.gc.ca)

BOX 2.2 ⁜ WOMEN'S RIGHTS: CHALLENGING BILL C-31

Ms. McIvor was not a registered Indian prior to 1985 and had married a non-Indian male. However, under Bill C-31, she became entitled to register as an Indian. She contends that she and her son, Mr. Grismer, are not in the same position as they would have been if she had been a male.

Unlike a male Indian in her situation, her ability to pass status to her grandchildren depended on her son parenting with a registered Indian. Children of her male counterpart had status prior to 1985 and so were registered under subsection 6(1) of the Indian Act. Any grandchild of this male Indian could be registered. Mr. Grismer, however, having only one registered Indian parent, was registered under subsection 6(2). And according to the 'second generation cut-off' rule, the fact that he had a child with a non-Indian meant that his child (Ms. McIvor's grandchild) could not be registered.

In 2007, a judge of the Supreme Court of British Columbia essentially agreed with Ms. McIvor and ruled that section 6 of the Indian Act (the section that sets out the rules for registration) violates the Canadian Charter of Rights and Freedoms, and . . . is discriminatory. The federal government claimed the judge erred and appealed the decision to the Court of Appeal for British Columbia. In 2009, the Court of Appeal found that section 6 of the Indian Act is discriminatory but in a more limited way than had the Supreme Court of British Columbia. To come to its decision, the BC Court of Appeal created a 'hypothetical brother' of Ms. McIvor and asked, 'What would happen to the child of his son?' Prior to 1985, the grandchild of the hypothetical brother would have lost status at age 21. However, under the 1985 Indian Act amendment, the grandchild was entitled to registration. In contrast, the grandchild of Ms. McIvor, equally the descendant of a non-Indian parent and grandparent, cannot be registered. The Court found these conditions discriminatory and declared paragraphs 6(1)(a) and (c) contrary to the Charter. However, the Court went on to say that it wasn't sure about whether more remote descendants of persons affected by the old rules should receive a remedy today in light of the complexity of the issues involved. As such, the Court of Appeal chose to leave it to Parliament to develop an appropriate remedy. The decision requires the government to take legislative action to remedy the discrimination in the Indian Act. Ms. McIvor appealed the decision but the Supreme Court did not hear the case.

Source: Adapted from *Discussion Paper: Changes to the* Indian Act *affecting Indian Registration and Band Membership*, at: www.ainc-inac.gc.ca/br/ls/mci-eng.pdf.

The BC Court of Appeal has given the government until the end of January 2011 to enact changes that will meet the issues raised in the *McIvor* case.

Thus, a new paragraph will be added to the Indian Act granting entitlement to registration to any individual (1) whose mother lost Indian status upon marrying a non-Indian man; (2) whose father is a non-Indian; (3) who was born after the mother lost Indian status but before 17 April 1985, unless the individual's parents married each other prior to that date; and (4) who had a child with a non-Indian on or after 4 September 1951.

Obviously, being or becoming 'Indian' is not always entirely as clear as self-identity, lifestyle, or who your parents and grandparents are. What is clear is that the federal government does not want to open up discussions about the Indian Act or act in a fashion that would be more inclusive. Nevertheless, under the new amendment to the Indian Act, nearly 50,000 young people would be newly entitled to become 'registered Indians', with less than 10 per cent being entitled to live on a reserve (INAC, 2010). However, one can see how the gender issue in First Nations affairs continues to be problematic.

Reflecting on Bill C-31

The actions of the federal government demonstrate that it insists on using the Indian Act as the basis for a solution to all issues concerning First Nations people. The Act is the core document upon which First Nation–government relations are based and is considered by the government as the 'scripture' that must be followed. The original Bill C-31 was intended to be gender-neutral in terms of eligibility rules (Clatworthy, 2006) and thus, it was thought, would not contravene the Charter of Rights. But it was an amendment crafted by the government and its bureaucrats, not by the First Nations, and the government could have accomplished removing the sex discrimination provisions in the Indian Act in any number of ways. For example, it could have given Indian women the same status as Indian men had under the old Indian Act to confer Indian status on their children. Rather than treat Indian women the same as men, however, it chose to place Indian men in a position similar to that of women under the old Indian Act (Barsley, 1999). A second issue is why does or should the government decide who is an Indian? The federal government has no similar legal rule to determine or delimit who is or is not a member of any other population group in Canada. In the end, the government chose to implement a bill that creates new 'castes' of Indians with dramatic long-term consequences. (See Chapter 12 for the demographic implications of such a change.)

Why would an individual care whether or not she or he is an 'Indian'? First of all, individuals—and groups of individuals, i.e., First Nations—argue that they, not the government, should be able to define who they are. An external, third party should not be able to tell people who they are or are not. Aboriginal people would agree they are Canadians. They are not looking to secede from the country and take on a new national citizenship.

At the same time, though, they argue that they should be able to define themselves (and govern themselves) as sovereign nations within Canada. In the federal government's view, however, being a 'legal Indian', which does have benefits, is a status that history, treaties, legislation, and the abject failure of the assimilation project have bequeathed to the present, and this is what it is objecting to. Put crudely, 'the only good Indian is one who is no longer a legal Indian.'

Second, as noted above, being a 'legal Indian' guarantees certain benefits: freedom from taxation of income earned from on-reserve economic activities; access to non-insured health benefits; various treaty entitlements; and eligibility for post-secondary education assistance. As such, registration embodies a set of rights and entitlements. Clearly, the federal government is interested in reducing these liabilities and one way is to reduce the number of people who have access to them—by legislative redefinition or, in some instances, through the comprehensive land claims process, as has been the case, for example, with the Nisga'a.

The settlement between the federal and British Columbia governments and the Nisga'a illustrates how change is occurring with regard to First Nations' quest for self-determination. Under the Nisga'a Final Agreement, enacted in 2000, the Nisga'a have the right of self-determination and self-government, and have authority over a variety of activities, including the management of welfare services, their land (about 2,000 square kilometres in the Nass Valley of BC, which is less than 10 per cent of the original land claim), education, the environment, and legal services. Their law-making authority operates alongside (not counter to) federal and provincial laws. At the same time, the Agreement excludes the Nisga'a from being involved in other activities, e.g., immigration. This comprehensive agreement effectively removes the Nisga'a from administration under the Indian Act to what is called the Nisga'a Lisims government, which is responsible for administering the nearly half-billion-dollar cash settlement for lands surrendered. Nisga'a law prevails and they have a constitution that spells out the structure and function of this Nisga'a Lisims government (Rafoss, 2005). However, under the Agreement they still are recognized as Aboriginal people under section 35 of the Constitution Act, 1982, and the Indian Act will only be of importance in that it defines who is an Indian. While the leaderships of other groups in BC, such as the Lheidli T'enneh and Maa-Nult, have agreed 'in principle' to similar settlements, the people have chosen not to ratify agreements at this time. The Lheidli T'enneh decision is partially based on a study carried out by the Native Nations Institute for Leadership, Management and Policy, which pointed out that the community was too small, with inadequate infrastructure, and that they needed more time to develop leadership and organizational structure (Cornell et al., 2004).

Consequences of Bill C-31

The initial impact of Bill C-31 has been a dramatic increase in the number of Indians in Canada. Nevertheless, Clatworthy (2001) finds that the demographic implications of this bill will be what the Assembly of First Nations calls 'Abocide'. Clatworthy uses current data with regard to the Indian population and looks at their mortality, fertility, and out-marriage rates, and develops a model projecting the population 75 years in the future. According to this model, for the next two generations (about 40–50 years) there will be an increase in the number of legal Indians. However, after that, there will be a dramatic decrease in the number of Indians, so that by 2075 there will be substantially fewer government-defined Indians in Canada than at present. This means that many individuals who live on a reserve and pursue an Indian way of life—e.g., attending sweats, participating in various societies, taking on appropriate society names, speaking a Native language, believing in Indigenous ways of knowing, practising spirituality on a daily basis—will no longer be considered Indians under Canadian law. Families will have some children who will be Indians while their siblings will not be. Individuals living on a reserve may no longer be considered Indian while those living in urban areas can be Indians. The complexity of this issue is confounded by the fact that bands have been given the right to define who can live on the reserve and they have chosen many different criteria to make that decision.

'Indians' and 'First Nations'

For some parts of this discussion we have talked about 'Indians' while in other cases we have talked about 'First Nations people'. 'Indian', as we have seen, is a legal term and has significant political and legal implications. On the other hand, Indian people have found the term to be demeaning and misapplied. Switzer (2000) argues that the term is still employed by older Aboriginal people because they have internalized and unconsciously accepted it over time. Beaudry (2000: 18) notes this when he states that '[a]sserting our rights in how we define ourselves is a priority but please do not correct an Elder when they are referring to themselves as Indians. Most elders attended the residential school system and that is what they learned. . . . Reclaiming our identities should be focused on our generation.' Under Canadian law only people who are registered under the Indian Act are 'Indians' with special rights. At the same time, it is recognized that individuals who are not 'Indian' may have the same cultural, social, and linguistic attributes (and a similar Aboriginal identity) as those individuals who are Indian.

Retzlaff (2005) states that the terms 'Native' and 'Aboriginal' should be used as modifiers, e.g., 'consultations with Aboriginal peoples' and not 'consultations with Aboriginals'. Yet, the popular media, e.g., newspapers and magazines, generally do not capitalize terms such as 'Native' or 'Aboriginal', taking their lead perhaps from the lower-case usage in the Constitution Act, 1982, but this can be argued as reflecting a non-recognition of First Nations people as distinct peoples/nations as well as a certain ignorance and disrespect. The Assembly of First Nations (2000) has published a fact sheet that indicates its desire to control identity. The AFN notes, for example, that one should avoid the phrase 'Canada's First Nations'. Given that many First Nations have 'nation-to-nation' relationships with the Crown, the diversity needs to be expressed. A more appropriate wording, according to the AFN, would be 'First Nations in Canada' or 'First Nations citizens'. This terminology reflects that for First Nations, Canada is theirs and not the fact that Canada 'owns' First Nations.

The origin of the term 'First Nations' is Canadian and dates to the 1970s when the National Indian Brotherhood (NIB) wanted to differentiate itself from other ethnic groups in Canada. It also wanted to differentiate itself from other Aboriginal groups such as the Métis and Inuit. It argued that it had special status, like Quebec, and as such needed a term that conveyed that special status. At the same time there was agreement that the term 'Indian' had become so debased and laced with negative stereotypes that it no longer represented the Indigenous population. 'First Nations' also conveys a political edge that the NIB wanted to present in the public forums. Thus, in 1976 the National Indian Brotherhood coined the term to refer specifically to status Indians (on/off, treaty/non-treaty) and became eponymous when the NIB morphed into the Assembly of First Nations in 1982. In addition to dealing with the 'two founding nations' issue of French/English Canadian history and politics, the Assembly of First Nations realized that such a new title was a powerful symbol that not only identified a subgroup of Aboriginal people but also has political cache in dealing with legal issues as well as identity. Within a short time, it became a public identification marker that allowed them to construct their political and social identity as they saw fit. As such, its first usage was to identify those individuals who fell under the jurisdiction of the Indian Act who lived on reserves and were represented by the Assembly of First Nations.

Since this time, 'First Nations people' has come to represent those who have status with the federal government and the term has gained widespread acceptance within the general public, Indian communities, and government. However, it needs to be pointed out that the term is only social, not legal, and generally conveys linkages to status Indians. Moreover, as the pejorative term 'Indian' is being replaced by 'First Nations', increasing numbers of people in Canada with some Indigenous heritage have come to acknowledge their identification with First Nations, though not all these people are status Indians.

'Aboriginal', 'Indigenous', 'Amerindian', and 'Native' have been gradually replacing the term 'Indian' since the 1970s, and 'Indian' has all but been removed from the discourse except for specific legal or historical contexts. After the coalition of Aboriginal groups emerged from fighting the White Paper of 1969, diverse Aboriginal groups such as the Métis, Inuit, and non-status Indians supported the use of the terms 'Native' and/ or 'Aboriginal'. However, after the 1982 constitutional changes, 'Aboriginal' took on a legal meaning (Burnaby, 1999). Today, even Indian and Northern Affairs Canada often uses the term 'First Nations'. This short history reveals that the 'Indian' label was given or taken away at the unilateral discretion of governments, and thus many people in Canada have attributes associated with 'Indianness' but are not legally considered 'Indians'.

Identity

Identity is actively shaped and reshaped. It is not something solely acquired at birth, remaining fixed and static. The fluctuation in the numbers of people claiming to be First Nations people also reveals that identities are multiple, unstable, and interlocking. Identities are not constant; their salience varies with situational and political factors. For example, when First Nations people struggle for access to resources, they present their identity differently from how they do in a non-competitive situation because they have learned to use different identities in different situations (Kymlicka, 2007).

The identity of First Nations people continues to be strong, and most see themselves as Blackfoot or Mi'kmaq first and then as First Nation Canadians, which indicates they still hold elements of traditional culture that are quite different from descendants of settlers and recent immigrants. How is this possible? Some people argue the strong human attachment to an ethnic group in turn produces a high ethnic identity. Others, however, argue that today's generation uses ethnicity because it has social significance and allows people to make distinctions between 'us' and 'them' with confidence. Jung (2009) agrees that human beings identify themselves as members of ethnic groups depending on the extent to which ethnic group membership has been vested with public and social significance. In the end, whether individuals perceive their identities to be mediated by ethnicity (or some other identity such as class, sex, race) reflects structural conditions in a society. She argues that ethnicity develops political importance when it is used as a marker of selective inclusion and exclusion by the state. As such, groups that have been created through exclusion and oppression have come to shape their identity because their members have suffered in common. And if they are in a position of inferiority, they feel they have grounds for redress that emerge from their own history (Jung, 2009).

This discussion forces us to think about two important dimensions of identity: behavioural and symbolic (Proulx, 2006). In the case of behavioural identity, individuals live their ethnicity by carrying out specific activities such as residence, language, and interaction patterns. On the other hand, many individuals feel they are 'First Nations' but their circumstances do not allow them to engage in the typical behavioural components of First Nations life. These might be individuals who have been removed from the reserve for some time, live in a nearby city, have lost the language but still feel a kinship to and try in small ways to practise a First Nations way of life. They might attend sweat lodge ceremonies, participate in drumming, and support, as a member of the audience, a variety of First Nation activities such as pow-wows and rodeos. They might also engage in more mundane activities such as braiding their hair, using sweet grass in the home, and adorning their bodies with 'Native' art such as earrings and bracelets. But these are symbolic aspects of First Nations culture.

When both behaviour and symbolic components of identity are present, the individual lives in a context that allows him/her to exhibit all of the ethnic components necessary to establish his/her ethnic affiliation with a First Nation community. Generally, these are individuals who live on a reserve and engage in First Nation symbology in everyday life. The space/place provides a sense of identity where the recognition of identity is given by the community (Peroff and Wildcat, 2002). This means that space/place extends beyond material objects to the relationships that underlie those objects. However, some people who do not live on a reserve wish to exhibit their First Nation affiliation (Brady and Kaplan, 2009). While we have identified the two ends of the continuum, it is clear that there are many variations in between. Ironically, neither of these conditions follows the rules or definitions inherent to the Indian Affairs register.

Like other multi-ethnic societies, Canada shows an implicit hierarchy of ethnic groups in which the dominant group receives a disproportionate share of society's rewards because it has power, authority, and control over the means of production. In order to enforce its power and sustain its privileges, various tools such as prejudice, stereotyping, and discrimination are employed to ensure long-term sustainability of ethnic inequality (Marger, 2006). In our case, First Nations people have been placed in the lowest niche within the hierarchy through a sustained effort of coercive actions that thwart the efforts of the people to move up the hierarchy. The examples are many, ranging over a long period of time. For example, in 1928, a joint Senate–House committee was set up to hear comments from First Nations people regarding the amendments to the Indian Act that prohibited the raising of money to pursue Indian land claims. The First Nations delegation that went to Ottawa to appear before the committee had seen a copy of the Indian Act that stated Indians were prohibited from raising money to pursue Indian land claims, but they did not have a physical copy of the Act. Spearheaded by MP H.H. Stevens, the committee accused the First Nations delegation of manufacturing their claim about Indians being prohibited from raising money to pursue Indian land claims. The First Nations delegation was required by the committee to produce the document—*Papers Connected with the Indian Land Question*—from which they were quoting. All members of the committee knew that the document had been deliberately withheld from the First Nation leaders and the conscious racist attitude belied the fact that there was a copy in the room but no one would tell them or provide them with the copy. Such tactics continue to be used as a means of stigmatization and rationalization for the actions taken against First Nations people. In a recent survey First Nations people were ranked lowest as potential marriage partners, as close confidants, as neighbours, and as co-workers in the workplace (Frideres, 2009).

Conclusion

Who is or isn't an Indian/First Nations person is a complex process, and definitions have changed over time and will continue to change in the future. Phenotypical attributes of an individual no longer indicate who is an Indian. Just because you 'look' Indian does not mean that you are or will be defined as one. Similarly, one can't make a judgement on the basis of lifestyle. Speaking an Aboriginal language and living on the reserve, which used to be pretty good indicators that an individual was an Indian, no longer serve as indicators of one's ethnicity or legal status.

Over the years the Indian Act has been controversial. Some observers say it is out of date. Others argue that it should be abolished. And still others argue it should be replaced with some forms of recognition of First Nations self-government. But it is also clear that the federal government has no intention of doing away with the Act. It has become the anchor of federal policy that reflects a deep resolve to maintain control over this group of people and to exercise influence with regard to First Nations' attempts to achieve self-government and independence.

Questions for Critical Thought

1. How has the Indian Act had an impact on the identity of First Nations people over time?

2. Compare the different types of First Nations identities and assess how that will impact today's relations with non–First Nations people.

3. When you meet someone, how can you tell if he or she is a member of a First Nations community?

Suggested Readings

Francis, D. 1992. *The Imaginary Indian*. Vancouver: Arsenal Pulp Press. The author provides a content analysis of media of all sorts to show how 'Indians' have been portrayed, which reveals the genesis of stereotyping and its continuing impact on how Canadians view Aboriginal people.

Guimond, E. 2003. 'Fuzzy Definitions and Population Explosion: Changing Identities of Aboriginal Groups in Canada', in D. Newhouse and E. Peters, eds, *Not Strangers in These Parts*. Ottawa: Policy Research Initiative. The author, who works for INAC, presents a detailed discussion on the identities of different Aboriginal people, how they have changed over time, and the consequences of such changes.

Nagel, J. 1996. *American Indian Ethnic Renewal: Red Power and the Resurgence of Identity and Culture*. New York: Oxford University Press. The author discusses the process of 'ethnogenesis', i.e., the development of an ethnic group. He shows how the Red Power movement in the US gave credence to Indian identity and the powers of such social movements.

Suggested Website

First Peoples: New Directions in Indigenous Studies
www.firstpeoplesnewdirections.org
   Four American university presses provide information regarding new research on Amerindians. They discuss new books and conferences where issues of Aboriginal people are the topic. The site also covers news and popular culture, and has a blog for those wanting to contribute.

3 Indigenous Ways of Knowing

Learning Objectives

- ⊛ To understand of the philosophical underpinnings of knowledge.
- ⊛ To be able to compare the axioms/postulates for both Western and Indigenous ways of knowing.
- ⊛ To gain a basic understanding of the Indigenous paradigm for knowing and its relation to Western ways of knowing.
- ⊛ To be able to identify implications for parties trying to communicate who have different languages, assumptions, and values.
- ⊛ To learn some points of overlap between the two paradigms.

Introduction

A general definition of Indigenous knowledge, presented by Battiste (2002), is that it consists of those beliefs, assumptions, and understandings of non-Western people developed through long-term association with a specific place. Or, as noted by Alfred (2009), it is the vibrant relationship between the people, their environment, and other living things and spirits that share their land. Alfred argues that it is knowledge contingent on the social, physical, and spiritual (not religious) understandings that have contributed to Native peoples' sense of being in the world and to their survival. In the past, the term 'Indigenous knowledge' was synonymous with terms such as 'primitive', 'wild', and 'natural'. As such, the entire field of Indigenous knowledge was viewed with skepticism, and scholars and policy-makers saw no need to seek out or explore this knowledge base for the insight it might bring to understanding the social behaviour of individuals and/or groups.

Proponents of Western ways of knowing claim that science is universal and that, in contrast, Indigenous knowledge relates only to particular people and their understanding of the world (www.livingknowledge.anu.edu.au). A full understanding of 'ways of knowing' will reveal that science and Indigenous knowledge reflect two different views of the world—science focuses on the component parts whereas Indigenous knowledge looks at the world from a holistic perspective. While some simply reject its validity, others acknowledge the existence of Indigenous ways of knowing but consider this a 'second tier' of knowledge—below science. They agree that traditional Indigenous knowledge can be an 'ethno' science and can play an informative role in knowledge formation, just as ethnobotany has added to the overall knowledge of botany and medicine. Despite a willingness to accept the value of Indigenous knowledge, there is a steadfast refusal to accept the worthiness of 'raw' Indigenous knowledge (Semali and Kincheloe, 1999). From a contemporary Western view, only if the knowledge can be tested and validated through the use of the scientific method can it be considered useful and/ or important. On the other hand, Lehner (2007: 23) points out that for millions of Indigenous people, this knowledge reflects how they have come to understand themselves in relation to their social and natural environment. Moreover, this knowledge is 'intellectually evocative and useful for a variety of purposes throughout their lives'. Indeed, Indigenous scholars find it strange that they have to explain how their ways of knowing are different from science while scientists need no such justification in order to conduct their research (Wilson, 2008).

Today, First Nation communities are crafting research guidelines and protocols for those who wish to engage in research on First Nations people or communities. Rather than simply reject these guidelines and requirements, we need to examine the historic conditions that have led these communities to such action. Increasing self-determination in education as well in other areas of life has enabled these communities to develop strategies that reflect their struggle for power. Until recently, First Nation communities have not had power to define what education is or should be for their children. They have not been allowed to influence or determine the nature of Indigenous knowledge in the contemporary world. As Lomawaima (2004) points out, for the past 100 years church groups, federal and provincial bureaucrats, and state-supported post-secondary educational institutions have determined what knowledge would be available to First Nations people in such areas as curricula, pedagogical practices, teacher training, and language instruction. These external determinations are now being challenged by First Nation communities.

Epistemological Questions, or How We Know What We Know

In addressing the issue of knowledge, the question arises as to how we know things. Any knowledge base is grounded in a set of basic assumptions— fundamental premises considered to be unproven and not provable, called axioms or postulates. Our intent here is to provide a basic understanding of Indigenous ways of knowing and how these relate to Western ways of knowing (Aikenhead and Ogawa, 2007).

To address the question of 'how do we know what we know', we need to enter the field of **metaphysics**, which focuses on ideas or posited reality outside of human sensory perception. It addresses the study of what cannot be achieved through objective studies of material reality. Within the general field of metaphysics, issues of ontology, cosmology, and epistemology are included. Cosmology is the general philosophy of the universe considered as a totality of parts and phenomena subject to laws. **Ontology** deals with the philosophical theory of reality, including consideration of the universe. When we talk about ontology, we are saying 'What is your belief in the nature of reality?' Thus, if someone asks you what you believe to be real in the world, the question is asking about your ontology. If you answer that only things that can be empirically demonstrated exist, then that is your belief about the world—your ontology. If you include in your belief structure the existence of spirits, then that is a different ontological paradigm. This can never resolved through research; in fact, such beliefs are unresearchable and empirically untestable assumptions that you carry around in your head. **Epistemology**, the study of the foundations of knowledge, examines the nature of these premises and how they work. Epistemology is how you think about that reality. It is the question of how do we know that something is true? How do we come to know something? How is knowledge structured and evaluated? In Western ways of thinking, positivism is the dominant epistemological paradigm.

Metaphysical ideas are not based on direct experience with material reality and thus sometimes collide with Western ways of knowing, which are almost entirely based on material reality. We will begin by outlining the basic premises of Western ways of knowing (science) and then consider the assumptions, ontology, and epistemology embodied in Indigenous ways of knowing. 'Science', here, is the point of comparison since nearly all non–First Nations people have grown up accepting science as the model to be used in understanding the world and providing explanations of any sort.

Western Ways of Knowing

We begin by looking at the cosmology, ontology, and epistemology that are bound up in science (Western ways of knowing). The origin and evolution of science has led to the creation and acceptance of a set of rules that emerged out of the ancient beliefs of Egypt and Greece. As the ideology of science moved into Europe, it was supported by the Renaissance movement. Hatcher (2007) points out that by the sixteenth and seventeenth centuries a number of 'natural philosophers' such as Galileo, Kepler, and Newton sought to establish a knowledge system based on the authority of empirical evidence, as opposed to the previous basis of knowledge, which was religion or the monarchy. Out of this perspective emerged the belief that science could exercise power over nature. And, if humans held the key to science, they would be able to control the forces of nature. This gave partial rise to the Industrial Revolution and it provided a new role for science. However, the natural philosophers of the time (the first scientists) were unhappy to see their work used for the sole benefit of entrepreneurs and industrialists and so tried to distance their work from the applied technology by insisting that their work was for the benefit of all, removed from the economic goals of entrepreneurs. The scientists argued they were only interested in pursuing 'pure science' that was universal in time and place. By the mid-nineteenth century, the last evolutionary phase of natural philosophy developed when science became a profession (Aikenhead and Ogawa, 2007). It was a label that set them apart from the entrepreneurs, the technologists, and those who embraced religion as the way of knowing.

Science is an organization of knowledge that depends on laws that have been established through the application of the scientific method to phenomena in the world. It typically begins with an observation, followed by a prediction that is then subjected to an empirical test. If your hypothesis is supported by empirical data, then you have the beginning of a 'scientific theory' or 'truth' about the world. However, in science, there are 'postulates' (assumptions) that structure your way of knowing. For example, one postulate is that nature is orderly. This assumes that there is recognizable regularity and order in the natural and social world and that events do not just occur haphazardly. It also encompasses a postulate that if there is change, it is patterned and thus can be understood. As such, the epistemological basis of the scientific revolution created two worlds: the known and the knower (or sometimes called 'matter' and 'mind'). Humans were considered outside the space of the known, the cosmos, and could operate outside of time and space in an objective fashion. Hence, operating in an objective fashion, the knower (what we now call the scientist) sets out on a neutral mission to apply abstract reasoning and an Aristotelian logic to understand the natural environment. Semali and Kincheloe (1999) point out that such a clear separation between the mind and matter establishes a division between the internal world of sensa- tion and the objective world comprised of natural phenomena. And, building on this **Cartesian dualism**, scientists argue that the laws of physical and social systems can be uncovered objectively by scientists operating in isola- tion from human perception with no connection to the act of perceiving. Anyone who does not subscribe to this view of Cartesian dualism perceives it as destroying their unit of existence (Aikenhead and Ogawa, 2007).

Other premises or beliefs also encapsulate the process and ideology of science. Among the more salient assumptions held by those who ascribe to the science model are (1) the need for data; (2) the necessity of reduc- tionism; (3) the subservience of nature; and (4) a commitment to a realistic or 'objective' quantifying view (Aikenhead and Ogawa, 2007).

Data. One must use 'data', and only sensory data (seeing, feeling, hearing) can be employed to assess the natural environment. These data must be objective and empirically based.

Reductionism. In order to fully understand the operations of the whole, it has to be fragmented by the scientist and reduced to its minimal constituent parts, analyzed, and then pieced back together according to the laws of cause and effect. As Aikenhead and Ogawa (2007) point out, Newton extended this perspective by arguing that space and time were an absolute, regardless of context. Thus, researchers could begin to predict the future—the accuracy would depend on how well one could understand the precise detail of the natural phenomena and the sophistication of instruments of measurement. It is important to remember that the concept of time is a recent phenomenon; previously, time was a personal, subjective concept measured in some macro-cyclical sense—the seasons, the appearance of the different shapes of the moon. For example, the concept of causality can only emerge if time is perceived as flowing in a **linear** fashion so that the *independent* variable (the cause) comes in time before the *dependent* variable (the result, which is being impacted by the independent variable).

The subservience of nature. Nature is assumed to be capable of manipulation by humans. In other words, it is subservient to humans, who are in charge and, at the same time, at the apex of nature and yet beyond nature. To science, on a linear scale, humans are above all other animals, plants, and the rest of nature. This perspective reveals a dichotomy between humans and the rest of nature; not only are humans above all others, but they have the right to control. This **positivism**, which is also part of science, frees the scientist from any world view or ideology. It employs inductive or deductive logic that is applied impartially to observations and to strict empirical methodologies (Aikenhead and Ogawa, 2007). This belief also spawns the belief in quantification and realism.

Realism. Science depersonalizes people, objects, and events. Moreover, these people, objects, and events are quantified, which allows scientific observations, descriptions, and explanations to exist outside the scientist. In other words, if you can measure some thing in a quantitative manner, it exists. Alternatively, if you can't measure it, you cannot establish a truth value about the person, object, or event. In the end, science sees reality as being comprised of objective mathematical relationships.

As noted earlier, the study of knowledge is epistemology. This involves studying the defining features of knowledge, the substantive conditions of knowledge as well as the limits of knowledge. For example, what is the source of knowledge? In Western ways of knowing, it would be either rationalism or empiricism. On the basis of these sources, Western ways of knowing are then said to be 'true' and the truth has some permanence. These postulates or axioms of science are basic assumptions that have no empirical/rational basis but are accepted as fundamental truths. They allowed Western ways of knowing to move forward and become the foundations of the logic and belief system of science. Western ways of knowing are embodied in the equation: Knowledge = justified, true belief. And, it is assumed, you know that something is justified if it has been obtained through the rigours of the scientific method that includes an 'objective' stance in assessing reality. It turns out that Indigenous ways of knowing are not that different from this equation. Nevertheless, in Western ways of knowing, truth and knowledge are ends in themselves.

While we have simplified the Western approach to knowledge, the above captures the essence of how scientists claim to know what they know. This view provides the researcher with a paradigm by which he/she approaches and perceives an object, person, or event, and spells out how one would go about establishing the 'truth' regarding the object, person, or event.

Indigenous Ways of Knowing

Indigenous knowledge comprises the complex set of technologies developed and sustained by Indigenous peoples (Battiste, 2002). Battiste notes that Indigenous knowledge is generally embedded in the cumulative experiences and teachings of the people. As such, it is a dynamic system based on people's skills and is adaptable to problem-solving strategies that change over time. It is a knowledge system of its own with a unique internal consistency and postulates (Daes, 1995). Daes posits that Indigenous knowledge has its own concepts of epistemology and its own 'scientific and logical validity', but these are not parallel to the concepts and assumptions of science. Moreover, Piquemal (2004) and Battiste (2002) point out that Indigenous knowledge consists of all knowledge pertaining to a specific people and their terri-tory, and the totality of this knowledge has been transmitted from genera-tion to generation. We also will find that Indigenous knowledge is linked to land where proper ceremonies, stories, and medicines are held. Thus, the structure and diversity of Indigenous knowledge reflect the stories of creation, and the psychological connectedness of these stories to the people's cosmology plays a determining role in how individuals vision themselves in relation to each other and to objects and events. Battiste (2002) notes that for those following an Indigenous way of knowing, knowledge is not secular; it is a process derived from creation and, as such, is sacred; it is inherent in and connected to all nature, including humans. Wilson (2008) notes that knowledge itself is held in the relationships and connections formed with the environment that surrounds us.

Thus we find that Indigenous knowledge is more than the binary opposite of Western ways of knowing but something quite different. What we need to know, then, is whether or not there are a distinct ontology and epistemology for Indigenous ways of knowing and, if so, what they are. Battiste (2002) shows that Indigenous epistemology is found in history, philosophy, and ceremonies. Indigenous knowledge is embodied in the songs, ceremonies, symbols, and art of a people, and there is a belief that all persons must have a healthy sense of spirituality for mental and physical health. As a result, Indigenous knowledge is difficult to distinguish between the empirical content and the moral message. Moreover, Indigenous knowledge is less like positivism and more like critical theory or **constructivism** (Wilson, 2008), which insists on more fluidity to 'truth' about reality than positivists admit. For Indigenous thinkers, reality is constructed by our cultural and social values. In the end, there are many realities, not merely one, and these realities are specific to people and the place of those people. In short, reality is what you make it to be; when researchers and subjects come together and create a natural world common to both them, that is reality. However, knowledge in itself is not seen as the ultimate goal. The goal is the change that this knowledge will bring about, and thus research must have some goal to improve the reality of the research subjects (Wilson, 2008).

Knowledge, for Indigenous people, is not a *thing* in the world awaiting discovery, for Indigenous knowledge is shaped and guided by human actions and goals. Knowledge is what we put to use, and it can never be divorced from human action and experience (Daes, 1995). In addition, Indigenous ways of knowing reflect different levels of knowledge. Indigenous scholars argue that in Western thought scientists work on the lower levels most of the time. Burkhart (2004) argues that what constitutes data is different between Indigenous and Western thought. In Western thought, ideas, observations, and experiences are the basis of data—the Cartesian bias—where the mind and body are two separate substances. Indigenous thought posits that all experience, not just that of the scientists, must be taken into account as data. Thus, an individual must take into account the experiences of others, including stories told from generation to generation, in order to fully understand social reality.

Battiste (2002) argues that Indigenous ways of knowing also assume that meaning exists in a specific context—it is not universal. As such, it is difficult to interpret a particular idea from an unknown or different context, and not understanding that context is to engage in misinterpretation. Indigenous knowledge emerges out of one's experience, and it is this *subjective* experience that forms the basis for an *objective* explanation of the world.

In considering the differences and similarities between Western and Indigenous ways of knowing, we need to acknowledge that translating terms from an Indigenous language to English is sometimes problematic. For example, the English noun 'knowledge' does not easily translate into a verb-based Indigenous language. The best we can come up with as a translation is that 'knowledge' is similar to 'ways of living' or 'ways of being'. So, we have a problem already. In English, 'knowledge' is a noun and something that can be obtained, gained, quantified, stored, and assessed, and the known can be differentiated from the knower. This is not possible in Indigenous ways of knowing. As Aikenhead and Ogawa (2007) conclude, a translation for 'knowledge' would seem to be 'coming to know'. But 'coming to know' is different from 'knowledge', which, as a noun, establishes a person, place, or thing. On the other hand, 'coming to know' is a journey towards wisdom and a final destination. As you can see, some differences in world view arise from the language itself.

We now turn to see if we can identify the postulates, world views, metaphysics, values, and epistemologies of Indigenous ways of knowing (Indigenous ways of living in nature) and what the counterparts are in Western ways of knowing. Again, drawing from Aikenhead and Ogawa (2007), the salient components have been identified.

Monism. Indigenous ways of knowing do not have a division of mind and matter, so that everything in the universe is alive. Both animate and inanimate objects have a life spirit. The unwillingness to separate the nature of the relationship between the world of matter and the world of spirit is an important attribute in Indigenous ways of knowing. Indigenous knowledge also assumes that every individual element of the world, such as a rock or plant, has its own unique life force. These life forces are an essential element of all forms of harmony and balance—well-being—as well as an expression of interrelationships.

As Aikenhead and Ogawa (2007) note, three overarching ideologies are at the basis of Indigenous knowledge. First, each person has certain skills that allow that person to engage in personal and social interaction. Second, a vision of social change that leads to harmony or balance, rather than control of the social or natural environment, is required for each person. Third, one accepts the spiritual dimension of the environment. In this ideology, knowledge and the knower are intimately interconnected. In the end, the coupling between the knower and the known is strong. As we noted earlier, in science, spirituality was removed from the discourse in order to distance science (and scientists) from religious and royal authorities. Finally, Indigenous knowledge makes a distinction between knowledge and wisdom. Westerners seek knowledge (a commodity) while Indigenous peoples seek wisdom, which is intimately and subjectively related to human behaviour.

Holism. Daes (1995) and Battiste (2002) point out that holism in Indigenous ways of knowing is the opposite of Western reductionism. In Western knowledge we noted there is the process of fragmentation or decontextualizing of knowledge. From an Indigenous perspective, this severing of the cultural connections destroys the meaning of the behaviour or context. Traditionally, scientists have a view of the universe that restricts the capacity to think in terms of holism, although this view is changing. Nevertheless, scientists have separated science from such areas as art, religion, and philosophy, while no such separate categories exist in Indigenous ways of knowing. As a result, both scientists and Indigenous people will know the name of a song and how and when it is to be sung, but without the proper ceremony and relationships the song will not be understood or achieve its goal. Holism leads us to a discussion of relationships.

Relations. In Indigenous culture, everything is animate; everything has a spirit and knowledge (Battiste, 2002). And if all things have spirit and knowledge then they are all part of the great circle of life. Thus, all things are in relationship. The animal gives itself to the hunter: a spiritual or sacred relationship exists between the two; the shooting of the animal is not simply a sporting or economic enterprise as a result of the hunter's technology and superior knowledge. This ontological belief means that in Indigenous ways of knowing, people travel through life in a relational existence. As such, First Nations people focus on relationships that encompass knowledge, people, and all animate and inanimate objects, participating fully and responsibly in such relationships (Aikenhead and Ogawa, 2007).

Moreover, Indigenous ontology does not allow an individual to own knowledge as in Western ways of knowing because this relationship is shared and mutual. Knowledge is regarded as coming from the Creator and hence it is sacred—although it also has other components, such as physical, mental, and emotional. All human experience and all forms of knowledge contribute to the overall understanding and interpretations of the world. As Wilson (2001) points out, rather than calling something an object or an idea, the important issue is one's relationship to the idea, concept, or object. In summary, relationships are more important than reality. In Western ways of knowing, empirical evidence is the key to knowledge and is superior to any other kind of knowledge. In contrast, the primary characteristic of Indigenous ways of knowing is the focus on relationships—all things are interconnected and therefore relevant (Wilson, 2003). Stewart-Harawira (2005) argues that a central principle of Indigenous ways of knowing has to do with the interconnectedness of all existence. Moreover, this principle governs relationships between all humans and other forms of life. Finally, in Western ways of knowing, knowledge is approached through the use of intellect while for Indigenous ways of knowing, one would approach it through the senses and intuition.

Reciprocity. Reciprocity is another central tenet of the ontology of Indigenous ways of knowing. This concept recognizes the dual nature of every action and reaction. Thus, as Newhouse (2004) points out, when a person comes into a relationship with certain knowledge he or she is not only transformed by it but must assume responsibility for it. Ceremony is one way in which that relationship is carried out with respect. And the proper performance of ceremony allows the learner to gain access to knowledge holders and perhaps allows the knowledge to be transferred from one person to another.

Reciprocity recognizes that nothing occurs without a corresponding reaction. As such, individuals need to fully appreciate this conceptualiza-tion of action and ensure that they remain in 'balance'. One does not, for example, over-hunt but takes only what the hunter and community need. As the anthropologist Harvey Feit (2004: 106) notes of the James Bay Cree: 'Hunting involves a reciprocal obligation for hunters to provide the conditions in which animals can grow and survive on the earth.' Sharing with the community and treating the products of the hunt with respect and even reverence are part of this requirement of and need for reciprocity and balance. It also captures the concept of 'dynamism' (which also is an integral part of Western ways of knowing) in that Indigenous ways of knowing are always aware that changes happen as a result of new evidence, creative insights, and ongoing interactions. Indigenous knowledge is more than repetition passed from one generation to another. Knowledge holders continually make observations and test the reliability of their knowledge as well as exchange information with others (Cajete, 2000; Aikenhead and Ogawa, 2007). Everything is continually being revised as time goes on. In some respects, Indigenous knowledge is just as empirically based as science. Indigenous knowledge holders are astute observers of the natural world, and the particulars are understood in the context of the whole. In the end, to live properly, one must live in harmony and balance with nature for the sake of the community's survival.

Inner/Outer Space As Ermine (1995: 124) points out, Western knowledge is 'seeing knowledge on the physical plane objectively and thus can only find answers through the exploration of the "outer space", solely at the empirical level.' However, he notes that in First Nation epistemology the individual can only understand the reality of being and experience harmony with the environment by turning inward. Indigenous knowledge is thus based on 'inner space', which means that the universe of existence within each person is equal to the spirit of the self. In other words, our existence is based on the belief that all the elements that make up the world are connected and that the individual is interconnected to the whole—bringing about a sense of inclusiveness. Thus, spirits that exist give meaning to existence and estab-lish the starting point for Aboriginal epistemology. This is, as Aikenhead and Ogawa (2007) argue, the mysterious force that connects the totality of existence. While Western knowledge focuses only on the exterior sources for gaining knowledge, Indigenous knowledge focuses on the inner but never forgets the exterior essence of the individual. So, to gain an understanding of one's world, one must explore his/her existence subjectively and place oneself in the 'stream of consciousness'. In brief, you need to tap into your 'life force' in order to understand yourself as a being and understand your relations.

This view, however, goes even further in that other life forms, e.g., plants, animals, and non-life forms—rocks, earth, water—also have life forces that are connected to the individual. Since all elements on earth are interrelated and connected, this provides a vast scale of energy that one can tap into to understand more fully the universe through understanding oneself. As Ermine (1995: 86) indicates, 'it is a subjective experience that, for the knower, becomes knowledge in itself and that experience is knowledge.' This way of knowing is quite different from those who follow Western ways of knowing, and it reflects a gap between the two manners in which knowledge is acquired or known. This focus on inner space, the concern with understanding the inner-world cosmology and with the 'inwardness' of knowledge has been evident for many years, through the language of First Nations people, the rituals and ceremonies they carry out, as well as their dreams. The exploration of that inner space continues to be the focus of First Nations people, and their communities are based upon this culture of using the 'life force' to better understand the universe. Indigenous people see all human development linked to the natural environment—soil, water, rock, plants, animals, landforms—and thus Indigenous ways of knowing are instilled with a sense of place. And, because Indigenous people's identities are imbued with a sense of place, place becomes a part of their 'inner space' (Ermine, 1995).

Rituals and ceremonies, such as sweat lodges, sun dances, pipe ceremonies, and healing circles, demonstrate that First Nations people continue to seek their inward journeys. Of course, these ceremonies are corporeal sacred acts that allow the individuals to continue their spiritual exploration and to continue to understand their inner space. First Nations communities engage in these ceremonies and thereby enjoy the collective energy of the community to explore their 'inner–worldness'. For those who continue the practice, these ceremonies serve as pathways into the inner world (Ross, 2008).

Science versus Indigenous Ways of Living in Nature

In Western ways of thinking, there is a belief that knowledge is something to be gained and thus can be owned by either an individual or corporation. In addition, in Western ways of knowing science is separated from art and religion. From an Indigenous perspective, on the other hand, knowledge is relational and is shared with all—with animals, plants, mother earth, even the cosmos (Wilson, 2008). Moreover, in Indigenous knowledge, these areas of knowledge are integrated. As such, the method for constructing knowledge is different because of the different epistemological foundations of Indigenous ways of knowing. Measuring things is not paramount, as it is in Western ways of knowing, but the key to understanding is found in the relations that exist between things, and this does not mean simply cause-and-effect relations. The key is trying to understand the influences upon the system as a whole. Thus, as Newhouse (2004) explains, a First Nations

researcher lives in a world of constantly reforming multi-dimensional inter-
acting cycles where all factors are influencing other elements in the world.
In the end, Indigenous knowledge, unlike Western knowledge, is not an
attempt to control the world through understanding causal relations but
rather seeks to understand a world defined by relationships and forces.

Cajete (1997) suggests that while science has contributed an element of
insight, it has substantial limitations in the multi-dimensional, holistic, and
relational reality of Indigenous people. In addition, Timpson (2009) points
out that if one uses an Indigenous research paradigm situated in tribal knowledge, it will not be **grounded theory** or **participatory action research**.
Rather, it will be a research method congruent with tribal epistemologies
that reflects the distinctive approach of Indigenous knowledge systems to
the generation of new knowledge. This new epistemology will be a more
organic, non-institutional approach to knowledge and will involve elements
of methodology foreign to Western ways of knowing (Cajete, 1997).

As discussed earlier, Indigenous ways of knowing offer no tidy division
between objective reality and spirituality. However, in science, the inclusion
of a spiritual element into ways of knowing is eliminated immediately and
is not considered part of the paradigm of knowledge. On the other hand,
the maintenance of a balance with humans' relationship to nature is the
basic paradigm for Indigenous ways of knowing. As Cajete (2004) argues,
in Indigenous ways of knowing, the aim is not to explain an 'objectified
universe', but rather to learn about and understand responsibilities and
relationships. The role of empirical evidence is considered more legitimate
than cultural knowledge in Western ways of knowing. As Wilson (2008)
explains, from this Western perspective, Indigenous knowledge is denigrated
and not seen as extra-intellectual; rather, Indigenous knowledge, such as
it is, merely reveals the superiority of written text over oral tradition, and
this view contravenes the epistemology of Indigenous scholars. Moreover,
in science, the individual is the source and owner of knowledge, which
makes the individual or object the essential feature. In Indigenous ways of
knowing, by contrast, relationships are the essential feature. Finally, the
issue of Western linearity and Indigenous circularity differentiates between
the two ways of knowing, although these are not diametrically opposed.

At the same time, there are points of congruence between Indigenous
and Western ways of knowing. Empiricism, observation, reliability, and
experimentation are solidly embedded in both paradigms. And both have
confronted the problems of doing research. For example, Tofoya (1995) has
identified the problem of the 'principle of uncertainty' by noting that it is
impossible to know both the context and definition of an idea at the same
time. The more closely you define or explain an idea, the more it loses its
context and vice versa. In science a similar uncertainty principle (Heisenberg
principle) refers to the inability to measure speed and place at the same time.

Cosmologies and Chaos Theory

Cosmologies are the stories about 'humanness', and each culture seems to have a different cosmology. What the cosmology consists of will be rooted in culture and since Indigenous culture is rooted in place, the nature of place is embedded in their language. Language, then, allows the physical, cognitive, and emotional orientation of a people in providing generation after generation with a 'map of the world', i.e., a cosmology. Individuals carry this map in their heads and transfer it from generation to generation as well as use it on a daily basis to stay alive. These cosmologies have important impacts on the world view that people have, and our discussion has clearly noted major differences between Western and Indigenous cosmologies. Indigenous cosmologies are evident in storytelling and songs, which are predominant in their culture compared to the relative lack of storytelling and traditional songs in contemporary Western ways of knowing.

Some Indigenous scholars link chaos theory with Indigenous ways of knowing. Cajete (2000) notes that chaos is the process through which everything in the universe becomes manifest. It is an evolutionary force that describes the way nature makes new forms and structures out of the potential great void. It also represents the unpredictability and relative randomness of the creative process. However, an ordering process results from chaos, which he calls 'order for free'. Even small things in chaos theory are important and can have subtle influences ('butterfly effects') on a larger system over time. Thus, a song or ritual may have a great impact on the larger system. Someone who prays for rain or participates in a rain dance, it is believed, may have an impact on the eventual rain that occurs. Chaos theory demonstrates that everything is related and everything has an effect, and even small things have an influence. As such, a single individual's vision may transform a society (Cajete, 2004). While chaos theory may be part of Western ways of knowing, it has yet to be systematically integrated into the structure of science. But, as things change, it may well be that science will embrace chaos theory and incorporate the basic tenets into its epistemology.

Indigenous ways of knowing have five components that are linked together. First, there is a belief in unseen powers in the world. Second, there is an acceptance of the fact that all things (animate and inanimate) are linked and dependent on each other. Third, relationships between people are of primary importance. Fourth, all individuals have the responsibility to both teach and behave in a moral and ethical fashion. Finally, Indigenous knowledge is passed on by scholars of the culture, although this knowledge changes as the environment changes.

Conclusion

Every knowledge system is built on a set of axioms or postulates. These are neither true nor false and they are not subject to empirical investigation; they are simply assumed. If we were to change any of these postulates, we would quickly discover that what we know would radically change. As Aikenhead and Ogawa (2007) point out, if we change one axiom in Euclidian geometry, we create a very different system of geometry that would provide a very different view of the world.

Indigenous ways of knowing have different axioms/postulates from those of Western knowledge. Indigenous epistemology is built upon relationships rather than on the things themselves. It is more than merely a way of knowing. It is based on the concept of relational accountability—being accountable to all your relations (Wilson, 2008). Thus, it should not come as a surprise that an Indigenous world view, using different axioms, is different from that of non–First Nations people. Anderson (2009) points this out when he examines the intent of the 'treaty annuity' as part of the treaties. He shows that both parties agreed that the annuity payments were to be an integral part of the overall treaty objective of providing livelihood assistance for First Nations and their descendants. However, governments perceived the annuity and other treaty livelihood assistance to be temporary means of support, while First Nations perceived the annuity payment as renewal of a nation-to-nation agreement whereby the terms of the relationship could be reviewed and readjusted as circumstances might warrant.

At the same time, practitioners in each culture have first-hand experience that their way of knowing has served them well and has provided the necessary answers to the questions they have about life. Indigenous people have been using their 'way of knowing' for more than 10,000 years and it has served them well, while science as we understand it today has been around for barely 500 years. Also, of course, the two systems in many instances, because of their different starting points, ask different questions.

An understanding of what Indigenous knowledge is all about is important for several reasons. First, by introducing the concept of Indigenous knowledge, people will begin to have an increased awareness and better understanding of First Nations culture. Second, Indigenous knowledge has provided Western ways of knowing with important insights into the workings of the world in a number of areas, such as medicine (Cajete, 2000) and relational or 'talking' therapies. McKinley (2007) argues that understanding Indigenous knowledge will result in healing and rebuilding sovereignty within First Nations cultures. Finally, an appreciation of Indigenous knowledge gives us a better understanding of the cultural influences on school achievement by students whose cultures and languages differ from our Eurocentric culture.

We end by noting that we should never lose sight of the fact that the reason for exploring ideas is to expand our understanding of the diversity of human thought and not to expand our own specific ways of thinking so that they encompass all others (Cordova, 2004). Moreover, we need to understand that knowledge of any sort originates in a people's culture, the roots of which rest in their cosmology. The cosmology is the contextual foundation for a philosophy, a grand theory of sorts that, by nature, is speculative. A cosmology seeks to explain the story of the universe, its origins, attributes, and essential nature. It also sets forth the paradigm of thinking that will guide how people search for and accept data as knowledge.

Questions for Critical Thought

1. What are the central differences between a First Nations and Western paradigm?
2. What are the consequences of different groups having different paradigms?
3. Can the paradigms of First Nations people be integrated with the paradigm held by scientists?
4. Does the existence of different paradigms of knowing mean that all knowledge is relative and one is not better than the other?

Suggested Readings

Aikenhead, G., and M. Ogawa. 2007. 'Indigenous Knowledge and Science Revisited', *Cultural Studies of Science and Education* 2: 539–620. The authors discuss three different paradigms for 'knowing', comparing and contrasting each perspective.

Battiste, M., and J. Henderson. 2000. *Protecting Indigenous Knowledge and Heritage.* Saskatoon: Purich Publishing. The authors, an educator and a law professor, address the central concepts that make up Indigenous ways of knowing.

Waters, A., ed. 2004. *American Indian Thought.* Malden, Mass.: Blackwell. The contributors to this edited volume discuss Indigenous ways of knowing from a number of different perspectives, e.g., philosophy, mathematics, education, and logic.

Suggested Websites

Hanksville
www.hanksville.org
This site provides an interesting index of Indigenous knowledge resources on the Internet. Its coverage is wide, including such diverse topics as biodiversity,

supernova petroglyphs in Chaco Canyon, Inuit astronomy, and Native American geometry.

Indigenous Knowledge Websites
www.kivu.com/wbbook/ikwebsites.html

This site presents a listing of some of the most important traditional knowledge websites to be found on the Internet. It is worldwide and covers traditional knowledge websites from various countries and organizations.

4

Aboriginal Residential Schools: Compensation, Apologies, and Truth and Reconciliation

Learning Objectives

- ⊛ To gain an understanding of what the Aboriginal residential schools were all about.
- ⊛ To learn why Canadians did not deal with the issue of child abuse in the residential schools for nearly a century.
- ⊛ To be able to critically evaluate the response of the federal government to the charges of student abuse in the residential schools.
- ⊛ To assess the impact of the federal apology and the significance of the Truth and Reconciliation Commission.
- ⊛ To understand the differences between 'corrective' litigation justice and 'restorative' justice procedures.

Introduction

The political scientist Alan Cairns (2003) describes the history between First Nations and the Canadian government as a storehouse of deception, arrogance, mistreatment, coercion, and abuses of power. Indeed, this characterizes how the government treated all minority groups in Canada in the nineteenth and early twentieth centuries. Only within the past half-century have we taken some interest in how we have treated minority groups. To be sure, the events of World War II were important sensitizers and created a climate that Canadians would use to reflect on their governments' treatment of minority ethnocultural groups. Prior to then, however, most Canadians were silent on the issue or simply focused on the 'peace, order, and good government' mentality that the federal state and the British North America Act espoused when taking over control of the territory and the people in what is now Canada. Specific conflicts and injustices involving First Nations people were recorded in the past, but they were characterized as anomalies and not seen as the general thrust of the government.

By the 1960s and 1970s, however, scholars began to investigate the mistreatment of minority groups, e.g., Japanese, Chinese, South Asians, and included a more systematic analysis of Canada's treatment of First Nations people. The Royal Commission on Bilingualism and Biculturalism of the sixties provided a reflective assessment of how immigrant and minority groups were treated in Canada. Book 4 of the Commission report focused on the cultural contributions of other ethnic groups, demonstrating that the building of Canada was not just the result of the French and English. It was a period of time when Canadians would be forced to review the treatment of minority groups. When the two-volume Hawthorn Report appeared in 1966–7, some Canadians recognized that there was indeed something wrong with how we treated First Nations. Although not a word about residential schools or abuse appeared in this report, a new ethos began to emerge in Canada with regard to how minority groups were treated.

As the twentieth century unfolded and came to a close, the initial response to the charges that governments had inflicted harm on First Nations people varied from justifying why such actions was necessary to rejecting the charges. How, then, has it come about that the Prime Minister of Canada, in 2008, issued a formal government apology to Aboriginal people in Canada? Our focus in this chapter will be on the Indian residential schools and the manner in which the government dealt with this issue.

A History of Residential Schools

At the end of the nineteenth century, the federal government, in its attempt to assimilate First Nations people and to implement its **assimilation** policy in the most cost-efficient fashion, found an ally in its efforts through the Roman Catholic Church. This was not a new alliance: the first missionary-operated schools in New France had been established in the 1620s, and other missionary schools were in operation in the early 1800s. However, in the late nineteenth and early twentieth centuries, formal partnerships were established with the Catholic Church and with the Anglican, Methodist, Presbyterian, and (after church union in 1925) United churches to build a nationwide system of **residential schools** for First Nations children. The federal government was responsible for funding and setting general policy for the school system, while the churches oversaw the day-to-day operations of the institutions (Llewellyn, 2002). By 1874 the Canadian government, under Prime Minister Alexander Mackenzie, began removing First Nations children from their families and communities and placing them in Indian residential schools in an attempt to assimilate them into Canadian society. The federal government argued that since it had responsibility for educating and caring for First Nations people, these people would need to learn English and adopt Christianity and white settler customs. In addition, it was assumed that this new lifestyle would be passed on to the next generation so that, within a generation or two, First Nation cultures would be dead. Initially, about 1,000 students attended 69 schools across the country.

Settlers also demanded that the government deal with the so called 'Indian problem' and thus their interests merged with those of the government. Since the First Nations people had been defined as wards of the government at the time of Confederation and became a financial burden on federal coffers, it was in the government's best interest to pursue their quick assimilation. The solution of residential schools would not only address the settlers concerns but also relieve the government of costs once these people no longer were 'Indian'. The Annual Report of Indian Affairs (1885) notes:

> If it were possible to gather in all the Indian children and retain them for a certain period, there would be produced a generation of English-speaking Indians, accustomed to the ways of civilized life, which might then be the dominant body among themselves, capable of holding its own with its white neighbours, and thus would be brought about rapidly decreasing expenditure until the same should forever cease, and the Indian problem would have been solved. (Quoted in Llewellyn, 2002: 5)

By 1920 the deputy superintendent-general of Indian Affairs made residential school attendance compulsory for all children aged 7–15, and by 1931 over 80 residential schools operated across the country (only New Brunswick and PEI had no residential schools). The authorities took the position that speaking an Aboriginal language in the school was forbidden and all Aboriginal cultural practices were to be suppressed, e.g., long hair for boys would be cut. It is estimated that about 150,000 Aboriginal children were removed from their homes and communities and forced to attend the schools over a century. However, it would not be until 1958 that a recommendation for the abolition of residential schools was submitted to the federal government. Even more surprising, not until 2010 did the federal government actually expunge residential schools from the Indian Act. Rather than closing the schools, the federal government ended its formal partnership with the religious organizations and began transferring control to the First Nation bands in 1970. The last residential school closed its doors in Saskatchewan in 1996. Today an estimated 85,000 former Aboriginal students of residential schools are still alive. Many of these schools still stand and have been transformed into other educational institutions, e.g., colleges.

It is difficult to generalize about a tragic history that spanned Canada's vast geography for more than 100 years, from before the introduction of the automobile until after the introduction of personal computers and the Internet. Some residential schools, to be sure, were better or, rather, not nearly as bad as others. But the essential fact remains: generations of Aboriginal children were robbed of their cultural and spiritual birthright, and many were abused.

Throughout their residential schooling years, First Nation students lived in substandard conditions and endured physical and emotional abuse (Furniss, 2000). Life in a residential school was without family and without vocational training, and students were subjected to total control by school authorities. A kind of military authority was forced onto the behaviour of children and they were subjected to physical, psychological, and sexual abuse—directly and indirectly—if they deviated from the norms established in the school that reflected the dominant culture. Food was scarce, limited in variety, and of low quality. Housing attached to the schools resulted in crowded conditions and students were limited in their physical activities. All students were subjected to strict dress and deportment codes such as requiring them to cut their hair and to stop using their mother tongue. And contact with family and community was cut off with the exception of one or two months in the summer when the student was sent home.

As Haig-Brown (1988) points out, when the students were sent back to their home communities for a short summer break, they often no longer were fluent in their mother tongue, they were detached from the culture and traditions of the community, and they had been imbued with new values and norms that were different from those of the community. Any communication between the school and the family was always in English, ignoring the fact that many of the parents did not speak or understand English. Finally, the students were segregated by sex, and only surreptitiously could the boys and girls interact. The end result was that subsequent family life and interactions with the opposite sex were awkward, and this would indeed come back to haunt them as the trauma spread over generations. Today we find that these adults are ill-prepared to deal with others, limited in their ability to parent, and incapable of coping with stress. As a result, violence—physical, sexual—in First Nation communities is endemic and extensive. Parents are unable to exhibit 'parenting' strategies to help their children develop healthy psycho-social identities and resilience in dealing with stressors. In short, the ability of residential school students to re-enter their First Nation communities was minimal since they had lost their language and culture. Moreover, since the training they received in school aimed to create a compliant manual labour class at the bottom of the occupational hierarchy—farm labourers, domestic servants—the 'skills' they learned did not prepare them to function successfully in urban centres even though they spoke English/French. For most, the possibility of upward socio-economic mobility did not exist, and the **colour bar** prevented them from entering the world of the 'whites'.

These 'total' institutions—like prisons, mental hospitals, and the military—imposed conditions of disconnection, degradation, and powerlessness on the students and prevented any outside influences from moderating the schools' influence (Dyck, 1997). Like prisons, residential schools permitted and sometimes even encouraged abuse in order to bring about a transformation of the children's behaviour and identity. Physical, spiritual and psychological abuse was rampant in the schools as a planned strategy to resocialize First Nations children into becoming 'civilized children'. Sexual abuse, too, was all too common in some schools. The harsh and arbitrary punishments meted out each day were a constant reminder to the children that their Indian culture was unacceptable. Those who did not personally suffer sexual or physical abuse were subjected to spiritual and psychological abuse. All were removed from their families, their communities, and their culture, language, and spirituality were substantially dismantled.

Reports of child abuse within these institutions emerged early on, but since the reports were by First Nations people they were largely ignored and rejected by government officials and the media. Little evidence suggests that anyone accused of child abuse at a residential school was reprimanded or released. At best, if the abuse was egregious, the person would be moved to another school. Thus, for over three-quarters of a century the abuse that took place in these schools was ignored and a veil of silence was maintained by both church and government officials (Furniss, 2000; Haig-Brown, 1998). However, in 1989 the Mount Cashel Orphanage scandal in St John's, Newfoundland, gained wide media attention across the country and prominent First Nation officials made public that they had been subjected to physical, psychological, and sexual abuse while attending the residential schools. This was the first crack in the wall of silence that soon opened the floodgates of claims of abuse.

Denial is a process by which people shut out or cover up certain forms of information. Over the years, Canadians and their governments have used literal denial, arguing that something did not happen or that the assertions being made are simply not true. For example, many officials and others have argued that while there may have been some abuse, it was minor and the result of an errant individual. They also have argued that First Nations children, when they stayed at a residential school, had a better quality of life than non–First Nations children. In other cases, the argument switches to interpretive denial, which does not deny the facts but gives them a meaning different from what seems apparent to others. For example, students in the residential schools were 'disciplined', not abused, and thus the impact is softened. Also, corporal punishment in the schools is justified by suggesting that the situation required such harsh methods, and that similar disciplinary measures were used in Canada's public schools at the time. Quite apart from the dubious value of physical punishment, which is no longer generally tolerated in our society, such an argument ignores a significant cultural difference: Euro-Canadian society broadly accepted corporal punishment as a means of control; First Nation cultures did not.

Attempts to Resolve the Issue

In 1991 the **Royal Commission on Aboriginal Peoples** was created to address concerns in regard to the relationship between Aboriginal peoples and the government and to make recommendations for improving the social and economic circumstances of Canada's First Peoples. Among other things, the Royal Commission, for the first time, gave a public voice to those students who were abused during their stay in the residential schools and gave credence and legitimacy to those claimants. In its final report (1996), the Commission presented several recommendations with regard to how this issue should be dealt with.

The federal government chose not to respond to the allegations of abuse and thus residential school students began to approach both criminal and civil courts in their quest for justice. As Llewellyn (2002) notes, many victims opted to file civil actions (in addition to or in place of criminal charges) against the federal government, the churches, and, where possible, against specific individuals who committed the abuse. She points out that the nature of the charges included assault, negligence, breach of fiduciary duty, vicarious liability, cultural deprivation, and cultural genocide. In response, the federal government rejected such claims and, in one instance, petitioned successfully to have an Indian band council joined as a third-party defendant on the grounds that they bore some responsibility as a result of their role on the governing board of a residential school.

By 1998, the rapidly mounting legal claims against the federal government and the churches had become a cause of growing concern. (The actual cost for the churches by 1999 was well over $10 million.) Indian and Northern Affairs Canada and the Department of Justice were asked by the government of the day to test, in collaboration with churches and survivors, the potential for using an alternative dispute resolution mechanism to reach a settlement, which would involve more sensitive and timely resolutions for cases involving abuse in Indian residential schools. This mandate of using an alternative dispute resolution mechanism to resolve Indian claims emanating from the residential school experience was renewed in 2000. Llewellyn (2002) notes that the idea was that there should be an alternative way of resolving abuse cases outside of litigation and to find a way for residential students to have a voice in determining how their stories were told and how their compensation was determined. In the end, an alternative dispute resolution process was created by the Department of Justice for dealing with the legal liability for abuse claims arising out of the residential schools. In 2001 Prime Minister Jean Chrétien shifted the responsibility for dealing with the residential school cases from Indian and Northern Affairs and the Department of Justice to the newly created Office of Indian Residential Schools Resolution under the directorship of the Deputy Prime Minister.

At the same time, the government published *Gathering Strength: Canada's Aboriginal Action Plan* (1998), a response to the Royal Commission on Aboriginal Peoples' recommendations. This document included a formal statement of reconciliation presented by the Minister of Indian Affairs, Jane Stewart, which signalled that the government was generally supportive of Aboriginal claims and was aware of their historical grievances. At the same

time, however, in the delicate politics of appearance, because this statement came from the minister rather than from the Prime Minister, the
symbolic message was that the government did not fully support the Royal
Commission on Aboriginal Peoples recommendations and believed that the
minister's apology was sufficient (Nobles, 2008).

In an attempt to allow former students a choice in addressing their claims,
the government created the national resolution framework that was made up
of a litigation strategy, an alternative dispute resolution, and health supports
(Macleod, 2008). The Office of Residential Schools worked with former
students of the Indian residential schools, church representatives, a number
of Aboriginal organizations, and the legal system to try to develop and
implement a settlement agreement. The government document *Gathering
Strength* proposed an alternative dispute resolution process for students who
experienced physical and sexual abuse or illegal confinement at a residential
school (Llewellyn, 2002). Later, in 2003, the government moved to implement an out-of-court resolution program to compensate the other survivors
of the residential schools. At the same time, the government set limits on
what it was willing to deal with in the alternative process. For example,
it refused to consider the concept of cultural genocide or loss of culture
as negotiable issues in discussions about compensation, and argued that it
would deal only with settlements that involved sexual and physical abuse
or other illegal actions. Aboriginal leaders tentatively supported the idea
because they thought that the alternative process being proposed would
provide a more humane and expedient process for victims.

Two years later only 147 claims had been settled, while more than 2,000
had been filed and were awaiting hearing or adjudication. The government mandated up to 27 pilot projects using an alternative dispute resolution process but only 10 actually operated. Kaufman (2002) was asked to
evaluate these pilot projects and concluded that they did not create efficien-
cies, did not shorten the decision time, did not allow the survivors to have
a voice, and did not reduce the costs. As such, the pilot projects were shut
down and a new avenue for trying to resolve the claims was investigated.
By this time, more than 12,000 claims had been filed and a number of
class action suits were implemented. By 2004, under the alternative dispute
resolution process, about 3,000 decisions had been made, at a cost of $157
million. By 2007, nearly 20,000 claims had been filed, with just over 7,000
of these resolved. For those 13,000 claimants in litigation, about half were
settled before trial or by trial with a total compensation value of $127
million. In the end, the alternative dispute resolution process was not a
successful strategy. Llewellyn (2002: 13) points out that this process 'did
not challenge the assumptions underlying the current legal system nor did
it challenge the theory of justice inherent in the current legal system and
as a result, did not provide a meaningful alternative to litigation for First

Nations individuals who were forced to participate in the residential school system.'

But external events overtook the efforts of individual lawyers and First Nations people. In 2004, the Canadian Bar Association adopted a resolution calling for the government to change the existing dispute resolution process and provide a single payment to all survivors of Indian residential schools. This recommendation was based on practical concerns in that the legal system would soon be 'jammed' due to the number of legal cases being brought forward (Canadian Bar Association, 2005). This also provided the government with another strategy for dealing with the issue of residential school liabilities.

Justice and the Clash of Cultures

In 2007 the federal government once again came up with a plan to address the claims from survivors of the residential school system. Canadian civil law, it should be noted, is based on the narrow grounds of **tort law** and conceptions of issues such as harm, wrongdoing, and compensation (Llewellyn, 2002). In the tort system involving residential school claims, a claimant has to file a complaint, complete a lengthy application form, and provide intimate details of all incidents of abuse he or she was subjected to while in school. The process of filing a charge is so daunting that only a few took up the challenge, and thus the existing system was ineffective for most First Nations people who were in residential schools. Even if they did decide to proceed, they had to pay for the services of a lawyer. Second, considerable time and money are required to sustain a successful claim. A third issue is that even when the documents are filed and the court process unfolds, not all the cases will be found in favour of the complainant.

Under Canadian criminal law only physical and sexual abuse issues are allowed, and any claims with regard to cultural appropriation or loss were summarily dismissed by the courts. Hence, only those cases involving sexual assault and battery were considered by the courts as legitimate claims. Moreover, given that the average age of former residential school students today is 60, at the current rate of processing the complaints, most of the individuals would be dead before their complaints could be heard. The government accepted the recommendation by the Canadian Bar Association that the 'law of torts' was an inappropriate tool to deal with the issue of residential school cultural abuse and that some alternative process was required to deal with the backlog of cases that was quickly closing the courts. Thus, the first reason for looking for a different route to solve the issues was a pragmatic one.

Nevertheless, even though the use of litigation is a daunting experience, Llewellyn (2002) discusses several reasons why this strategy for resolving disputes was undertaken by some First Nations people. First, people rely on the courts because they are considered the core of legitimacy in Canadian society. Second, winning in court vindicates the claimant and publicly demonstrates that the individual was harmed in some way. Moreover, in the litigation system, if the plaintiff wins, he/she can be given a 'damage award' that demonstrates that the individual's rights were violated and the law provides compensation for those wrongdoings. Third, the courts, it is believed, will provide protection for the less powerful and help to rectify the power imbalance between a First Nations individual and the government (or church). Fourth, First Nations individuals consider the use of the courts because of its public nature. Court proceedings are usually public and the media are allowed to report on the details of the case. As such, there is a feeling that if the claimant went to the courts, the abuse and degradation of the individual within the residential school system would become public information—with the hope that the public would find such actions repugnant and demand that the courts provide compensation for the individual who had his/her rights diminished. The final advantage for using the courts is that they are familiar and known by First Nations people. Given that about 70 per cent of First Nations persons have been involved in a court procedure by the time they are 30, they have some understanding of what happens in court.

At the same time, First Nations people have many concerns about using the courts—after all, their incarceration rates, especially in western Canada, are far above the national average—and thus they, and their leaders, were receptive to an alternative dispute resolution mechanism. Factors such as the cost of litigation, the time it takes, and the adversarial nature of the court system are all powerful disincentives. Moreover, the current legal system has a narrow conception of 'harm' that is restricted to the harm suffered by an individual. A family or community cannot be brought into the litigation system to claim harm. Finally, the current legal system—civil and criminal—focuses on 'winners' and 'losers'; engaging in compromise is simply not part of the process.

In the end, an unholy alliance between the Canadian Bar Association and the Assembly of First Nations (AFN) agreed that a new resolution procedure had to be established—the AFN hoping that a more **restorative justice** approach would be chosen. As a result, external and internal pressures on the government resulted in a meeting with the Assembly of First Nations to develop a package of restitution for school survivors. In effect, the government gave up on the **corrective justice** model but did not, at the same time, fully embrace a restorative justice model. To have done so would have precipitated events that were ideologically unacceptable to the government.

The corrective justice system of our current litigation process creates winners and losers. When the plaintiffs and defendants enter the court, they are adversaries and the conflict between the two sides intensifies as the process unfolds. The goal of the plaintiff is to establish liability, and the winner takes all. Charges and counter-charges between the two parties are commonplace and compromise is not likely to be the end result of a court case. In the case of the residential school abuses, the current system was sorely inadequate in dealing with the issue of harm for First Nations individuals (Llewellyn, 2002). Under current criminal/civil law there is a claim by one party (in criminal law, the state; in civil law, the individual) that he/she has been harmed by wrongdoing of the other party. In short, this system addresses the claim that one person or party has interfered with the rights of the individual victim. In turn, the defendant claims that he/she did not violate the rights of the plaintiff. Corrective justice, then, takes the position that justice is served by taking from the wrongdoer (freedom, fines, damage payment) and, in the case of damage payment, returning it to the victim. The objective, insofar as possible, is simply to return things to the way they were before the wrongful act—the status quo.

The problem with this system is that it has difficulty addressing non-material harm. How do the courts compensate an individual for abuse, loss of language, loss of family life, loss of a childhood? In the civil suits, the former residential school students could obtain financial compensation, but the courts could do little to deal with the issues of non-material harm. Moreover, the churches took the position that if they were forced to pay, they would go bankrupt, which would mean that they would be worse off, materially, than the students who would gain financially; the government would have to find monies from other programs to pay the students, and the non-material components of the former students' lives would not appreciatively change. To varying degrees, they still would be without their language, their religion, their families, their communities, their lost lives. Given these issues and the factors discussed above, the decision to jettison the corrective justice system to resolve the issues emerging out of the residential schools appears to have been correct.

The government chose to resolve the issue through a very different process, but not one that could be called restorative justice. The primary focus was on the settlement of the legal dispute rather than on dealing with other underlying issues between the parties—the broader relationships between government and First Nations. As Llewellyn (2002) points out, the problem is not with settlement per se but rather with settlement as the central goal in dispute resolution. Indeed, it would seem that the government was interested in settlement even at the expense of justice. It took the expedient route of offering a compensation package of $2 billion, with no questions asked, if the individual claimant met the nominal criterion—having gone to an Indian residential school.

In 2004, Prime Minister Paul Martin suggested that Canada was willing to embark on a new collaborative relationship with First Nations people. He stated that no longer would Ottawa engage in 'top-down' policy formation and discuss policy with First Nation leaders only after it was formed. He offered a 'principle of collaboration' that would be the basis of a new partnership under his leadership. Moreover, as he noted, the route chosen by the federal government to address residential school abuse had never directly involved non-Aboriginal Canadians in the process. The government, however, had worked with the churches in determining their degree or percentage of financial responsibility—the Anglican Church, in 2002, was the first to reach a settlement, for $25 million—and the churches, with the exception of the Roman Catholic Church, had made full apologies in the 1990s (Dickason with Newbigging, 2010: 246–7).

The Aboriginal peoples grudgingly accepted the government's proposal for settlement, but this was not the resolution they wanted. The abuse suffered by the students was a result of a relationship of inequality, oppression, and disrespect evidenced by the churches and the government, and this poor relationship was what Aboriginal leaders had hoped to see addressed through a process of restorative justice. These issues were raised by residential school victims during presentations to the Royal Commission on Aboriginal Peoples as well as in contributions to the Working Group on Truth and Reconciliation and in exploratory dialogues that took place in 1998–9. The settlement offered by the federal government does not deal with this. In the dialogues a number of principles were set forth by First Nation participants. They argued that whatever process was to be used, it had to be holistic and spiritual. Moreover, it had to allow for all relevant issues to be dealt with and there would be recognition of the 'connectedness and interdependence' of all things. For example, they insisted that the abuse experienced by a student could not be addressed in isolation from the context of the residential school system, the legal system, the economic system, and the relationship between First Nations people and non–First Nations people. Claimants wanted the government to concern itself with relationships, to move towards relationships of mutual concern, respect, and dignity (Llewellyn and Howse, 1998; Hughes and Mossman, 2005). Victims sought a form of restorative justice and the issue of compensation was only of secondary interest. The government rejected these principles and chose a strategy that would allow it to sidestep these issues and focus on the settlement. The government reversed the order of importance and focused on the compensation as a one-time payment that would mean the issue is resolved—forever. There is no recognition that what is at issue is more than the settlement of individual legal claims. Any commitment to restoring relationships of equality between the two parties has been ignored and remains part of the legacy of governments' relationship to First Nations people—they are not equal to non-Aboriginal people in the eyes of government.

First Nations people were looking for a restorative means of addressing a history of abuse that went far beyond the specific residential schools issue or settling an individual claim. What they wanted was similar to what was proposed by the Royal Commission on Aboriginal Peoples, the Assembly of First Nations, and the Law Commission of Canada—a process of restorative justice (Younging et al., 2009). Restorative justice is founded on the idea of restoring social relationships of equality. Moreover, as Llewellyn (2002) notes, in restoring relationships all parties must be concerned with both the harm and its relevant contexts and causes. If the relationships among the parties are to be restored, you need to expand your assessment beyond the single dispute at issue. The underlying conflict has to be addressed and resolved. The aim of restorative justice is thus an ideal of social equality. As such, restorative justice deals with restoring the relationship between the wrongdoer and the victim while accounting for each person's rights to equal dignity, concern, and respect. The justice objective is not to restore the relationship to what it was before the wrongdoing but to restore it to an ideal of social equality (Ross, 1996).

For the federal government to have taken a restorative strategy would have required the admission of a position of inequality that allowed the abuse at the residential schools, and then the thorny issue of establishing a relationship of equality between First Nations people and non–First Nations people would need to be tackled. This, of course, would entail rethinking the linkages and operations of institutional orders—tort law; the Indian Act; federal government ministries such as Indian and Northern Affairs and the Department of Justice; economic assistance programs; indeed, even Canada's penal system—to determine how they could (and must) be changed to facilitate the social equality between government and First Nations. Moreover, this would have to involve all Canadians, not merely their government. Clearly, this did not take place, and non-Aboriginal Canadians are once again uninformed bystanders, unaware of the issues and only hearing that it is costing them $2 billion to resolve this issue.

The Settlement

In 2005 the government and the Assembly of First Nations signed an agreement-in-principle in which the government offered a solution to address the legacy of the residential schools. Representatives from the government, churches, AFN, and legal counsel for former residential school students reached the agreement-in-principle for providing compensation to former residential school students. In May 2006 Parliament approved the agreement and in 2007 the $2 billion Indian Residential Schools Settlement Agreement came into force. There are many components to this settlement. First of all, it financially compensates residential school survivors. Against the advice of First Nations people, the government refused to provide compensation to families of residential school attendees who had since died. Nor would there be any compensation to families or communities. Second, individual and collective programs address the legacy of the Indian residential school system. A Truth and Reconciliation Commission and a commemoration fund were established, and an Aboriginal Healing Foundation was created. Finally, the churches, through negotiated settlements with the government, contributed $100 million in cash and services towards healing initiatives.

Under this agreement, residential school students are entitled to a single payment of money called the 'common experience payment', which compensates for the harm that resulted from the school experience. Each student who spent at least part of one year living at a school (and can document it) is eligible for a payment of $10,000 plus $3,000 for each additional year. As of mid-2008, nearly 100,000 applications for the common experience payment had been made and payments had been made to nearly 70,000 survivors. In addition, survivors could receive up to $275,000 for specific sexual and physical abuse and, if they so desired, could take their cases to the courts independent of the agreement. As part of the statement of reconciliation, the Minister of Indian Affairs created the $350 million Aboriginal Healing Fund (over five years) to help those impacted by the residential schools.

There are still unresolved issues facing survivors. For example, if the students were in schools funded directly by churches (over the years, an estimated 25,000 students attended these schools) rather than the federal government, they are not included in the settlement. These survivors are required to enter an 'independent assessment' process where they are eligible for compensation for varying degrees of abuse. It is like the alternative dispute resolution process but more fairly balanced. The compensation can be up to a maximum of $430,000. Survivors are able to choose where they want to hold the hearings, and the cases are heard in front of independent adjudicators. An established set of criteria are used by the adjudicators and there are no differences across provinces. It is a more liberal test to award compensation, and claims through this process can address what are called opportunity losses—the impact on earnings. In addition, a complex set of criteria deals with cases of physical or sexual abuse as well as persistent abuse.

The Apology

Reconciliation agreements and apologies are not new. Governments for centuries have used these political strategies for a variety of reasons. Canada made an apology and payment of money (to a foundation instead of individuals) for the internment of Japanese Canadians in World War II, and more recently apologized to the Canadian Chinese community for the early twentieth-century head tax and for exclusionary immigration policy during the first half of the last century. Churches, corporations, and other entities also have engaged in apologies of various sorts. Maple Leaf Foods issued an apology for introducing contaminated food into the grocery stores and Toyota apologized for having faulty parts in its cars. So, apologies are not unique but they are unusual. Apologies, however, are not always forthcoming. The Canadian government has refused to offer an apology to the Ukrainians or Doukhobors for alleged mistreatment dating back nearly 100 years. Similarly, Australia, like Canada, refused to issue an apology to its Aboriginal people until 2008, while Japan continues to refuse to apologize for the enslavement of Korean women for the sexual 'comfort' of troops during World War II, and modern Turkey steadfastly denies the role of Ottoman Turkey in the deaths of more than a million Armenians during World War I. As mentioned above, the Protestant churches apologized formally for their past treatment of residential school students: the Anglican Church in 1993; the Presbyterian Church in 1994; and the United Church in 1998. The Catholic Church has not, although a small Assembly of First Nations delegates met the Pope in Rome in 2009, at which time he expressed his 'sorrow' for the Church's part in the harm caused by the residential schools (Dickason with Newbigging, 2010: 247).

Both the churches and the government were extremely careful to ensure that any 'apology' they issued could not then be used to sue them in court as an admission of liability. The result, as Llewellyn (2002) suggests, was a somewhat two-faced position in that they acknowledged and apologized for their actions outside the court but denied responsibility and liability in court. In cases where abuse has been a focus of litigation, neither the churches nor the government has denied it happening. Their strategy has been to deny responsibility by claiming the other party was liable.

As noted earlier, Canada made a public statement of reconciliation towards Aboriginal people in 1998. Ten years later the Minister of Indian and Northern Affairs, Chuck Strahl, travelled across the country stating that an apology would not be part of a multi-billion dollar compensation package for former students of Aboriginal residential schools. Others in the Conservative government hinted there might be an apology but not until after the Truth and Reconciliation Commission had tabled its final report. However, Strahl was convinced that it was the morally correct thing to do and a prominent Conservative senator (who had helped broker the deal to merge the Canadian Alliance and the Progressive Conservatives) began to lobby Prime Minister Stephen Harper to offer an apology. In addition, Canada had given two other recent apologies (Chinese head tax and Maher Arar), and the Australian government had recently apologized for its treatment of Aboriginal people—apologies that were positively received by their citizens. No one wants to live in a country where atrocities are committed against a people, and if such things have happened, then a majority of people want their governments to say they (and you) are sorry for past actions (Nobles, 2008). It makes for feel-good optics and, more importantly, it's the right and decent thing to do.

On the other side of the equation, First Nations argue that serious injustices have been perpetuated by the dominant group through their past actions and policies. Broken treaties, residential schools, fiscal injustices all call for apology and compensation. International law and norms buttress domestic Indigenous mobilization, and First Nations people for many years have sought to use the international arena to support their demands for their rights—from the Six Nations Iroquois at the League of Nations in the early 1920s seeking recognition of their right to self-governance, to disenfranchised First Nations women achieving intervention from the United Nations in the early 1980s for recognition of their rights as Indian women, to the James Bay Cree joining with international environmental groups in the 1980s and 1990s to halt the expansion of the James Bay hydroelectric project. They argue that they are unique peoples with distinct values and claim that this does not justify a two-tiered approach to human rights, either collective or individual. Finally, First Nations have used morality as an appeal, noting that in Canada many reserve populations have a quality of life and socio-economic opportunities similar to those of impoverished people living in the poorest less developed countries in the world, and that government is accountable for this state of affairs. First Nations people also argue that denial and minimizing historical injustices have long neutralized the potency of their claims while undercutting any government attempts to remedy the wrongs. The official declaration of an apology acknowledges the wrongdoing and allows for meaningful change to begin.

The reconciliation was a brokered process that involved lobbying by Aboriginal groups, non-governmental organizations (NGOs), churches, welfare advocates, and professional associations, and most of this happened behind the scenes. Moreover, Canada invoked 'sovereign immunity' before issuing the apology, meaning that the admission of wrongdoing could not be used in a court of law. Finally, the government had to be clear about what it was apologizing for. Was it apologizing for loss of land, for lack of respect of First Nation cultures, or for forcing students into residential schools? (See Box 4.1 for excerpts of the formal apology.)

Of course, apologies need to be more than words. In this case, the apology is attached precisely to the historical injustices that resulted from forcing young Aboriginal children into government-supported residential schools. The apology also suggests that new political arrangements will be put in practice since the old ways of doing things produced the actions that precipitated the apology in the first place. Apologies have to involve compensation because this represents an earnest good faith and sincerity on the part of the

Box 4.1 ❖ Canada's Apology

The government now recognizes that the consequences of the Indian residential schools policy were profoundly negative and that this policy has had a lasting and damaging impact on aboriginal culture, heritage and language. . . . The legacy of Indian residential schools has contributed to social problems that continue to exist in many communities today . . . the government recognizes that the absence of an apology has been an impediment to healing and reconciliation. To the approximately 80,000 living former students and all family members and communities, the government of Canada now recognizes that it was wrong to forcibly remove children from their homes and we apologize for having done this. It will be a positive step in forging a new relationship between aboriginal peoples and other Canadians, a relationship based on the knowledge of our shared history, a respect for each other and a desire to move forward together with a renewed understanding that strong families, strong communities and vibrant cultures and traditions will contribute to a stronger Canada for all of us. . . .

Source: Indian and Northern Affairs Canada, at: www.ainc-inac.gc.ca/ai/rqpi/apo/sig-eng.pdf.

party making the apology (Nobles, 2008). A political apology such as this is an acknowledgement and moral evaluation of wrongdoing. In summary, these apologies are admissions of past injustices that can be used by the government, which now says there will be changes in the content and direction of First Nation policies, and by First Nations, who can now demand changes by noting that the government has publicly agreed that past policies and programs were wrong.

But apologies are not legally binding. Even if you apologize, there is no legal consequence if you renege on promises made in the apology. At the same time, apologies are extremely public and remain in the public consciousness for considerable time, and in the public domain 'for as long as the sun shines and water flows'. Finally, apologies do not assign collective guilt. The general idea is that apologies can achieve reconciliation—a positive change in emotional dispositions. Reconciliation means not only more harmonious societal relations but also changes in political, economic, and legal arrangements. Thus, political leaders can use apologies to change public policies. Research (Nobles, 2008; Mathews, 2005) has demonstrated that when apologies are perceived as genuine, they can reduce the risk of litigation and help resolve legal disputes once they arise. In short, they instill a bit of trust into the relationship. To a certain extent, the official Canadian apology was based on this philosophy. The relationship between First Nations people and government is burdened with distrust and an increasing spiral of litigation has emerged over the past quarter-century. In an attempt to attenuate this upward spiral, an apology was proposed. Perhaps even more important is the ideological position that political actors and parties have on group claims and their understanding of national history and its moral burden.

In the present case it was agreed that an apology to Canada's Aboriginal peoples would be issued and it was linked to some concrete action taken by the federal government. The government's views of citizenship and related constructs of national history, and especially its moral obligations, were paramount for Prime Minister Harper. From the First Nations perspective, the apology puts historical loss and restoration at the centre (Nobles, 2008).

On 11 June 2008, Prime Minister Harper issued a historic apology in Parliament to former students of residential schools and their families, with the leaders of national Aboriginal organizations and residential school survivors in attendance. The leaders of Canada's other federal political parties also offered their (in some cases more personal) apologies, and the Aboriginal leaders each responded. Box 4.1 presents several brief excerpts from the government's apology.

Opponents of apologies have argued that Canada does not have to live in a permanent condition of guilt, repentance, and shame. Moreover, how do you establish a hierarchy of 'deserving sufferers' who require an apology? For example, when will the Acadians who were expelled from the Maritimes in 1755 and 1758 get their apology? Others argue that an apology will lead the recipients to dwell on the grievances of the past. Opponents of apologies say that past bad practices, if we judge them as such today, do not obligate government to agree now with the current demands of those, such as First Nations people, who seek redress for wrongs of the past. Many times government officials reject giving an apology because they argue that today's generation has not inflicted the injustices of the past and therefore don't feel guilt or responsibility for actions taken generations ago. In other cases, people suggest that the negative side of history is just one small part of the overall history of the country, much of which is positive. Thus, to give an apology implies that nothing good was done by the dominant group and they refuse to accept that reasoning (Mathews, 2005).

Perhaps most important in the decision to offer an apology is the political worth of such action. What does public opinion tell the officials? Will an apology result in being rewarded or punished by the electorate? Polls prior to the apology showed that 75 per cent of Canadians supported the government making an apology. In the end, a public apology is both symbolic and concrete: it acknowledges the harm of past government action and implicitly or explicitly promises that the wrong will not be repeated. In this case, it establishes a new standard of behaviour towards First Nations people, but as others have pointed out, an apology is just a speech. Any positive effect depends on the acceptance of the apology by the First Nations people and the actions to be taken by the government in the future. One of the goals is to 'bear witness' to what has gone before in the hope of creating a collective memory and shared understanding that will benefit First Nations and non–First Nation people in Canada.

Truth and Reconciliation Commission

The Truth and Reconciliation Commission was established by the final agreement between the government and Aboriginal peoples. The truth-seeking dimension of the Truth and Reconciliation Commission is to establish the wrong that was done in suppressing the history, culture, and identity of First Nations people, Métis, and Inuit. Reconciliation—restoring goodwill in relations that have been disrupted—is the second component.

The Indian Residential Schools Truth and Reconciliation Commission was formed in May 2008 with the appointment of Justice Harry S. LaForme of the Ontario Court of Appeal as its head. It is charged with the tasks of helping Canadians know and understand the 'truth of our Indian residential school legacy' and to promote reconciliation. It also is to address the general deleterious effect that the residential schools had on First Nation communities. The three-member Commission was given a five-year mandate and a budget of $60 million. Unfortunately, the original Commission soon foundered: none of the members would move to Ottawa where the offices and support staff were located; and internal disagreements immediately arose among the members on a number of issues, notably regarding whether the focus should be on 'truth' or 'reconciliation'. Justice LaForme, a man of First Nation descent, resigned in October 2008; the other two members clung to their positions until early 2009 before finally stepping aside, having accomplished nothing.

A second round of candidates was considered and in June 2009 a new Commission was put in place. The current three members are the chair, Justice Murray Sinclair, who was the first Aboriginal judge appointed in Manitoba, Wilton Littlechild, an Alberta regional chief and lawyer, and Marie Wilson, a noted journalist, broadcaster, and Northwest Territories public servant. They began their job by moving the office from Ottawa to Winnipeg (so as to better represent the school survivors, who are mostly from the West), hired new staff, and held their first public event in Winnipeg in mid-2010. The Commission's stated principles (Box 4.2) are based on rebuilding and renewing Indigenous relationships and the relationship between Indigenous people and non-Indigenous Canadians, with a focus on justice, fairness, respect, and the needs of victims (Flisfeder, 2010).

According to the Canadian government, the Commission will research and examine the factors that brought about the Indian residential schools legacy. Moreover, it will be an opportunity for people to tell their stories about

Box 4.2 ❖ Five Principles of the Truth and Reconciliation Commission

1. To discover and formally acknowledge the past abuses. Canada has to accept the fact that it engaged in harmful activities and to acknowledge the suffering it imposed upon First Nations people. Canada has to take responsibility for that suffering. So, to uncover the truth is a joint process and to make public what happened, why it happened and to try and prevent it from happening again.

2. To respond to specific needs of victims. The commission has to address the needs of the victims. Collectively First Nations people have to feel that their suffering has been recognized and acknowledged. This is a kind of social justice that affirms that the victims were damaged, it was wrong and the victims were right in noting it was wrong.

3. To contribute to justice and accountability. Canadians have to accept responsibility for those who perpetrated and benefited from the violence. This then establishes a 'moral compass' for the rest of Canada and establishes the boundaries of what is acceptable and not for today and tomorrow. This can be achieved if the process of healing is public and with acknowledgement from the national/provincial political, church, industry and other leaders in Canada.

4. To outline institutional responsibility and recommend reforms. This aspect of the TRC will be to establish how the institutional orders, e.g., judiciary, political, education, have conspired and benefited from the treatment of First Nation people The TRC is to make recommendations about how the structure of Canada might be changed to ensure that this does not happen again. The TRC will need to publicly identify systemic changes that will address the unequal relationship between First Nations and non–First Nations people.

5. To promote reconciliation and reduce conflict over the past. The last role of the TRC is to bring former adversaries to a common understanding of their history and reduce the potential for future conflicts.

Source: Truth and Reconciliation Commission of Canada, 2008, at: www.trc.ca/websites/trcinstitution/index.php?p=7.

a significant part of Canadian history and thereby create a more accurate and public historical record. The Commission will create a comprehensive historical record regarding the operations of the residential schools, establish a permanent research centre, host several national events in different regions of the country, support community events, support a commemoration initiative, and, of course, report to the government with recommendations regarding the legacy of the residential schools and how reconciliation can provide a basis for a new relationship between governments and First Nations people and between the Aboriginal and non-Aboriginal populations of Canada (see www.nativejournal.ca, 'Indian Residential Apology', 2008). While the Commission will cross the country to speak with former students and Aboriginal organizations, it is not a tribunal and is separate from the claims settled by the Indian Residential Schools Settlement Agreement. Originally there was an elaborate schedule of events and a wide scope to its mandate, but since the new commissioners have been appointed it is unclear what their schedule of events will be or what the time frame of their mandate is. In any case, the Commission is intended to serve as a form of restorative justice that aims, broadly, to heal the relationship between offenders and victims.

One might argue that colonialization is now over and is past history. However, First Nations people continue to experience oppression as a legacy of European colonization. Just because an apology has been offered and survivors of the residential schools have received some money, this does not mean that the system has changed or that the relationship between First Nations people and the government has fundamentally altered. Indeed, as noted in Chapter 1, one of the first acts of the Conservative government when it took office in 2006 was to scrap the recently signed Kelowna Accord that sought to establish a new relationship between government and the First Nations. There must be recognition that First Nations people are not (and never were) like children who needed to be treated as wards of the Crown and 'civilized' and 'assimilated' by a 'superior' settler society. Because of the destruction of First Nation cultures and the legacy of abuse they have experienced, First Nations people must deal not only with anger towards their adversaries, but also with internalized colonialism, self-hatred, and ongoing abuse in their families and communities.

Flisfeder (2010) points out that while the Truth and Reconciliation Commission is an admirable idea (one drawn from the South African and Rwandan experiences), for it to be successful it has to involve more than just the First Nation communities. It has to incorporate the non-Aboriginal people and communities as well as the private sector. As he notes, reconciliation is about healing relationships and building trust, not simply 'forgive and forget', which is how many Canadians have interpreted the apology and the compensation program for residential school survivors. Flisfeder argues that reconciliation means restorative justice—a restoration of relationships—which in turn means that First Nation communities ought to be restored to the condition they would have been in if the wrongs perpetuated against them had not happened. Moreover, the extent and nature of the harm have to be examined to ensure that all of the implications of that harm are dealt with. The Commission can make the issue public, identify the harms, and make recommendations on how to mend the social relationships and bring about reconciliation between the two parties. However, it cannot enforce the recommendations, and if history is any indicator, the recommendations will not become the basis for any new, overarching legislation to help to fundamentally alter relationships. Critics who point out that rage and frustration will be the result will be correct if that is the case, and the Commission will not have brought about reconciliation.

How the Truth and Reconciliation Commission intends to bring about reconciliation between Aboriginal people and non-Aboriginal people remains unknown. At minimum, the Commission will need to engage non-Aboriginal Canadians at a deeper level in order to work towards reconciliation, but there is little evidence they plan to do so. The focus thus far is strictly on First Nation communities across the country. The result is that the average Canadian is not even aware of the Commission or its activities. So, one of the functions the Commission could play in potential reconciliation will be to teach non-Aboriginal Canadians about the extent and nature of the residential school legacy through various public and media forums. The commissioners will need to make it more understandable for non-Aboriginal people if they expect the two-way process to unfold. Moreover, reconciliation will not magically happen in the limited five-year period that the Commission is in existence. That is a project the Commission can begin, but it will need to be continued—by First Nations and non–First Nations Canadians—in myriad small ways over many years for it to succeed.

Conclusion

Why did Canadians and their leaders for so many years largely ignore or deny the abuse—personal and cultural—that was taking place within the residential schools? A constructed definition of reality by the government and the churches ensured concerned Canadians that the schools were working just fine and that the goal of assimilation was moving forward as planned. While there certainly were some problems, they were presented as minor, relative to the overall goal, and any 'Indian problem', however that might have been constructed, was not near the top of the public agenda—Canadians had wars to fight (and many First Nations men saw action in the two world wars), prospective immigrants to welcome or to turn away, a Great Depression to survive, an economy to nurture and grow, cities to build. Residential schools, and what went on within them, simply did not seem very important. Issues of abuse, cultural genocide, and spiritual death, to the extent they were even considered by public or church officials, were viewed as collateral damage that one could expect from such a massive undertaking. Since the goals were admirable and desirous, or so it seemed, Canadians did not have to be informed of the day-to-day issues. As a result, this secret was contained for nearly a century before it came to the foreground and reached the public agenda. A number of factors were instrumental: a few First Nations leaders spoke of their own experiences; a few survivors and researchers published personal accounts; the Royal Commission on Aboriginal Peoples called attention to the damage the schools had done to individuals and communities; and, not inconsequentially, a growing self-awareness and empowerment of First Nations people had begun four decades earlier in the First Nations response to the federal government's White Paper on Indian Policy.

Today, some will still argue that the abuses were not so significant, and others will claim that the schools benefited First Nations people. They point to former Assembly of First Nations National Chief Phil Fontaine, a product of the residential schools, and suggest that he was able to overcome the adversities of sexual abuse and become a role model and leader in the community. In resolving the residential school legacy, the federal government chose a practical strategy that allowed it to focus on the settlement of the claims and to sidestep the underlying issues that produced this legacy. Essentially, the Indian Residential Schools Settlement Agreement is the largest class action settlement in Canadian history. Along with an apology, the government largely considers the issue closed and resolved—without having to deal with messy issues such as social equality and restorative justice except in a piecemeal, divide-to-conquer fashion. At the same time, First Nations people feel, once again, that they have been denied justice. It remains to be seen whether the Truth and Reconciliation Commission can change this in a positive way by grabbing and holding onto the public attention—as Justice Thomas Berger did in the 1970s by taking his Mackenzie Valley Pipeline Inquiry to remote Aboriginal communities and seeing that the media were there to report the stories of the people.

Questions for Critical Thought

1. Why did the government, churches and Canadians deny the existence of abuse happening in residential schools for First Nations children?

2. Why did the government establish residential schools for First Nations children?

3. Why did the government choose to make a settlement with survivors of the residential schools rather than deal with the issue through a restorative justice process?

4. How important is it that the government of Canada issued an apology to First Nations people?

Suggested Readings

Blackstock, C. 2007. 'Residential Schools: Did They Really Close or Just Morph into Child Welfare?', *Indigenous Law Journal* 6: 71–8. The author looks at current First Nations schools as well as changing policies by government with regard to child welfare.

Flisfeder, M. 2010. 'A Bridge to Reconciliation: A Critique of the Indian Residential School Truth Commission', *International Indigenous Policy Journal* (Spring). The author presents a brief history of the residential school settlement but challenges the belief that the Truth and Reconciliation Commission will be able to meet its mandate. (The *International Indigenous Policy Journal* is an online publication. To find the article, type the journal title into the search engine of your computer.)

Furniss, E. 2000. *Victims of Benevolence*. Vancouver: Arsenal Pulp Press. The author, an anthropologist, presents a case study of what went on in one residential school.

Llewellyn, J. 2002. 'Dealing with the Legacy of Native Residential School Abuse in Canada: Litigation, ADR, and Restorative Justice', *University of Toronto Law Journal*, 52: 253–300. The author, a legal scholar, defines the limits of tort law and its application to the residential school claims.

Nobles, M. 2008. *The Politics of Official Apologies*. New York: Cambridge University Press. The author provides an extensive cross-cultural comparison of apologies given by governments over the past half-century. She discusses the questions of why, to whom, and what for.

Suggested Websites

Aboriginal Canada
www.aboriginalcanada.gc.ca
This official government Aboriginal Canada portal has information on the history and settlement of the residential school tragedy. Also provides a listing of various statistics, publications, and other information on the residential school issue.

Indian Residential School Survivors Society
www.irsss.ca
This is the site for the Indian residential school survivors. Survivors present, from their perspective, the history, settlement, and impact on their lives. Also has some interesting links to other sites.

Indian Residential Schools Truth and Reconciliation Commission
www.trc.ca/websites/trcinstitution/index.php?p=3
The website for the Truth and Reconciliation Commission includes history, short biographies of the commissioners, a listing of all the known government-funded residential schools, and information on the Commission's current and future activities.

5 Intergenerational Trauma

Learning Objectives

- To understand trauma and intergenerational trauma.
- To learn how trauma impacts people's lives and the lives of subsequent generations.
- To discover the costs of intergenerational trauma.
- To see how Canada has responded to the issue of trauma and intergenerational trauma.
- To find out how the Aboriginal Healing Foundation has dealt with trauma within a First Nations community.

Introduction

Denham (2008) defines **trauma** as an extreme, important event against a person's body or self-concept. It is an injury that does serious harm and challenges a person's self-healing ability unless measures are taken to counteract the injury. However, it is important to remember that traumatic events do not always result in psychiatric distress. As Denham points out, because people in different societies vary in how they experience, process, and remember events, distress may not be due solely to the traumatic event per se, but the response attributed to or meaning derived from the trauma experience. Moreover, there are individual differences among people as to how they process and deal with traumatic events.

Intergenerational trauma was first recognized in the mid-1960s by clinicians working with the children of Nazi Holocaust survivors. Today the evidence is clear: intergenerational transmission of trauma indeed exists. Empirical evidence from the Holocaust, the Vietnam War, rape victims, the Indian residential school experience (both in the United States and in Canada), and more recent events in Iraq and Afghanistan have shown that trauma and its after-effects are real. Early reactions of society at large to those who had suffered trauma were not sympathetic and this had a significant negative impact on their post-trauma adaptation. What is today known as post-traumatic stress disorder, a common debility experienced by those, for example, who have experienced military combat, was commonly called 'shell shock' during the wars of the twentieth century, and those who suffered from it were about as likely to be dishonourably discharged or even executed for desertion as they were to be treated medically. The response of many Canadians to trauma survivors, then and now, has been to 'let bygones be bygones' and to suggest that sufferers 'need to get a grip and get on with their life.' Or it is met with stony silence in that the stories being told by the survivors are so horrifying that they simply could not be true. In other cases, blaming the victim is the strategy to deal with the survivors—for example, 'your parents should have sent you to a public school and then you wouldn't have had to go to the Indian residential school.' In any case, no one took the stories of atrocities against First Nations people seriously until recently, and for many people who attended (or were incarcerated in) the residential schools, the shame of the abuse led them not to talk about it. Interestingly, the same silence was common among soldiers returned from the two world wars. In general, in regard to the Indian residential schools, a conspiracy of silence and denial lasted for nearly a century.

The Role of Culture

Culture makes our life predictable. We live in a social context that provides us with rules, norms, and sanctions. We understand that to not follow the rules can mean that negative sanctions will result. With the expectation of those negative sanctions, most people conform and we all can go about our lives. However, when extreme behaviour continues to exist with no societal sanctions, our cultural defence mechanisms are lost. Thus, when there is pronounced and continuous social discontinuity in the order and predictability of life, individuals may experience trauma. The subsequent cultural disintegration and the shock that it creates for individuals and communities lead to trauma that few who experience it can fully understand. As deVries (1995: 56) points out, when people experience cultural disintegration, 'a lack of trust turns into paranoia, aggression becomes the dominant response and identity confusion leads to a lack of clear self-concept.' Social capital is reduced and the community often becomes chaotic and dysfunctional. So it is not just the individual who is affected but also families and communities.

The rapid succession of traumatic events sometimes prevents an adequate period of grieving and bereavement. The establishment of Indian reserves created a loss of territory and lifestyle, but also destroyed the institutional structures that had been established in communities and bands. Loss of relationship to their traditional environment was also a severe spiritual and psychological injury. And, finally, to continue the colonization process, Canada attacked the core of their identity—language, family, and spirituality. Duran, Duran, and Yellow Horse Brave Heart (1998) have coined the term 'soul wound' to describe the historical trauma as the Aboriginal peoples of North America lost their lands, their lifeways, and their cultures.

They argue that the 'soul wound' and its effects are complex, extend over generations, and are cumulative. This trauma, they suggest, is a result of historical and cumulative cognitive/spiritual wounding that has occurred over time—over a lifespan and across generations. Soul wounding is intensified if commensurate times of mourning are not allowed. Moreover, this soul wound will impact children from birth onward. Unresolved trauma is intergenerational, so that succeeding generations also are impacted by the experiences of the previous generation who have been 'soul-wounded'.

Trauma and Intergenerational Trauma

Trauma

Neurological research has found that the persistence of traumatic events is stored in the brain differently from normal day-to-day occurrences. Memory depends on three things: the magnitude of the event, the salience of the event, and the context of the event. The stored information, though in the deep recesses of the mind for normal experiences, can be brought to the foreground unexpectedly. For example, when people are exposed to threat, their bodies react by producing stress hormones that help them deal with the situation. Having been sexually abused as a child certainly fits the criteria of magnitude, importance, and context. In the case of people who are abused, the individual is likely to feel helpless, overwhelmed, and panicky, and these intense emotions interfere with what we call memory—the ability to remember and think about an event and 'make sense' of it as part of our stored information. Traumatic memories may be pushed out of awareness but when they return, they are intense and unchanged as if the event was happening in the present (Castellano, 2006). In the end, people with post-traumatic stress disorder are unable to properly integrate memories of the trauma and, instead, are mired in the continuous reliving of the past. The past, of course, is painful, and one way to deal with this, as we know all to well, is to escape reality through drugs and alcohol.

So, what is this condition of trauma? Each of us has an identity that involves the interaction of multiple systems—the interpersonal, the biological, the ethnic, the religious, and the list goes on. Danieli (1998: 58) suggests that 'each of these dimensions dynamically coexist along a time dimension that allows you to create a continuous memory of your life from past to the present and allows you to think about the future.' Thus, you are able to see yourself as the same person today as you were yesterday. There is, she says, a kind of free-flowing access and movement within all these systems at all times. However, when you are exposed to trauma, it causes a rupture or a kind of being 'stuck' at a certain point in this complex free-flowing structure, a condition she calls 'fixity'. In short, the traumatic event (or events) that you experience causes a rupture to your identity. Moreover, the nature and intensity of this rupture will determine the extent of disorganization and disorientation, or level of 'fixity', the individual experiences. For many former students, the experience of residential schools not only ruptured self-continuity but also ruptured all existing support structures. In addition, the conspiracy of silence after the children left the residential schools continued the rupture and did not allow people to heal.

The Aboriginal Healing Foundation (2006) has demonstrated that trauma is associated with a long procession of cumulative losses such as the loss of culture, spirituality, language, traditions, family, and community as a consequence of the physical, psychological, and sexual abuse that students experienced. At the same time, numerous barriers, such as denial, lack of resources, racism, geographic isolation, healer fatigue, poverty, and unsupportive leadership, have stood in the way of healing.

World views are embedded in deeply held values and shape how the world is experienced and explained. World views incorporate our perceptions about the nature of life, how we interact with one another, and how we act with the natural world. They are shared and, therefore, cultural. However, culture is dynamic and influenced by changes in the physical and social environment, so culture changes over time. Indigenous world views can be described as holistic and cyclical, process-oriented, and firmly grounded in a particular place. Wholeness, balance, connection, harmony, and growth are foundational concepts of an Indigenous way of knowing, as are the values of sharing, respect, and spirituality. As the Canadian Institute for Health Information (2009: 168) notes, 'a holistic approach involves more than just the individual; it includes relationships with and balance with the family, community and nature.'

Intergenerational Trauma

Time, it is said, heals all, so one might imagine that there really isn't anything substantive about 'intergenerational trauma'. But there is. Yellow Horse Brave Heart (2003: 159) defines historical trauma as the 'cumulative emotional and psychological wounding across generations originating with a group trauma experience'. Yellow Horse Brave Heart and DeBruyn (1998) argue that while there is general agreement that historical trauma can be passed from one generation to the next, little empirical study has examined the 'generational trauma response'. That is, how does the next generation respond to the trauma their parents experienced? They suggest that First Nations people suffer from 'historical unresolved grief', which provides some insights into such behaviours as domestic violence, substance abuse, and suicide. Children of survivors have consciously or unconsciously internalized their parents' trauma experiences into their lives. Like their parents, the children of survivors manifest similar behaviours. Not only did the extra-familial conspiracy of silence happen, but it dovetailed with the intra-familial silence.

Intergenerational trauma is when events and maladaptive responses become embedded in shared memories of the community and are passed on to successive generations through storytelling, patterns of parenting, and memories. Even if the specific events are not fully remembered, behaviour is rooted in collective memory and this persists in community life, becoming the backdrop for interpreting and responding to current reality (Castellano et al., 2008).

While the focus of early research on intergenerational trauma was on Jewish Holocaust survivors and their children, by the 1980s new research on post-traumatic stress disorders emerged on the social, psychological, and physiological effects on survivors as well as on their family members in other contexts where people had undergone repeated traumatic experiences, such as the Vietnam War. Van Ijzendoorn et al. (2003) found a difference in psychological well-being and adaptation between second-generation Holocaust survivors and members of a comparison group. Danieli (1998) points out that the effect of significant trauma is passed to the children, even those born after the traumatic experiences of the parents. Other research by Wolfe (2002) and Dion et al. (2003) has shown that survivors with alcohol or drug dependencies or anger management problems are clearly prone to disrupt the development and life adjustment of their children and other family members. As Portney (2003: 132) notes, 'parents who are reliving their own trauma, dealing with pain by emotional numbing or detaching themselves from reality cannot help a child develop a reasonable sense of safety.' Thus, when these children encounter normal events that bring on developmental challenges, traumatized parents are unable to help the child make sense of what is happening. In the end, parents who suffer from post-traumatic stress disorder have difficulty in helping the child have a healthy sense of identity, self-reliance, and emotional balance (Castellano, 2006). Danieli (1998) also indicates that the family is a main purveyor of both conscious and unconscious values. Consequently, the family is a major institution by which a child is taught adaptive and maladaptive ways of defining and coping with society.

How have First Nations people been traumatized and what has been the impact? The impacts of European colonialism were pervasive and affected nearly every First Nations person. Were they all traumatized? No, but the impact was extensive and few escaped the impact of language loss, family and community disruption, and loss of social organizations. In the case of the residential schools, it would seem reasonable to suggest that of the 150,000 students who went to residential schools, all were exposed to some trauma although many exhibited **resiliency** and were able to deal with the experience in a positive manner. Also, by no means were all Aboriginal students repeatedly subjected to physical, sexual, or purposeful psychological abuse. Research suggests that the principal of the school set the tone for what went on in each school. However, principals—and policies—changed. A reasonable, and conservative, guess would be that half of the students in the residential schools experienced trauma of one sort or another, and if each of these abused people married and had three children, this would result in 225,000 second-generation survivors, and if these children married, there would be even more. Such figures, of course, do not account for the extra-familial impacts on communities and individuals who did not personally experience trauma, or whose parents/grandparents did not personally experience trauma. Nor does such accounting consider the more general loss of culture that all students who spent more than a few months at a residential school would have experienced, which, if not specifically traumatizing for the individual, was life-changing nonetheless. Thus, the impact on the original abused students, in fact, on all students, has a far and long reach.

Sochting (2007) shows that parents, grandparents, siblings, and other family members, as well as entire communities, suffered psychological and emotional losses with the removal of the children, something today we call complex post-traumatic stress disorder (Herman, 1992). This disorder is linked to conditions that have resulted in a series of 'blows' to the developing child in the form of abuse in a context where there is inadequate social support. Moreover, the impact of abuse has more impact if the perpetrator is a person of trust, such as a priest, teacher, or parent. Duran and Duran (1995) have shown that both individuals and communities undergo several phases of post-traumatic stress disorder over time. Only in the later stages can healing take place. Once the individuals and community realize they have been affected by the process of colonialism they can begin the process of deconstructing colonialism, first within themselves and then within the community.

This theory of historical trauma describes the consequences of multiple stressors experienced by entire communities over generations. Images of traumatic events and maladaptive responses become embedded in shared memories of the community and are passed on to each new generation through community interaction, patterns of parenting, memories, and storytelling. Even if events are not fully remembered, behavioural patterns rooted in collective memory persist in community life, becoming the backdrop for interpreting and responding to current reality (Castellano et al., 2008). The results of such chronic traumatic events (sometimes called revictimization) show up as self-destructive behaviours, impairment in establishing and regulating emotional attachments, self-perceptions of guilt, shame, inability to trust and enjoy emotional intimacy, and lost faith in existing belief systems or in the value and meaning of one's life.

The Cost of Trauma

The magnitude of the problem is far beyond what the ordinary Canadian thinks. The cost, in social and economic terms, is enormous. The impact on the actual survivors was direct and immediate. As a result, these individuals were unable to participate in the social institutions of Canada in a meaningful and productive way. Their maladaptive actions led them to alcohol and drug addictions, to withdrawal from society, and/or to severe mental problems. As for economic costs to the larger society, a recent study of homelessness in California indicates that it costs $300,000 per year to deal with each homeless person (Quigley et al., 2001). If Canada had dealt with the issues of education and assimilation of First Nations people differently at the time (or even in the past 20 years), the savings today would have been tremendous. Instead, the negative impacts on these children and later generations were allowed to continue. Canadians (including First Nations people) now are having to pay the price of inaction by government officials.

First Nation communities experience extremely high suicide, drug and alcohol addiction, and mental illness rates when compared to the general population (Sochting, 2007). Moreover, Aboriginal people account for 17 per cent of homicide victims and 23 per cent of those accused of committing a homicide. Overall, Aboriginal people are 10 times more likely to be accused of homicide than non-Aboriginal people (Statistics Canada, 2006). Historically, these notable differences were seen to be a result of the genetic makeup of the First Nation population. Later, explanations referred to the unwillingness of these people to assimilate, and more recently a cause was identified in the 'dependency' that emerged through colonialization. Today we are forced to focus on the lack of integration into the educational and economic institutional order of Canada, partially brought about by the traumatic experiences that First Nations people experienced. Others are now suggesting that the link between a childhood abuse history and subsequent sexual abuse or psychiatric problems is a key factor. The Aboriginal Healing Foundation now focuses on communal post-traumatic stress disorder or what some would call intergenerational trauma.

Consequences of Trauma

The government of Canada, in its zeal to assimilate First Nations people, engaged in a program that had positive but also many negative impacts on the students and, in years to come, their children. Providing First Nations children with an education seemed to be an admirable goal, but the truth is that deculturation and assimilation were the government's primary goal. How were the survivors to know how to relate to others? How did they know how to parent? How did they know what to do when confronted with family issues? In short, what had they learned in the residential schools? The answer for many of the children was to look at their own experience and use that as the proper response. In other cases, those who were convinced that the lessons learned in the residential schools were wrong simply didn't know how to respond. One way of dealing with the inability to make a reasoned decision is to use brain-numbing substances such as drugs and alcohol. It should not come as a surprise that many school survivors began to live their lives in such a manner. As one survivor noted at a healing session in 2008, 'I thought the appropriate way to deal with stress was to get drunk or high. When it came to disciplining my children, I thought you should just beat the shit out of them and they would learn.'

Although many former students did not experience direct personal abuse, they did experience other forms of trauma, as we have seen. Moreover, harm that occurs to children within institutions is not restricted to the victim alone. As Wolfe et al. (2002) point out, other children, who might not have experienced direct abuse, were often aware of the abuse and in a state of continuous fear that they would become the next victims. Children who witness ongoing abuse of other children are likewise harmed by such exposure and can have trauma of equal severity to that of the victims themselves (ibid.).

Confronting Trauma

Three concentric circles reflect different levels of analysis and understanding (or lack thereof) in regard to the residential schools. The largest circle represents the larger society with its institutional orders and inter-linkages; in the middle are First Nation communities; and in the centre, the smallest circle represents the individual(s). At all levels, there was a conspiracy of silence. The larger society refused to address the events that produced the trauma, and to a certain degree still has not faced the issue. The First Nation communities mirrored this silence, and while they continue to exhibit trauma there has been little discussion or attempt to deal with it. And, finally, at the individual level, at least until very recently, there has been little reflection or discussion on the events that brought about the trauma. Only when one can break through all three levels of silence can the issue be dealt with.

The Aboriginal Healing Foundation, as part of the settlement of residential school abuse, was created in 1998 with $425 million to support it in its work of funding local healing initiatives. The Foundation proposed several strategies for addressing the issue, although it noted that the amount of money and the time frame were unrealistic. The Foundation has claimed that all Canadians need to begin the healing process by acknowledging the harmful acts and admitting these were wrong. Then, there has to be some redress or compensation for those individuals who were wronged. As we have seen, the federal government provided a fund to pay each of the survivors of the school system. The next step, according to the Aboriginal Healing Foundation, is the development of strategies to create 'balance' (to use a First Nation term) in individuals, families, communities, and the nation with regard to the physical, mental, and spiritual healing that must take place. This is the restorative justice that First Nations people are looking for. And this is where the government, as noted earlier, has drawn the line. While the government was prepared to 'pay off' the residential school survivors, it is not interested in getting into discussions about social equity, the repair of relationships, trust-building with First Nations, and other exercises aimed at building social relationships. Flisfeder (2010) argues that, consequently, the Healing Foundation could not achieve the objective of reconciliation.

Figure 5.1 illustrates the framework for understanding trauma and healing related to residential school abuse that has been employed by the Aboriginal Healing Foundation. Situated below historic trauma are the program elements that support the healing process, and at the bottom are the strategies used to bring about healing. Wesley-Esquimaux and Smolewski (2004) show that the aim of therapies is to help traumatized people move from being distressed and immobilized by the past to focusing on the present and future. The general model employed by projects funded by the Aboriginal Healing Foundation employs the three pillars shown in Figure 5.1: reclaiming history, cultural interventions, and therapeutic healing (Archibald, 2006). The specific programs implemented varied considerably over the country although all used this framework. This approach is quite different from viewing health from a Western perspective, which emphasizes individualism, independence, and self-reliance. Finally, activities that address spirituality are a distinguishing feature of the holistic approach to well-being for First Nations people. This approach recognizes that the first task of recovery for the traumatized individual is to establish the survivor's safety. This takes precedence over all others, for any therapeutic work cannot succeed if safety has not been adequately secured.

The actual nature and organization of the various ceremonies to bring about healing are very different as one goes across the country (see Box 5.1 for one example). Overall, two ceremonies have been identified as being effective tools for healing: a 'Letting Go' ceremony (held at the site of a former residential school) provides the structure for acknowledging and then releasing the pain associated with traumatic memories; 'Welcoming Home' ceremonies formally welcome survivors back to the community and those who did not return are remembered.

At the most objective level, the Aboriginal Healing Foundation, which did not receive any new funding in the 2010 federal budget, funded 1,346 contracts to support various healing initiatives across the country. Those projects dealt with over 110,000 participants in healing processes and another 30,000 people were provided training to continue the work within

The Need for Healing: Historic Trauma

Intergenerational impacts of the loss or undermining of language, culture, spirituality, traditions, and belief systems; loss of family and community members through war and disease; loss of political autonomy, land, and resources; loss of children to residential schools; and widespread physical and sexual abuse of children in residential schools. At a macro level, these losses can be seen as the root cause of the dismal social, economic, and health status of Aboriginal people. At the individual and community level, the nature and extent of the losses and the resulting trauma vary greatly.

Promising Healing Practices: Necessary Elements

Aboriginal Values/Worldview
Programs reflect Aboriginal values of wholeness, balance, harmony, relationship, connection to the land and the environment, and a view of healing as a lifelong journey.

Personal and Cultural Safety
Establishing safety is a prerequisite to healing from trauma. This includes ensuring physical and emotional security and providing services in a setting that reflects participants' culture and traditions.

Capacity to Heal
Promising healing practices are guided by skilled healers, therapists, Elders, and volunteers who are non-judgemental, know their own strengths and limitations, and are well-respected in the community.

The Three Pillars of Healing

Reclaiming History
Understanding and awareness of the intergenerational impacts of the residential school system; acknowledging Aboriginal history; and understanding current conditions in a historically accurate way. This allows personal trauma to be understood within a social context and reduces self-blame, denial, guilt, and isolation; can be a catalyst for healing; and can also lead to mourning what was lost, a recognized stage in the healing process.

Cultural Interventions
Recovery of cultural pride and identity; increased understanding of history, ceremonies, language, art, philosophy, and traditions. A positive, empowering experience that provides a secure base from which to launch personal healing. Also promotes healing (culture is good medicine) and a sense of belonging that supports individuals on their healing journey. Informal social activities (feasts, pow wows, cultural events) facilitate this sense of belonging.

Therapeutic Healing
A broad range of traditional and Western therapies and combinations that address individual trauma. The overall therapeutic approach is holistic and culturally relevant. The various approaches and therapies recognize that healing from severe trauma, especially sexual abuse, can be a long-term undertaking.

Environment

The conditions that influence both the need for healing and the success of the healing process, including individual experiences, strengths, resources, motivation, and relationships within the family; community-level social, political, and economic conditions; community culture, traditions, language, history, resources, and governance; the degree of leadership support for healing and community capacity and access to skilled healers and therapists.

FIGURE 5.1 A Framework for Understanding Trauma and Healing Related to Residential School Abuse

Source: Aboriginal Healing Foundation (2006: 18).

BOX 5.1 ❀ HEALING CEREMONIES FOR SURVIVORS: BUFFALO RIVER DENE NATION, DILLON, SASKATCHEWAN

Despite a history of involvement with the Roman Catholic residential school system, the Buffalo River Dene have maintained much of their traditional hunting and gathering lifestyle. September's annual moose hunt is supplemented by year-round lake fishing, and many people catch fish to add to the winter's food supply. This traditional self-reliance has formed the foundation of Buffalo River's approach to community healing.

Twelve years ago, a decision was made to invest the band's resources into the process of healing. Community meetings were held. People were encouraged to tell their stories. This began a process of healing in the community, to which many remain committed to this day. This is the context into which the Aboriginal Healing Foundation project was introduced.

Both the healing project and some community activities play a strong interactive role in the community's healing. Two counsellors organize activities and events related to healing. Each year, hundreds of people attend the Residential School Remembrance Weekend where honour is paid to those who attended the schools. The survival of those who have returned is celebrated, as is the survival of culture and tradition. Of the two counsellors hired by the project, one speaks Cree and one speaks Dene.

A therapist works with individual clients to develop problem-solving skills for dealing with issues related to past abuses and negative relationships. The band council portfolio holder for the AHF conducts sweats and other traditional approaches to healing. Attendance at these events is continually growing. A sense of cultural identity is thus built into the sense of personal identity.

Evidence of success. Thirty-five people have been trained in suicide intervention, 25 people in Native family systems and hundreds more in addiction prevention and treatment activities. Between 40 and 50 men and women take part in the healing retreats. In addition to conducting group and family work, the therapist has seen over 100 children and adults. Ten boys are currently participating in a youth values group. The community now has a 40 per cent employment rate, as well as a lot of private business ownership. Ongoing healing is a part of life and is celebrated regularly.

Strategies contributing to success. The Buffalo River Dene Nation made a decision many years ago that it was time to begin the process of healing. The chief is supportive of the project and encourages the integration of healing procedures with the development of cultural and spiritual practices. The involvement and support of the chief has proven to be invaluable in the success of this project.

The councillor cares about the project, which is evident in his involvement on a day-to-day basis and in the ways in which he works with the community during his spare time. The project co-ordinator is involved in the development of traditional strengths within the community. He also documents the world as it once was through videotapes.

Source: Aboriginal Healing Foundation, *Final Report of the Aboriginal Healing Foundation, Vol. III: Promising Healing Practices in Aboriginal Communities*, 192.

the various communities. The prescription the Foundation took was that the community services should be 'culturally appropriate' and thus no single program was employed in all communities. The only criteria were that the programs had to address the trauma produced by the physical and sexual abuse in residential schools, be accountable to survivors and the community, be consistent with Canada's Charter of Rights and Freedoms, and otherwise support their communities in dealing with the trauma. When community proposals were submitted, the Foundation assessed whether the proposal was meeting a community need, that the proposal was feasible, that a team with the ability to carry it out was available, and whether or not the community could ensure the safety of the participants. As such, the Foundation met its quantitative objectives.

The Foundation also has alerted us to other issues that have not been discussed by government or First Nation communities. For example, a process focused on the abuse of First Nation students within residential schools by other First Nation students needs to be established. Moreover, the Foundation points out that First Nation communities need to design programs to deal with the abuse of returning children by the adults who were left behind when the children were placed in residential schools. They also need to design a process for dealing with current family violence and sexual abuse, that is, the consequences of intergenerational trauma.

The Aboriginal Healing Foundation has noted that the issue of violence currently taking place in First Nation communities is being met, in some cases, with a wall of silence. The silence is evident within families as well as within the communities. As Ross (2008) points out, while most of the abusive priests, nuns, and teachers have died or moved into obscurity, fellow students that abused school survivors are very much alive and in many instances live in the same community as the abused survivor. He explains that if people disclose abusers in the community, these accusations may well be defined as personal attacks and further exacerbate existing animosities within the inter-family politics of dysfunctional First Nation communities. These abuses, in many cases, have been kept secret for many years because no one in the community wanted to hear about them or admit to them. But, as Ross notes, keeping silent may only perpetuate the inter-family antagonisms that plague current community education, housing, and politics. If not exposed, this normalization of sexual abuse and the degree to which it is tolerated stands as perhaps the darkest secret needing to be dealt with by First Nation communities.

At a subjective level, we need to know if programs sponsored by the Aboriginal Healing Foundation were able to bring about individual or community healing. The Foundation's mandate identified five goals. First, it wanted to promote awareness and understanding of the legacy of the Indian residential schools. This was partially accomplished. By providing a social context for what was previously viewed as individual problems, the issue was placed in the public arena where it belonged. Moreover, the education about the legacy of the schools, which was central to the projects, provided a framework for addressing the survivors' needs. The funded projects did raise awareness and understanding of the legacy of residential schools for First Nation communities.

A second goal was to enhance the capacity of First Nations people to heal others. Communities receiving funding from the Foundation were able to train people in the skills to support healing within their families and communities and to effectively manage crises that will emerge in the future. Teams in the community are now better equipped to address the legacy with tools and training for victims and offenders. Moreover, these teams will now be able to train others to help in dealing with the legacy.

A third goal was to meet the needs of various communities in terms of providing programs that would address the legacy issue. Nearly all of the projects offered in First Nation communities had full enrolment, and in many cases they were over-enrolled. The result is that survivors, their families, and the communities are fully engaged in the process of healing. However, it is estimated that over 130,000 First Nations people still would like to participate in these programs. With the termination of federal funding to the Aboriginal Healing Foundation in 2010, the communities now will need to find their own financing and administrative structures to continue the programs for those not able to participate in the initial programs. A fourth, related goal was to develop strategic planning for other projects and with other agencies to focus on healing. Yet, a strategic therapeutic plan such as this depends on a long-term commitment to its support. Thus far, there is no long-term plan by the government or the communities to continue funding these programs. Overall, evaluation of the projects shows that immediate and short-term goals were achieved. What remains to be ascertained is whether the projects have developed any lasting healing for the individuals and their communities. Considerable anecdotal evidence suggests that the projects were successful, but a more systematic and long-term evaluation of the projects will need to be undertaken. Has domestic violence in those communities with Foundation programs diminished? Have suicide rates decreased? Has alcohol and drug abuse declined? These will be just some of the indicators that will need to be assessed over the long term.

Nevertheless, it would seem that the government, as is often the case, looked for a quick fix. In this instance it was a pilot project originally envisioned for five years that encompassed well over 600 communities: an expenditure of less than $300 per person for each of the five years. The assumption is that once the programs were put in place, people would go to one or two healing sessions, be healed, and then they would begin to heal others. At the end of the process, all would be healed and the government could set this issue aside and move on to other issues in other domains.

Conclusion

From the beginnings of the residential school system in late nineteenth- and early twentieth-century Canada, First Nation individuals, groups, and families fought against and sought to counteract what they rightly recognized as trauma and as an attempt at cultural annihilation. Parents protested; children ran away from the schools or, failing that, stole food and even committed arson within the schools; families pitched their tents just beyond the grounds of schools to be near their children and to facilitate visiting them (Dickason with McNab, 2009: 308–9). No one in a position of power listened, or chose to acknowledge what this policy truly meant to Canada's First Peoples. Defeat and begrudging acquiescence set in for many First Nations people. And silence shrouded the hard truths of what the schools were doing to children, families, and communities. For those who still objected, little if any resolution to problems was forthcoming.

By the 1980s, however, some historians and former residential school students had begun to publish accounts of what the schools were like and what they had done to people (e.g., Sluman and Goodwill, 1982; Barman et al., 1986; Brass, 1987; Haig-Brown, 1988; Johnston, 1988). Not all reports and all experiences were darkly negative, but a silence began to be broken. The efforts to break the wall of silence around the residential school system moved forward in 1993 when the RCMP created the Native Residential School Task Force to examine all residential schools in operation from 1890 to 1984. One year later the former Chief Justice of New Brunswick directed an investigation into student abuse at five Nova Scotia residential schools, some of which were directly funded by churches. In its 1996 *Report*, the Royal Commission on Aboriginal Peoples addressed the issue and broke the taboo against speaking about Indian residential schools, revealing the extent of the abuse suffered by First Nation children.

The research over the past three decades clearly reveals that post-traumatic stress disorder is a medical condition that impacts some people. The research on child abuse documents the multiple effects that can linger into adulthood and carry on into the next generation. Wolfe et al. (2002) conclude that children who have been repeatedly abused experience depression, anxiety, and low self-esteem and have other somatic problems. They also exhibit self-destructive behaviour. In addition, these children are at risk of being unable to control impulses or regulate their emotions, and have a lack of empathy. Adult survivors of childhood abuse, Wolfe et al. explain, become depressed and anxious, creating a cycle that can reach into the third generation.

The work of the Aboriginal Healing Foundation was extensive and affected First Nation communities across the country. Survivors, families, and communities who participated in projects funded by the Foundation discovered that a better tomorrow might be possible but that things will never be the same. Ultimately, that was the point of the Foundation. The Foundation projects in some cases acted as a catalyst for other community activities, while in other communities the projects started the process of healing.

Questions for Critical Thought

1. How have some school survivors come to view their tenure at the residential schools as positive while others were traumatized by the school experience?

2. Can the experiences of Holocaust survivors be compared to the experiences of students who attended the residential schools? Explain.

3. How can healing projects, such as those sponsored by the Aboriginal Healing Foundation, have a mediating impact on the trauma experienced by school survivors?

Suggested Readings

Danieli, Y. 1988. *Intergenerational Handbook of Multigenerational Legacies of Trauma.* New York: Plenum Press. Traces the chronology of how the medical profession began to accept the concept of 'trauma' as a legitimate illness and one that could be passed from one generation to the next.

Duran, E., B. Duran, M. Yellow Horse Brave Heart, and S. Yellow Horse-Davis. 1998. 'Healing the American Indian Soul Wound', in D. Yael, ed., *International Handbook of Multigenerational Legacies of Trauma.* Albany: State University of New York Press. The authors, who first introduced the concept of intergenerational trauma, provide a good definition of the term. They also introduce the concept of 'wounded soul' to express the impact of colonialization on First Nations people.

Yellow Horse Brave Heart, M., and L. DeBruyn. 1998. 'The American Indian Holocaust: Healing Historical Unresolved Grief', *American Indian and Alaska Native Mental Health Research: The Journal of the National Center* 8: 60–82. The authors present the argument that the colonizing impacts on First Nations have not allowed them to grieve and come to terms with the changes they have experienced.

Suggested Website

Aboriginal Healing Foundation
www.ahf.ca
 The Aboriginal Healing Foundation supported numerous research projects, community-based projects, and discussion papers on the impacts of the residential schools. All of these are available at the Foundation's official site.

6 'Hear' Today, Gone Tomorrow: Aboriginal Languages

Learning Objectives

⊛ To understand the environmental context for language and language use in the world.

⊛ To appreciate the current Aboriginal language use and viability of languages throughout the country.

⊛ To know some current strategies that enhance the role of Aboriginal languages in communities.

⊛ To understand the factors related to language use.

⊛ To project the viability of Aboriginal languages in Canada.

Introduction

Throughout the twentieth century, the disappearance of languages seemed to be accelerating. Norris (2009) notes that only about a third of Indigenous languages originally spoken in Canada have a chance of survival and less than half will be spoken in half a century. The normal interpretation is to use numbers of people speaking the language as the basis for making a projection, and on this basis some authorities have suggested that only three Aboriginal languages in Canada—Cree, Ojibway, and Inuktitut—are viable in the long term. However, others, including Norris, point out that other structural factors contribute to the retention of language. In Alberta, for example, the Blood are a small group but their language is thriving and viable because they have invested time, money, and energy in ensuring that the next generation has the language. Consequently, middle-aged Bloods are taking language training because the language is being taught in their schools to small children and the older generation is already fluent.

Turcotte (2006) points out that despite the value of speaking a second language, children tend to lose their ancestral language quickly if it is not fostered and supported by family and community. He also found that the higher the levels of education and income of the parents, the less likely they were to pass on their mother tongue. We also know that daycare centres and schools prefer that children learn one of the two official languages as quickly as possible. This results in the child coming to believe that the home/mother tongue has little or no value and is not necessary for achieving success in Canadian society. Moreover, Pacini-Ketchabaw and Armstrong de Almeida (2006) found that in their analysis of school policies and among teaching professionals, English and monolingual students are privileged over minority languages and bilinguals.

The forces of globalization increasingly threaten Indigenous languages through the standardization and homogenization of peoples and cultures (McCarty, 2005). At the same time, globalization stratifies and marginalizes minority groups (Borgoiakova et al., 2005). Today, 90 per cent of the 6,000+ languages of the world are spoken by about 10 per cent of the population (Hall and Fenelon, 2009). Thus, both Marti et al. (2005) and Wurm (2001) suggest the trend of language (both national and tribal) disappearance (sometimes referred to as **language shift**) will continue and accelerate. They argue that by the end of the twenty-first century, 90 per cent of all existing languages in the world will have disappeared (Grenoble, 2008). Even though there are some attempts to reintroduce Aboriginal languages through the mass media, e.g., the Aboriginal Peoples Television Network and Aboriginal newspapers, the argument is that this will not override the impact of ubiquitous English-language programs on the radio and television. However, some communities have introduced the First Nation language in the schools and also provide adult language courses for people who never learned the language. In these cases, language viability has increased as the number of speakers increases.

As the size of a population speaking a particular language is the primary criterion for predicting language maintenance, one can see the reasonableness of predictions regarding language loss. This concern for the retention of languages applies to First Nation languages in Canada. We will look at the implications of language loss through the structural and community factors that seem to be related to First Nation language use and retention as we look further ahead into the twenty-first century and assess the likelihood of language survival for the more than 50 Aboriginal languages in Canada (Skutnabb-Kangas, 2004; Nettle and Romaine, 2000; Krauss, 1992). Over the past century in Canada, nine Aboriginal languages have already become extinct and experts predict that many more are on the brink of disappearance (Norris and Jantzen, 2005).

Socio-demographic factors such as fertility, language transmission, age structure, migration, **exogamy**, community participation, **group vitality**, use of language in the home and at work, and other factors influence language continuity (Boermann, 2007; Slavik, 2001). Others have noted additionally that the number (percentage) of speakers in a community; official status of the language; institutional support for the language; loyalty towards the language; external economic, political, and social pressures; and the dispersion of a language community all will have profound impacts on language resiliency and continuity (Norris and Snider, 2008).

Language and Culture

What are the implications and consequences of language loss? First of all, the beliefs and culture of a people are embedded in their language and are given expression by it. Grimes (2000) argues that the key to identity and retention of culture is one's ancestral language. Language is one vehicle for a network of cultural values that operates below the level of consciousness. Thus, as Rahman (2001: 78) notes, 'language is central for the transmission of ideas, values and perceptions of reality that make up one's cosmos or world view.' Others point out that through the production of discourses groups create and express their belief system, and thereby the basis by which they judge everything (Pitawanakwat, 2009). Linguistic power used in a community can be either pragmatic or symbolic. Pragmatic power is based on the ability to communicate with others; symbolic power refers to a language that has a value (whether positive or negative) in the mind of the perceiver (Rahman, 2001).

The form and structure of First Nation languages are quite different from Euro-Canadian languages. Thus, they also shape the relationship between the mind of the speaker and the person, thing, or event being described by language (Canada, 2005). As Romero (2004: 18) points out, languages are not alienable 'products'; rather, 'they are active processes in the here and now with deep ties to a people's past.'

Linguists studying First Nation languages find that they focus on relationships as well as on understanding relationships, not on proving a point. Language is used to establish connections and negotiate relationships with the goal of living in balance. As a result, First Nation languages establish the relationship between the subject and object of a phrase differently from English or French. For example, most First Nation languages permit the speaker to focus not only on the identities of the objects but also on the relationship between them. On the other hand, English places a focus on an awareness of oneself and what that person has to say (Canada, 2005).

Little Bear (2000: 182) argues that 'language embodies the way a society thinks and through learning and speaking a language, an individual absorbs the collective thought processes of a people.' He points out that First Nation languages are, for the most part, oriented towards process and action rather than towards objects. As such, they are rich in the use of verbs and aimed at describing happenings rather than objects. You could speak in Cree for five minutes and never invoke a noun or pronoun, something that is virtually impossible in English/French. Finally, First Nation languages are relatively free of dichotomies, e.g., either/or, black or white, alive or dead. Even in translation, the following Cree story—told to small children about a spider—demonstrates the use of action and process, a lack of dichotomies, and the open-endedness of much First Nations narrative.

The spider crawled across looking for a place to spin a web. In a little while she found an opening where no webs had been built. Although she wasn't sure exactly how the web would turn out, it had to begin with the first strand. So, anchoring the first strand of the web securely to the framework of the lodge, she dropped into the empty space. Hanging, suspended in midair she wasn't sure where the wind or the other passing creatures would take her but she placed her faith in the forces of nature to take her to a spot where she should tie off her first strand. Finally, it blew her to a place where she could tie off her first strand. Then she started the whole process over again. On and on she worked, and the web took shape: sometimes through her own efforts, sometimes redirected or assisted by those around her, sometimes guided by the forces of nature. As she spun, some of the old strands were cut or broken, and she replaced them or resecured them. She never knew in advance what the final shape of her web would be. As her web developed she took time to appreciate what she had done and a pattern began to emerge. In the end, after long effort, she had spun something unique and beautiful. Her web was firm and flexible. It filled the openings that she had found.

Stories in a First Nation language, because they are quite sparse relative to those in European languages, encourage the imagination. Moreover, words carry the content of messages as well as a sense of continuity, history, and linking of the past, present, and future. First Nation languages are associated with the themes of infinity and perpetuity. Euro-Canadians tend to see these words as 'hyperbole', in part because of the analytic, objectivistic traditions of Western thought (Einhorn, 2000). The rhetoric of Western language deals with finite movements, with beginnings and ends, with causes and effects. For example, French and English are clear in differentiating between speakers and audience: speakers deliver messages; audiences receive them. Moreover, Western languages have little tolerance for ambiguity, incompleteness, and inconsistency. You are expected to present complete, consistent messages, and clarity and precision are highly valued. Language in First Nation communities is not about a discourse that assumes completion or expects an ending. The open-ended language of First Nations reflects beliefs in letting people contemplate answers; and First Nation speakers purposely avoid being directive to allow the listeners to infer the meaning and implications of what is spoken.

First Nation languages stress the existence of invisible/spiritual worlds while many Westerners, with a more pragmatic and materialistic belief system, often cut themselves off from the spiritual world, considering it suspect or unreal (Caduto and Bruchac, 1989). Western science, as we saw in Chapter 3, is not interested in 'invisible' or supernatural forces, and thus, in Western science and in Western society generally, you can't say 'the devil made me do it.' You have to have a measurable force. What can't be measured is of less value—spirits are relegated to specific domains in life and even those are suspect. In conversation, even the invocation of a spirit will make you pause. If someone starts telling you that your behaviour or his/ her behaviour is a result of spiritual forces, you likely will walk away shaking your head. This is not so true in First Nations belief systems and world views, and the languages reflect this difference.

Finally, Canada's two official languages—French and English—are representational. Words represent reality. However, in First Nation languages words are considered presentational. That is, words bring reality into being or present the being of things. Viewing words as presentational may explain why First Nations people consider language as standing for reality. Thus, words are intrinsically powerful, magical, and sacred (Einhorn, 2000). In sum, language shapes one's perceptions of the world, reaction to the environment, and responses to issues and problems. In the end, languages provide their users with a world view that is created, in part, by their language. The loss of a language brings a new world view to the holder and requires adaptive techniques to bridge the change. At the same time, as the language shift occurs, tensions will be created within the community between those who retain their ancestral language and those who do not (Kroskrity and Field, 2009).

Aboriginal Peoples and the Future

Since the mid-nineteenth century, Canadians have thought that First Nations people would disappear through assimilation, intermarriage, or disease. However, as Romaniuc (2008) points out, this prediction has not come to pass. The growth of their population in Canada has been phenomenal over the past half-century and exponential within the past decade. The total Aboriginal population has increased by 45 per cent over the past 10 years compared to an 8 per cent increase in the general Canadian population, and much of the latter has resulted from immigration (Travato, 2008). The First Nations sector of the Aboriginal population increased by 29 per cent over that 10-year period and now makes up about 800,000 people (Goldman and Delic, 2008; Taylor and Bell, 2004; Verma, 2008).

During the past century, certain indicators suggested that First Nations people were becoming more and more urbanized. Again, it was predicted that First Nation communities would be decimated by the increasing exodus from reserves into the urban centres. Data showed the increasing urbanization of First Nations and such a prediction seemed to have been confirmed. In the last three decades, however, increasing numbers of individuals have returned to their 'homelands' and fewer individuals are leaving their First Nation communities (see Table 12.3).

Similar predictions have been made about First Nation languages. Since the middle of the twentieth century, some have assumed that First Nations people would become so thoroughly assimilated through inter-marriage, education, and integration that they would have largely lost their languages by the twenty-first century, and that by the fourth generation, assimilation would be so complete that First Nation languages would make up an insignificant portion of the non-official language speakers. However, while there has been some loss of language over the years, the predictions have proven incorrect. One major reason for the preservation of languages is that Indigenous identity is critical to 'personal relationship' networks (integrative function) for maintaining community (Morita, 2007). Indigenous identity is affirmed by using the Native language. In addition, many First Nation languages are now offered as a 'credit' subject in primary, secondary, and post-secondary schools across the country. Enrolment figures reveal these classes have bloomed over the past decade.

If the language is so important, why don't the parents teach it to their children? Ali and Kilbride (2004) have found that it is difficult for parents to teach their language and culture to young children without the support of external agencies. Albanese (2009) notes that other impediments to teaching language to children include the lack of time and money to socialize with others from their own ethnic and language background. Cech (2010: 67) indicates that among First Nation communities 'silence is valued' and that 'children tend to converse with other children rather than with their elders.' While this is true, children certainly are not isolated from their parents. In fact, parents take their children everywhere and the children listen and learn. Another possible factor in language learning is that the actual speaking between First Nations adults is sparse by Western standards. In other words, we feel we have to talk; they don't. Also, the lack of cultural representation in the media and school curricula are strong impediments to language transfer and retention, although, as noted above, this is beginning to change as more First Nations take control of their own education systems and include Aboriginal language in the curriculum.

Besides these various factors that can work against language learning and retention, one of the most important reasons why parents don't teach their children their ancestral language is that they have lost the ability to speak the language. Through the strong, forced assimilation of First Nation students over the years, many First Nations people have lost their language and thus are unable to teach their children. Today, in many First Nation communities, these same middle-aged people are learning their ancestral language for the first time.

The Link between Social Structure and Language

Figure 6.1 depicts the overall linkages between structure and language as suggested in the literature. This model is dynamic and accepts that the various dimensions may change over time. That is, as fertility rates change, the number of speakers may change and the change in these variables will directly or indirectly influence the language use within a community. Furthermore, the relative impact of the specific factors may change over time. For example, in Canada, First Nation language use was forbidden for many years in schools. However, these attitudes and restrictions have been removed and have provided greater opportunities for First Nations people to learn and use a First Nation language.

The model first addresses the role of language in the community, e.g., is it **instrumental** or **integrative**? The instrumental reasons also are called 'pragmatic', 'rational', 'objective', or 'utilitarian' (Rahman, 2001) and focus on the individual's ability to obtain a better job, increase income, or further participate in society. On the other hand, the 'integrative' or 'non-rational' or 'subjective' reasons reflect personal, emotional, or hedonistic bases. These integrative aspects refer to the dimension of our needs that cannot be measured in terms of better jobs or a higher income (ibid.) and reflect the subjective, affective, and emotional aspects of language. On the other hand, it does not mean that these integrative objectives are less valuable than instrumental goals.

If the language community is marginalized and not fully participating in the larger society, then the role of the language can be both instrumental and integrative. It is instrumental in that residents will need the ancestral

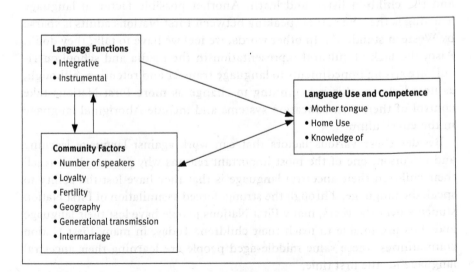

FIGURE 6.1 Structural Factors Related to Language Use and Retention

language to function within the community and to carry on interactions, community activities, and various economic transactions. At the same time, it provides them with an integrative function in their community. However, there are external pressures on First Nations people to enter mainstream economic and social activities. This puts pressure on a First Nation language to lose its integrative component (because you can use another language to function in the community in various dimensions, e.g., political, economic, social) and a language shift occurs that is solely instrumental in nature. When the language group is fully participating in the mainstream society, then the Indigenous language has already given in to the language loss and the remaining linguistic use is only its integrative function within the First Nation community.

Figure 6.1 also shows that other demographic/structural factors impinge on a linguistic community and have an impact on language use and on retention. For example, in Canada, language prohibition was universal for many years so this factor is a 'constant' within the analysis. Moreover, factors such as the official status of a language as well as the 'death/dispersion' of First Nation communities also have impacted all First Nation communities.

Language Shift, Continuity, and Fluency

Language continuity refers to the extent to which a group of people are able to continue using a language in their everyday life over time. An **index of continuity** has been the major indicator of **language viability** that scholars and politicians alike use to make predictions about how long the language will continue to be used. This index represents the ratio of the number of people who use a language at home relative to the number of people who have that language as their **mother tongue**. A ratio of 1.00 represents a complete reproduction of the language and suggests high viability for the language. Anything less than that value suggests that there is language 'loss' and that over time the language will be lost. Scholars have used an index of 0.30 as the threshold for determining the viability of a language. Table 6.1 provides a profile of some of the First Nation languages as well as the viability of these languages.

Well over a quarter of a million people now report an Aboriginal language as their mother tongue (a language first learned and still spoken). The three largest language families today are Algonquian (e.g., Ojibway, Innu-aimun, Cree), Eskimoan (e.g., Inuktitut), and Athapaskan (e.g., Dene, Dogrib). Table 6.2 shows the distribution of Aboriginal mother tongue throughout Canada. It clearly reveals substantial differences among provinces. Of those who claim an Aboriginal mother tongue, two-thirds live on reserves. Also, nearly 4 per cent of those individuals who have an Aboriginal mother tongue are not registered Indians. Today, the general language continuity rate for

TABLE 6.1 Number of Mother Tongue Speakers, Continuity Index, and Viability of Language, Selected Aboriginal Languages, Canada, 2001

Language	Mother Tongue	Continuity Index	Viability
Cree	80,075	0.62	large
Ojibway	23,520	0.45	large
Innu-aimun	9,890	0.91	small
Algonquin	1,860	0.30	uncertain
Mi'kmaq	7,650	0.65	small
Blackfoot	3,025	0.56	uncertain
Malecite	825	0.33	uncertain
Dene	9,595	0.81	large
Dogrib	1,925	0.70	small
Carrier	1,445	0.34	small
Salish	1,920	0.21	endangered
Gitksan	1,000	0.31	uncertain
Nisga'a	600	0.23	endangered
Mohawk	425	0.08	uncertain
Iroquoian	245	0.08	uncertain
Haida	165	0.06	endangered

Sources: Norris (2006, 2008); Statistics Canada (2008); Canada (2005).

TABLE 6.2 Percentage of Aboriginal People Claiming an Aboriginal Mother Tongue by Province/Territory, 2006

Province/ Territory	Per cent with Aboriginal Mother Tongue
Manitoba	38
Saskatchewan	34
Quebec	34
Alberta	27
Ontario	24
Nunavut	19
British Columbia	15
NWT	7
Nova Scotia	5
Newfoundland	2
Yukon, PEI, NB	2

Source: Statistics Canada, 2008, at: www.statcan.ca/english/freepub/11-008-XIE/2007001/pdf/11-008-XIE20070019628.pdf.

all Aboriginal languages is 0.64 (home language/mother tongue), a decrease of over 10 per cent since 1981. On the other hand, the continuity rate is 1.20 if we reconceptualize the numerator as 'knowledge of an Aboriginal language' and the denominator as 'mother tongue'. Norris (2003) refers to this as the 'index of ability'. The numerator reflects the ability to speak and understand an Aboriginal language in a normal conversation. This indicator suggests that overall there has been a gain of language capacity in some Aboriginal communities. However, this broad categorization does not take into consideration the differences among the three groups of Aboriginal people—First Nations, Métis, and Inuit.

Focusing only on First Nations, we find that some have flourishing languages. For example, in over 10 per cent of First Nation communities more than 80 per cent of the people are fluent in the language and are able to read and write the language. An additional 18 per cent of communities have 'enduring' languages, which means that over 60 per cent of their population is fluent in their language. On the other hand, in 28 per cent of the communities less than 50 per cent of the population (adults and some youth) are speakers of their language. Thirty per cent of the communities where less than 50 per cent of the adult population (and no youth) are speakers of a First Nation language reveal a decline in language continuity. Overall, most of the First Nation communities have language continuity rates that suggest they are viable over time. However, we also know that 11 per cent of the communities in Canada have fewer than 10 adult speakers of a particular Indigenous language, revealing that these are indeed endangered languages.

According to the 2001 census, less than one-quarter of the total Aboriginal (Indian, Métis, and Inuit) population said they had knowledge of or ability to converse in an Aboriginal language. At the other end of the spectrum, between 13 and 18 per cent of the Aboriginal population claim to most often speak an Aboriginal language in their home. These statistics need to be placed in the context of the work of Norris (2006), who found that the number of young people (0–19) speaking an Aboriginal mother tongue is decreasing. She also found that, in the past two decades, the percentage of Aboriginal people knowing an Aboriginal mother tongue declined from 41 per cent to just over 30 per cent. Nevertheless, during the same time frame, the percentage of adults aged 55 and older with an Aboriginal mother tongue increased from 12 to 18 per cent. This overall picture includes First Nations, Métis, and Inuit. If we compare the three different Aboriginal groups, there are major differences in language use and mother tongue knowledge. For example, Inuit have a mother tongue rate of 66 per cent while Métis (speaking Michif) have a rate of 4 per cent mother tongue continuity.

As discussed above, scholars have developed typologies for determining the 'viability' of languages, ranging from 'viable' to 'uncertain' to 'endangered' to 'extinct'. The main criterion seems to be the size of the population using a First Nation language. For example, Cree, with over 80,000 speakers in 2001, is rated 'viable', while Tlingit, with 105 speakers, is rated 'endangered'. Another basis for determining which category the language will be placed in is based on the ratio of home use to mother tongue speakers. However, we find that some small language groups, e.g., Blackfoot (4,000), Malecite (<700), and Dogrib (2,000), have extremely high continuity indexes and are considered 'viable' languages into the near future

(Table 6.1). This divergence among ratings suggests that, besides the mere size of a population or the 'continuity index', other structural factors (Barrena et al., 2007) impinge on language communities and have an impact on language use and continuity.

Nevertheless, the index of continuity for all Aboriginal languages decreased throughout the twentieth century: e.g., 0.91 in 1951, 0.76 in 1981, and 0.65 in 1996. Into the twenty-first century the index continued its decline, but then in 2006 it began to stabilize and perhaps even actually increased slightly. The data show that for on-reserve First Nations, the index is 0.93; for off-reserve it is 0.73. Thus, while the data in Table 6.3 reveal a steady decrease in the percentage of all Aboriginal people having an Aboriginal mother tongue, there has been an increase in the knowledge of an Indigenous language for on-reserve First Nations people. As well, a strong correlation exists between language continuity and where one lives, e.g., reserve vs. city. Only 10 per cent of Aboriginal people living in a city have an Aboriginal mother tongue. Four per cent of Aboriginal people in cities have an Aboriginal home language and only 14 per cent of these city-dwellers reported knowledge of an Aboriginal language. These figures are low compared to the national figures of 26, 18, and 29 per cent, respectively, with regard to Aboriginal mother tongue.

TABLE 6.3 Percentage of Aboriginal People Claiming an Aboriginal Mother Tongue, 1986–2006

	All Aboriginal	On-Reserve	Off-Reserve
1986	28.6	46.6	15.7
1991	26.9	50.3	18.3
2001	21.4	58.2	11.2
2006	19.8	62.6	9.2

Sources: Statistics Canada (2006); Statistics Canada, *Aboriginal Peoples Survey 2001 Initial Findings: Well-being of the Non-Reserve Aboriginal Population* (Catalogue no. 89–589–XIE); Royal Commission on Aboriginal Peoples, *Report*, vol. 4 (Ottawa: Minister of Supply and Services, 1996).

Another way of determining the language viability of a group is to assess the extent to which a language is used in the home. The census of 2001 reveals that for the total Aboriginal population, 75 per cent of the people spoke English at home while less than 4 per cent spoke French. The remaining 21 per cent spoke an Aboriginal language at home, which is slightly lower than the proportion with an Aboriginal mother tongue. Table 6.4 indicates the home language of the major divisions of the Aboriginal population as well as the ability of an individual to carry on a conversation in that language (Aboriginal knowledge).

These data demonstrate major differences with regard to residence (on- or off-reserve). Just over half of on-reserve First Nations people have an Aboriginal mother tongue, 41 per cent use the language at home, and 55

TABLE 6.4 Home Language and Knowledge of Aboriginal Language by Residence, 2006

| | First Nation Residence | |
	On-Reserve (%)	Off-Reserve (%)
English, home use	57	84
French, home use	2	4
Aboriginal, home use	41	9
Aboriginal knowledge	55	19

Sources: Norris (2008, 2009); Norris and Snider (2008); Statistics Canada (2006).

per cent understand an Aboriginal language. In regard to children of ages 0–14 living on-reserve, 39 per cent speak an Aboriginal language, up from 36 per cent in 2001. On the other hand, for off-reserve First Nations people, only 16 per cent have an Aboriginal mother tongue, 9 per cent use their Aboriginal language at home, and 19 per cent have a working knowledge of an Aboriginal language. Those First Nations people living in the city have even less facility with an Aboriginal language, with only 9 per cent with an Aboriginal mother tongue, 3 per cent who use an Aboriginal language in the home, and 12 per cent who have a working knowledge of an Aboriginal language. Of young children (0–14) living in the city only 6 per cent speak an Aboriginal language, down from 8 per cent in 2001 (Bougie et al., 2010).

Table 6.5 shows the age distribution for those who claim to have a working knowledge of their Aboriginal language. The data illustrate that overall there has been a growth in the numbers of speakers who can carry on a conversation in an Aboriginal language, primarily through learning the language in school, e.g., acquisition of a second language. This suggests that some languages are gaining speakers at a faster rate through second-language acquisition than through mother tongue transmission (Norris, 2006).

TABLE 6.5 Percentage of First Nations People Who Have Knowledge of Aboriginal Language, by Age Group and Residence, 2001 and 2006

| | 2001 | | | 2006 | | |
	Total	On-Reserve	Off-Reserve	Total	On-Reserve	Off-Reserve
Total	30	50	14	29	51	12
0–14	21	36	8	21	39	6
15–24	25	44	10	24	43	9
25–44	33	58	17	30	56	13
45–64	45	71	26	39	67	21
65+	57	81	32	51	81	25

Source: Statistics Canada, Aboriginal People in Canada in 2006: Inuit, Métis and First Nations, 2006, p. 49, Table 23.

As the statistics in the preceding tables suggest, the forces of assimilation and the Indian Act had a dramatic impact on language use, retention, and resiliency. This, in turn, has created uncertainty in the lives of First Nations people. Their culture, their traditions, and their view of the cosmos have become shaded and ill-defined. Such personal and cultural uncertainty has affected their view of the world, of government, and of non-Aboriginal peoples. It is not surprising that they would have little trust in what governments say and do. If people told you that English was a foreign language, evil and worthless, that if you spoke it in public you would be publicly humiliated, and that you had to speak 'Templanese', how long would you hold out? And furthermore, you would not be allowed to visit with your parents over long periods of time and would not be allowed to use English within the confines of the camp you would be forced to live in. Only when you reach your teens, or later, would you be released. This would have a tremendous impact on your self-concept and self-worth, yet this effectively is what the residential schools did to several generations of First Nations young people. Seen in this light, the figures noted above regarding language retention and use demonstrate a remarkable resilience on the part of First Nations people.

The Future of Aboriginal Languages

The results of assessing the impact of structural/demographic community factors (Figure 6.1) are shown in Table 6.6. On the basis of a literature review, a number of structural variables are identified as possible correlates of language use/sustainability. An examination of Statistics Canada's community profiles allows for assessment of the correlations between various structural conditions in First Nation communities and the community's language use/knowledge.

Employment, the first variable, is categorized as 'employed' and 'unemployed'. Biddle et al. (2008) show that a correlation between socio-

TABLE 6.6 Correlation between Selected Community Variables and Language Facility in First Nation Communities

| | Language Facility Adults | | |
	Mother Tongue	Knowledge*	Use at Home
Employment	0.07	0.02	0.09
Mobility	−0.41	−0.36	−0.41
Education	−0.33	−0.29	−0.46
Pop. size of community	0.09	0.03	0.08
Per cent speakers	0.57	0.51	0.45
Geography of reserve	0.56	0.41	0.53
Average age on reserve	0.63	0.39	0.49
Median income	−0.12	−0.23	−0.17
Intermarriage	−0.83	—	−0.38

*Knowledge refers to the ability to conduct an everyday conversation with another person in an Aboriginal language.

economic status (SES) and speaking an Indigenous language at home is relatively high. While a composite SES profile is not shown in Table 6.6, we do have separate measures with regard to employment, income, and education. Employment can be used as a proxy for measuring the 'integrative/instrumental' aspect of language use. Those communities with high unemployment, we might assume, have little or no use for non-Aboriginal language because they are unable to integrate into the larger economic system that requires English and/or French. They presumably would reflect high levels of Aboriginal language use and knowledge and subsequent language continuity, yet the data do not confirm this reasoning. The correlations reveal that communities with higher rates of unemployment have only slightly higher rates of Aboriginal mother tongue use—both knowledge of and use of an Aboriginal language at home—than those with lower rates of unemployment.

Mobility ('Have you moved in the past five years?') is the second structural variable, and can be used as a second proxy measure of mainstream participation. Those communities with high levels of mobility reflect lower levels of Aboriginal language maintenance, thus supporting the idea that the need for knowledge of and use of Aboriginal languages is limited to those communities that have displayed low levels of mobility. Mobility may mean movement within the First Nations community but more than likely reflects the individual's decision to move out of the community and then back to the First Nations community (since the data were gathered within First Nation communities).

A third proxy measure of participation in the mainstream society is education. Higher levels of education also are related to language use: the higher the level of education in the community, the lower the level of Aboriginal language use, mother tongue knowledge, and use at home. Thus, all three of these indicators suggest that an Aboriginal language plays an important integrative role in a First Nation community that is stable, has a low average education, and has a high rate of unemployment. These communities do not see the need to acquire one of the official languages because they do not participate in the social, economic, and political structures of Canadian mainstream society. On the other hand, those communities that have high employment also have high mobility rates as well as higher educational achievements and use English as the functional language for integrating into the mainstream society; thus, they see less need for an Aboriginal language.

A small correlation exists between language use and community size. As for the percentage of people within a community who can speak an Aboriginal language, not surprisingly, this correlates highly with mother tongue knowledge and use at home. This may suggest that Aboriginal language learning as a second language contributes, in the long run, to the larger number of individuals with an Aboriginal mother tongue.

Geographic location of the First Nation community also is thought to have some importance in language maintenance (Slavik, 2001). Based on the coding scheme devised by Indian and Northern Affairs Canada (urban, semi-urban, rural, remote), a substantial correlation is found between community location and language use/maintenance. First Nations people in remote/special access regions have a much higher percentage of Aboriginal mother tongue speakers than those in rural or urban First Nation communities. This confirms a strong connection between the geographic residence and the number of people having a First Nation mother tongue (Norris, 2003). Urban First Nation communities are much more likely to have low rates of Native language knowledge, use, and the possession of that language as a mother tongue, while isolated communities tend to have high levels of language use, knowledge of, and possession of their mother tongue.

The age of a First Nation community (as a proxy for 'generation') has been suggested as an important factor in language use/continuity (Slavik, 2001). Norris (2006) found that the average age of the mother-tongue population was highly correlated to an 'index of language continuity', which reveals that the older the age of the mother-tongue population, the higher the index of continuity. However, this has an 'expiration date' attached to it: as the cohort continues to age, the aging population begins to die off. At that time, if a replacement cohort of younger people is not also obtaining an Aboriginal language, the language will become extinct. The current data show that the median age of the First Nation community is strongly related to the Aboriginal language being the mother tongue, but less so for language knowledge and use at home. This suggests that while younger members of the population are not acquiring an Aboriginal mother tongue, they are acquiring an Aboriginal language through some means of second-language acquisition.

In regard to the income level of the community, the median income of First Nation communities and its impact on language use were considered. The data show a modest inverse relationship—the higher the median income, the less an Aboriginal language will be used at home, the less the community will have knowledge of an Aboriginal language, and the lower the rate of Aboriginal mother tongue. Again, these results may reflect the linkage of the community to the mainstream society.

As might be expected, the association within a language group between the percentage of individuals in a mixed marriage (where one partner speaks an Aboriginal language and the other does not) and language use indicates that marriage outside one's language group works against maintenance of the minority language. One study, based on an examination of 30 languages, found that linguistic intermarriage is more likely to identify a contemporary instance of group disaffiliation than is ethnic intermarriage, and the effect on the next generation is much more likely to be final (Stevens and Schoen, 1988). Moreover, earlier research suggests that the persistence of non-English languages is more common with those individuals who are poorly educated and have low incomes. The results show a negative correlation of −0.83 for mother tongue. This confirms that in mixed marriages there are considerably lower rates of Aboriginal language use. These data also suggest that the non-Aboriginal marriage partner, as a rule, is not interested in learning an Aboriginal language. However, this factor is inextricably intertwined with the issue of on- or off-reserve residence. The question now is how Bill C-31 will impact the rate of mixed marriages and thus influence language continuity. This strong correlation supports the contention that language use and continuity are highly related to language facility by both parents.

We can see, now, that out-marriage is associated with diminished continuity of language—a strong inverse relationship between language continuity and exogamy. A similar relationship is found when mother tongue is linked to exogamy. However, the correlation is reduced to −0.38 when the dependent variable is 'use at home'. Overall, endogamous families (both parents speak an Aboriginal language) result in the highest language continuity for their children. This level of continuity is followed by lone-parent families, and the poorest language continuity outcome is for exogamous marriages.

Conclusion

Historical factors, such as the discouragement of Aboriginal languages in the public schools as well as in residential schools, have ruptured the transmission of language from one generation to another, so that First Nation communities are dealing with the lack of mother tongue transmission. For example, today, 12 per cent of Cree speakers have acquired the language through second language learning, thereby reflecting an interest in the community to retain the language. Moreover, language classes are being offered in First Nation communities across the country at all levels of educational institutions. In addition, new courses are being developed in First Nation communities for mid-generation adults who were unable to learn (or prevented from learning) their language when they grew up.

First Nations people are no more a homogeneous ethnic group than others; indeed, in important ways, such as language and lifeways, they are less homogeneous than other ethnic groups. No single set of cultural practices represents 'Aboriginalness'. The colonial experience, the generational trauma, and the marginalization that First Nations people have experienced over the past century have resulted in three different types of Aboriginal identity: (1) those who emphasize speaking an Aboriginal language, have knowledge of and participate in Aboriginal ceremonies and rituals, and are linked with other Aboriginal people; (2) those having two Aboriginal parents who stress the knowledge of ancestral history and are conscious of Aboriginal networks and blood-ties; they may speak/understand some Aboriginal language but not at a fluent level; and (3) those who have been raised in Canadian–Aboriginal families and their central indicator of Aboriginalness is having Aboriginal ancestors as well as having some symbolic knowledge or understanding of Aboriginal culture and ceremonies. They are not able to converse in an Aboriginal language but may have some knowledge of words and phrases they can use at appropriate times.

Thus, we find that structural factors differentially impact language continuity and use. This leads to the issue of the need for language use to sustain Aboriginal identity. The Irish people largely adopted English yet retained their identity. The new generations of Jews in North America lost their Yiddish yet retained a sense of community and identity. Ukraine has experienced a similar history of language restriction yet Ukrainians retained their language and culture as part of their national identity and in the ethnic identities of emigrants. These histories suggest that language, while important, needs to be examined in the specific historical and cultural context of the group being studied.

Predictions of precipitous population declines among First Nations people and of increasing migration to the cities were confirmed facts in the 1970s. However, it is clear that these predictions have been moderated by values and structural conditions impinging on First Nations people. Out-migration from rural reserves has now shifted to in-migration and urbanization has stalled. While death rates for First Nations people have decreased substantially, birth rates have not made a commensurate change. At present, First Nations people have a birth rate twice that of the general population and today we find that nearly 50 per cent of the First Nations population is under the age of 29. The interaction of a young population with language use and continuity remains to be seen.

Language is a symbol of identity for many First Nations people, and it provides a focal point for mobilization for both integrative and instrumental reasons. Those who promote language retention and rediscovery are well aware of the linkage between language and identity. They resist assimilation, rhetorically, by investing in learning their own language, which may not be empowering, at least in the beginning. However, in the long run, they may expect further changes that would allow their language to be given official recognition. In other cases, people learn an Aboriginal language because it has some symbolic significance. Integrative reasons such as pride and awareness of Aboriginal identity also are important in language retention. In this respect, learning and teaching an Aboriginal language may be symbolic resistance to the domination of the majority.

In the end, as Laitin (1998) points out, all social groups change behaviour over time. In the present case, we are referring to language use/sustainability. The **tipping point** for the loss or retention of a language occurs because people's choices about their actions are based partly on what they think others are going to do. It means that people will lean towards learning an Aboriginal language to the extent that they believe that other people in their reference group are changing. Thus, tipping towards learning an Aboriginal language happens when a community feels that it would empower the group. Moreover, the learning of an Aboriginal language may also serve a political purpose—one of consolidating and empowering a dominated group; the individuals may learn an Aboriginal language for either symbolic or political reasons (Galley, 2009).

Questions for Critical Thought

1. How important is maintaining an Aboriginal language for First Nations people?
2. Should the public schools offer Aboriginal languages as an option for students to take in primary and secondary schools?
3. Should those languages classed as 'not viable' be allowed to become extinct or should public monies be used to ensure they continue to exist?

Suggested Readings

Norris, M. 2007. 'Aboriginal Languages in Canada: Emerging Trends and Perspectives on Second Language Acquisition', *Canadian Social Trends* 83: 20–8. The author assesses the viability of languages and makes a projection as to whether or not they will still be in existence by the next decade.

Pacini-Ketchabaw, V., and A. Armstrong de Almeida. 2006. 'Language Discourses and Ideologies as the Heart of Early Childhood Education', *International Journal of Bilingual Education and Bilingualism* 9: 310–41. The authors identify how first languages that are different from English or French are important for the academic success of students.

Turcotte, M. 2006. 'Passing on the Ancestral Language', *Canadian Social Trends* 80: 20–6. Using census data, the author reveals the level of use and continuance of Aboriginal languages in Canada.

Suggested Websites

Aboriginal Canada
www.aboriginalcanada.gc.ca
   The Aboriginal Canada website of the federal government has statistics and maps regarding Aboriginal languages in Canada.

Aboriginal Languages and Cultures
www.edu.gov.mb.ca/ab_languages/index.html
    This Aboriginal language and culture website focuses on the teaching and
    learning of Aboriginal languages in western and northern Canada and includes
    web links with regard to language issues in this part of the country.

7 Well–Being and Health

Learning Objectives

- ⊛ To understand why First Nations people are reluctant to participate in the mainstream society's biomedical health-care system.
- ⊛ To know about the health and well-being of First Nations people.
- ⊛ To identify some of the determinants of health status for First Nations people.
- ⊛ To learn about the health-care system of Canada as it relates to First Nations people.

Introduction

This chapter includes **well-being** in its title as it is more encompassing than just 'health' and allows for a more general assessment of how well First Nations people are doing in Canada. As noted in the Aboriginal Peoples Survey (2006), well-being is a multi-dimensional concept that encompasses the mental, emotional, and physical as well as the spiritual aspects of life. Well-being involves the attributes of an individual as well as the physical and social environment in which he or she lives. This conceptualization fits well into many First Nation communities who use the medicine wheel, a symbol of holistic healing that embodies all of these elements. As noted by O'Donnell and Tait (2004), for First Nations people the natural world is a crucial part of individual well-being because of the linkages and inter-relationships between people living close to the land and that physical environment. For First Nations people well-being results when a balance or harmony among these elements is established by the individual and/or community. Once measures of well-being have been established, policies might be developed and directed towards achieving the needs and aspirations of First Nation communities. Not all communities have the capacity to incorporate policies to achieve well-being; thus, special attention needs to be given to those communities that first need to build their capacity in order to take on the job of enhancing their well-being. Because the level of social capital in communities differs, this becomes an important factor in the well-being of any community.

Etiology in Society

People who are vulnerable and socially disadvantaged have less access to health resources, tend to be sick more often, and generally die earlier than those who are not socially disadvantaged (Richmond, 2009). All of these conditions apply to the ill health experienced by Aboriginal people. However, research also has pointed out that societies having high-quality social environments, trusting relationships, and social support offer a protective effect on the level of illness experienced by the group. How do we explain this paradox of a First Nation community that is perceived by residents as having a high-quality social environment, is high in trust relationships, and is defined as having high levels of support, yet still shows low levels of well-being? Part of the explanation is that social support has both positive and negative properties that operate in conditions of poverty. We also know that social support operates at different levels—individual, family, and community—and thus social support may differ at each of these levels, in some cases negating the positive support produced at another level. For example, if you want to stop drinking and your friends continue to drink, they will soon abandon you and isolate you from their group and their friendship. Social support is offered only to those who drink. If you can develop another social network, you can compensate for the loss of this social support but it takes time and the individual may not find a comparable network.

When thinking about First Nation communities, we need to consider well-being in physical as well as in mental and spiritual dimensions. Moreover, definitions of disease and illness or health have a social as well as pathological component. For most people, the physical condition of an individual must be defined as one of illness before the individual can perceive that she or he is ill. If the group, neighbourhood, or community defines the condition as an illness, then certain steps are taken to correct the condition. On the other hand, if the condition is not defined as an illness by the individual's reference group, the individual would not consider it appropriate to assume a sick role and would not seek treatment (Kane et al., 1976). Thus, the definition of illness in a community will determine the norm of health or state of well-being considered normal for its members. A First Nation individual living in a First Nation community is most likely to interpret his or her own health status relative to others in the community. As a result, what constitutes illness or sickness will be determined by the definition of the group and the group's reaction to people who exhibit certain symptoms or behaviour (ibid.).

At the same time, professional health-care practitioners reflect middle-class, Western values with regard to health and health-care, and Western medicine, for well over a century, has viewed the human body as a machine of various distinct parts or mechanisms, rather like an automobile. If one part—a badly broken leg, a tubercular lung—can be brought back to a state of health by medical intervention, then everything is assumed to be fine again. Any patient not sharing this perspective, these Western values, is at a distinct disadvantage. Health-care practitioners often do not understand the attitudes and lifestyles of patients from a different culture. These professionals, socialized in a middle-class milieu to accept Western biomedical care, are ill-prepared to deal with patients whose behaviour does not conform to middle-class values. For example, they assume that First Nation patients share their perspective on illness, health-care, and well-being and that they have access to the same resources as the middle-class patients or the medical professional. In reality, however, First Nations people generally are poor and can manage only the barest of material necessities: heat, food, and clothing. Thus, their immediate concerns are for obtaining food and housing. Middle-class notions of health and well-being are a remote dream.

The end result is that in the practitioners' day-to-day experiences with First Nations people, the behaviour of patients clearly reinforces the notion that they do not follow the directions of the practitioners in order to heal themselves. As such, First Nation patients are defined as unwilling or incapable of carrying out orders or taking responsibility for themselves. The negative attitudes of professional medical practitioners are expressed more or less openly, making encounters with health-care providers unpleasant for many First Nations people. Every time they return to the health-care facility, they must undergo this humiliating experience. The common strategy employed by First Nations people is to avoid the unpleasant situation by not returning to the practitioner or facility and seeking out alternative health practices.

Moreover, First Nations people prefer to deal with medical practitioners who take a more holistic, inter-connective perspective that accounts for all the dimensions of the individual. However, the health-care system of the dominant society has an elaborate division of labour: nurses are interested only in one aspect of the patient, the X-ray technician in another, the orthopedic surgeon in still another. First Nations people find this a foreign experience that is both confusing and frustrating. They also perceive the rational, objective, and unemotional manner of health-care professionals not as the mark of a good professional, but rather as an indication of a cold, heartless person, unsympathetic to the patient.

Just as contemporary health-care typically is focused on isolating the one cause within an individual's body, the locus of cause tends to be focused on the individual. Thus, Canadians are encouraged to view health-care and health risks in terms of the individual, rather than in the context either of society or of the actions taken by vested interest groups such as the Canadian Medical Association or multinational corporations. This individual-centred conceptualization of well-being has led to a strictly curative or controlling, rather than preventative, orientation, in which technical biomedical solutions are offered to solve the individual's problems while the social, economic, and political causes of ill health are ignored. As Segall (1989) points out, this position obscures the extent to which health and illness depend on socially determined ways of life. The provision of health-care services follows a Euro-Canadian model that stresses the individual nature of disease and treatment. Individuals are responsible for their health and the subsequent treatment of those ailments. Moreover, only specified individuals such as doctors and nurses have the right to engage in health treatment and the provision of drugs.

The lack of cultural connection is frequently cited as a primary cause of many of the social and health problems facing First Nations communities. For example, the lack of health-care specialists who cannot speak an Aboriginal language can be problematic in diagnosing a health problem or in dispensing a cure. The insistence on a model that focuses only on biological genesis and ignores all other 'causes' is equally problematic in that First Nation individuals use a more 'holistic' approach to health and health-care. In addition, spiritual aspects not condoned by Euro-Canadian medicine may be invoked in the traditional cure. Having a white, middle- and upper-class view of well-being and health obscures the extent to which health and illness depend on socially determined ways of life. Less advantaged classes in the mainstream culture may have attitudes, needs, and social environments more similar to those of Native peoples. Moreover, the current medical system is resistant to accepting any alternative form of 'medicine' other than what has been approved by the Canadian Medical Association.

Recent research has shown that we must investigate the importance of the social environment to understand why some people stay healthy and others get sick. This perspective rejects the conceptualization that illness is strictly within the realm of the individual to control and alerts us to the importance of a social context (Marmot and Wilkinson, 1999). As noted above, the social behaviour exhibited by people is shaped by such factors as patterns of social control, norms, and mores, which facilitate or reduce opportunities to engage in specific behaviours and present different coping strategies for dealing with well-being.

In general, First Nations' belief systems define health as 'living in balance' with other systems of which the individual is a part. A health-care system that is sensitive to First Nation culture must be holistic, flexible, and responsive to the individual, the community, and the disease/illness. Thus, for First Nation individuals, all aspects of life must be lived in 'balance and respect' in order to achieve wellness. Health is holistic because it integrates the physical, spiritual, mental, and emotional aspects of the person with his/her physical environment (RCAP, 1996). However, with the rapid social change impacting First Nation communities, these beliefs and values have become increasingly difficult to practise and are not considered important by the dominant biomedical health system in Canada.

Wellness difficulties of First Nations people cannot be separated from their spiritual beliefs because they believe that healers can only be effective if they seek the aid of spiritual forces. First Nation healers define wellness as having one's head and heart in congruence. Unwellness (or what we call illness) is when there is a disruption of the essential harmony of life or an imbalance of various elements. People must keep in balance if they want to be healthy and well. At the same time, it should be noted that First Nations people do not totally reject Western medical or psychological concepts; they just see them as limited in their healing forces (Herring, 1997). A major concern expressed by First Nations people is that mainstream medicine is a reflection of the monocultural and ethnocentric perspective of the dominant society. For example, in most First Nation healing practices, power and responsibility rest with the healer, not the person needing healing. The First Nation person expects the healer to know the problem and how to deal with it (ibid.). Another example is how First Nations people use silence as a sign of respect, especially with authority figures. Neither do they engage in eye contact, which can be interpreted quite differently when using a mainstream lens. These issues point out that not only are the curative activities by mainstream society misperceived by First Nations people but also the delivery of those services may be defined as inappropriate.

Today in Canada we have increased our level of well-being so that we are ranked in the top 10 countries of the world. However, if the focus is just on First Nation communities, the results turn around and we are in the bottom 10 per cent of the countries in the world. In other words, First Nation communities have levels of well-being equivalent to the world's least developed countries. Why is this the case? First of all, Canada has developed a basic infrastructure that has brought clean water, all-weather housing, and a sewage treatment process to most of its citizens. It is well known that in developing countries, these are the three most important factors in increasing the level of well-being, decreasing mortality, and enhancing quality of life. In First Nation communities, many do not have clean water, appropriate housing, or proper sewage treatment.

Finally, cultural continuity has an impact on the well-being of an individual. Chandler and Lalonde (2008) argue that when circumstances occur in such a way as to undermine self or cultural continuity, then a sense of ownership of the past is lost and the future becomes irrelevant. They point out that if the 'temporal course' of one's individual or cultural identity is destroyed (in part or whole), those individuals will no longer be interested in participating in their community and will engage in destructive behaviours, e.g., alcohol, drugs, violence, suicide, since there are no connecting points that give the individual enduring personhood or cultural continuity.

They found that communities scoring high on cultural continuity factors (self-government, control over education, health, police and fire departments, land claims achieved or in process) had much higher rates of well-being than those that scored low on these dimensions. They also found that the number of women in community government and control over child services contributed to higher levels of community well-being. In summary, those communities with high **social capital** had high levels of well-being.

The Health System

At the beginning of the twentieth century, Canada did not have any kind of co-ordinated effort to address the health crisis First Nations people were experiencing due to the introduction of a number of deadly diseases. Settlers coming to Canada were of a genetic strain that had been exposed to these diseases for centuries and had developed immune systems that moderated the impact or made them resistant. First Nations people had not been exposed to these diseases; the introduction of smallpox, measles, tuberculosis; and other communicable diseases had a devastating impact. It is estimated that during the first 500 years of European settlement in North America, nearly 90 per cent of the Indigenous population died of various diseases introduced by the settlers. Initially, health-care provisions for First Nations people were, like for other Canadians, dependent upon family, friends, and voluntary organizations for support. Not until 1945 was the Department of National Health and Welfare created to help with health-care for First Nations people. This department supported all Canadians since the federal government argued that it did not have any statutory or treaty obligations to provide health services to First Nations people. However, in 1962—86 years after the Treaty 6 provision of a 'medicine chest'—the federal government created the Medical Services Branch that consolidated all federal agencies having anything to do with health services for First Nations people when normal provincial services were not available.

Health-care in Canada is largely under provincial and territorial jurisdiction. Nevertheless, the provinces and the federal government have argued for many years about who covers First Nation health issues and to what extent. Today, much of the health-care provided to First Nations people is provided by the provinces, but many disputed areas result in First Nations people having difficulty or finding it impossible to obtain certain health services. In 1967 a new Indian Health Policy was implemented. At this time the government noted that this policy was based on a special relationship the federal government had with First Nations people, and that the new 'health policy for First Nation people flows from constitutional and statutory provisions, treaties and customary practice' (Health Canada, at www.hc-sc.gc.ca/ahc-asc/brainc-dirgen/fnihb-dgspni/fact-fiche-eng.php).

This statement is a complete reversal of what had been said 20 years earlier. The government's new policy stated it has a 'commitment to First Nations people to preserve and enhance their culture and traditions and it recognizes its legal and traditional responsibilities to First Nations people.' Finally, it encouraged First Nation communities to pursue their goals using existing Canadian institutions.

The federal government, since the 1970s, has argued that its policies were to be built on three pillars and this commitment has not changed to the present. The first of the three pillars is to promote community development through social and economic development in First Nation communities. This pillar is based on the assumption that poverty prevents members of the community from achieving a state of physical, mental, and social well-being. The second pillar is that the federal government will act as an advocate for First Nations people in order for them to achieve their aspirations. This will be achieved through the development of First Nation community capacity. For example, they will be more involved in the planning, budgeting, and delivery of programs in First Nation communities. Finally, the third pillar focuses on the Canadian health system. Given the complexity of the system, which involves federal, provincial, territorial, and private interests, the federal government agrees to co-ordinate this system so that health promotion, the detection and mitigation of hazards to health, and other public health activities in First Nation communities will be seamlessly provided.

In the 1970s the Medical Services Branch started to work towards transferring control of health services to First Nation communities and organizations. After the *Report* of the Royal Commission on Aboriginal Peoples was released in 1996, the federal government introduced a new 'action plan' for dealing with health issues in First Nation communities, focusing on high-risk diseases such as diabetes and tuberculosis. Then, in 2000, the Medical Services Branch was renamed the First Nations and Inuit Health Branch. This reconstituted agency provides support for the delivery of community-based health programs on reserves. In addition, it provides drug, dental, and ancillary health services to First Nations people regardless of residence. It also 'provides primary care services for First Nations people who live in remote and isolated areas where provincial services are not provided and deals with non-insured health benefits, providing dental, vision, prescription drugs, medical supplies, transportation and mental health counseling for First Nations people' (Health Canada, at: www.hc-sc.gc.ca/ahc-asc/ branch-dirgen/fnihb-dgspni/fact-fiche-eng.php).

Today the Strategic Policy, Planning and Analysis Directorate provides policy and planning advice on health related issues and initiatives. Four divisions within Health Canada focus solely on First Nations health issues: Health Information and Analysis Division, Office of Inuit Health, Policy Development, and Strategic Policy and Planning. These offices analyze health information about First Nations people, carry out research on health issues, develop strategic policy and planning, and prepare the First Nations and Inuit health system to respond to medium- and long-term challenges. They provide community programs, such as the healthy child development, youth suicide prevention, addictions prevention and treatment, disease/injury risk factor prevention, and community capacity-building initiatives (Health Canada, at: www.hc-sc.ca/fniah-spnia/pubs/aborig-autoch/2009-stats-profil/10-culture-eng.php). The First Nations and Inuit Health Branch of Health Canada also contributes to the funding, delivery, and assessment of public health and health promotion services to First Nation communities. In sum, all of these departments examine health issues related to First Nations and propose solutions to address problems. They fund over 500 health facilities across the country, and currently have involved in these programs nearly 700 nurses, 22 physicians, 60 substance-abuse treatment centres, 75 nursing stations, home and community care in 600 communities, primary health-care in 200 remote communities, and well over 220 health centres. While the health provision capacity of Health Canada is quite comprehensive, it remains ironic that First Nations people have the poorest health in Canada.

Level of Well-Being

With such a sophisticated infrastructure of health delivery, how can it be that First Nations people do not give evidence of well-being? A partial answer is that we have not invested in the necessary infrastructure that would build the foundation for good health. For example, nearly 80 per cent of First Nation reserves do not have safe, potable water, have substandard housing, and do not have adequate sewage treatment systems (Harden and Levalliant, 2008).

In 2005 the Commissioner of Environment and Sustainable Development issued a report called *Drinking Water in First Nations' Communities*; it showed that First Nation communities have no regulations or legislation regarding drinking water. While there are administrative guidelines and policies with regard to safe water on reserves, they are not being implemented and do not deal with the realities on the reserves. Frequently, members of a First Nation community have to be airlifted from their community because of the lack of water or of sewage services (most recently, Kashechewan in Ontario, Fort Chipewyan in Alberta, and Yellow Quill in Saskatchewan). Each year over the past decade, more than 100 First Nation communities lived with a 'boil water' advisory—some for as long as 13 years before action was taken to provide the community with safe drinking water. This situation is the culmination of years of neglect and the absence of effective programs to provide safe drinking water for First Nation communities. As one First Nations person noted, 'I wonder how different the response would be if the residents of Vancouver were without access to clean safe water?' Clatworthy (2009) found that about half of all homes in First Nation communities suffered from at least one form of housing deficiency—four times higher than that of the general Canadian population. More than one-third of the houses in First Nation communities require major repairs and 20 per cent of all households are overcrowded. To deal with these conditions, major investments of time, money, and energy are required to deal just with the standing problems, and more of those same commitments are needed to help with the ongoing problem and to maintain improvements, once these are made.

We noted earlier the tension between the biomedical concept of health imposed on First Nations people and their own conceptions of health, which provides another explanation for poor health. Finally, poverty in itself leads to poor health. Well-being is a composite of several individual indicators that tell us the extent to which First Nations people are integrated into the social, economic, and political spheres of the country. Some researchers have argued that community control, community engagement, and cultural continuity are the key indicators of well-being (Lalonde, 2005). Whether suicide rates, neonatal death rates, poverty, overcrowding, or length of life, the Canadian media all too often call attention to the low level of well-being in First Nation communities. While Canadians theoretically want all people to have good health, their concern about First Nations people is muted, first, because they do not have to deal with such living conditions and may not even realize what First Nations people have to deal with, and second, because even if they know about it, they do not know what they can do about it. From the First Nation perspective, the impact is direct and every day.

This situation leads to feelings of **relative deprivation**. First Nations people compare their health with the well-being of other Canadians and know that they are living a life that is much poorer than others. The ubiquitous nature of mass media in even remote First Nation communities has fostered this sense of relative deprivation. First Nations people have come to see and experience the differences between their lives and those of other groups in Canada and the comparison has led them to the conclusion that they are not worth as much as other Canadians. In fact, it can be argued that, at a societal level, all of us are lessened by the deprivation and poor health in our midst. Several studies have shown that the health and well-being of a society is largely dependent on socio-economic equity throughout the society, not on how wealthy and well-off the 'average' person is. In other words, the wider the gap is between the rich and the poor, the poorer the health and well-being of society as a whole (see, e.g., Clarke, 2008: 50–2).

At an individual level, this may result in a lack of self-respect that leads to intra-group conflict and self-abuse such as drug and alcohol use. As Beavon and White (2007) point out, those who share history and culture,

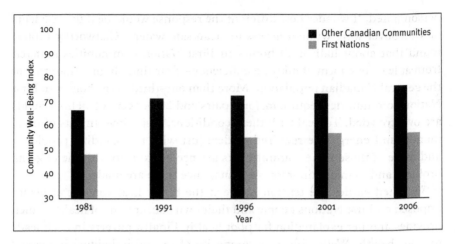

FIGURE 7.1 The Well-Being of First Nation and Non–First Nation Communities
Sources: Census of Canada, 1981, 1991, 1996, 2001, 2006.

who become bound together in groups, will begin to assess that they are not treated fairly. Collective responses that confront mainstream Canadians with regard to relative deprivation become a challenge to the fabric of this country. Another outcome of the relative deprivation is conflict at different levels. For example, in 2007, the Assembly of First Nations and the First Nations Child and Family Caring Society of Canada filed a complaint with the Canadian Human Rights Commission seeking compensation for Canada's funding policy for First Nations children—a policy that has been in place since 2000 (Blackstock, 2007).

Martin and Guimond (2009) have developed a summary measure of progress in a Registered Indian Human Development Index that combines life expectancy, adult literacy, school enrolment, and per capita gross domestic product (GDP). On the basis of this index, they find that while there was some improvement in well-being of First Nations people between 1980 and 1990, this improvement had slowed by 1990; and, since then, despite some increase in well-being, the gap between First Nations and other Canadians has not closed. Indian and Northern Affairs Canada has developed a different community well-being index and its data confirm previous findings: in 2006, First Nation communities showing the lowest community well-being scores were located in the Prairie provinces (where the largest proportion of the Aboriginal population lives). Figure 7.1 compares the well-being of First Nation and non–First Nation communities.

Recently (2001–6) there has been a dramatic decrease in the well-being of First Nation communities while other Canadian communities have shown a stable or increased well-being index. The well-being scores of First Nation communities reveal a low mean, 57 out of 100, as well as a wide range of scores: 37–77. Non–First Nation communities have a much higher mean (77) with a much smaller variation: 64–87. These data show that, on a measure of well-being, among the bottom 100 Canadian communities 96 were First Nations. And on the reverse end of the scale, among those top 100 communities in Canada, only one was a First Nation community.

State of Health

Entire books have been written addressing the state of health of First Nations people. Here, we can only begin to look at some of the structural factors that contribute to health. Then, we will look at two components of health: subjective, **self-rated health**—how First Nations people see their health status—and the objective assessment of health—the extent of disability and the incidence of selected health conditions, such as diabetes, tuberculosis, and causes of death.

Community Structure

O'Sullivan (2006) set out to determine the impact on well-being of the structure and nature of the reserve. She wanted to know how the index of well-being for First Nation reserve communities compared with nearby non-Aboriginal communities. She also wanted to know if the attributes of the reserves, for example, their size and geographical location, have anything to do with the people's well-being. She gathered data from across the country to address this question. First, she found that the absolute community well-being scores for reserves and non–First Nation communities had increased over the past two decades. Only a few communities of both types had a lower community well-being score at the beginning of the twenty-first century than before. She also found that while the well-being gap between the two types of communities had decreased somewhat, the real change appeared in the 1996 census data; but in the subsequent 15 years, there has not been any reduction in the gap. O'Sullivan projects what the level of well-being will be in both First Nation and non–First Nation communities in 2041. She finds that the average community well-being score for First Nations communities will fall about 6 points below the level seen in other communities in 2001 and decrease between 2011 and 2041, implying that improvements will level off in 2021 when First Nations have achieved only a moderate level of well-being. At the same time, the non–First Nation communities will continue to improve in their well-being to 2041.

White and Maxim (2007) also looked into the issue of whether special attributes of reserves have an impact on well-being. Their research design paired reserves with non-reserve communities that were comparable and looked at their respective levels of well-being. They also compared the difference in well-being between all reserves and all non-reserve communities to the differences between paired reserves and their 'comparable' non-reserve communities. In their unmatched analyses, where all reserves were compared with all other Canadian communities, reserves scored significantly lower on community well-being. In fact, reserves scored nearly 20 per cent lower than non–First Nations communities. This finding is in agreement with O'Sullivan's findings and confirms that living in a First Nation community means you will have a lower well-being score than other Canadians. Even when First Nation communities were matched with non–First Nation communities, the differences remain.

However, these findings do not address the question of whether some First Nation communities have better 'well-being' than others and, if so, what special characteristics are linked to that better well-being. For example, one might predict that isolated reserves or smaller reserves would have lower well-being scores than more urbanized reserves or larger reserves. When various attributes of the reserves were taken into consideration, the authors found that the differences did not disappear; confirming that such structures as the size of the First Nation community had little impact on the well-being scores of the community. However, they did find that the level of well-being was related to geographical location. In the more isolated First Nation communities the level of well-being was low, while in the more urbanized reserves the level of well-being was higher. Overall, the important variable linked to well-being was whether or not the community was a First

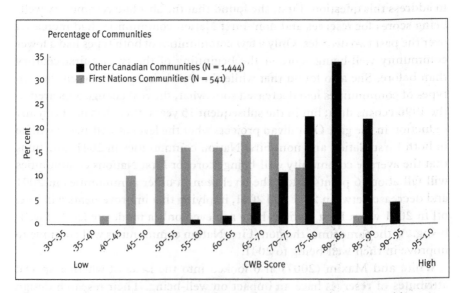

Figure 7.2 Community Well-Being: First Nation and Other Canadian Communities, 2001

Source: Adapted from McHardy, M. and E. O'Sullivan. 2004. First Nations Community Well-Being in Canada. Strategic Research and Analysis Directorate, Ottawa, Indian and Northern Affairs Canada, 10.

Nations one. In short, something about the organization, structure, and operation of a First Nation community produces a lower level of well-being than what happens in a non–First Nation community. Further research will need to delve into this question as to what factors (and combinations of factors) produce communities with higher or lower levels of well-being.

While the community well-being score cannot be interpreted to represent all aspects of well-being, it does give us some sense of how healthy communities are in Canada. Figure 7.2 compares First Nation and other Canadian communities with regard to their well-being (McHardy and O'Sullivan, 2004). As the scores range from 0 (extremely low levels of well-being) to 1 (extremely high levels of well-being), Figure 7.2 graphically displays the disparity between First Nations and other Canadian communities. These data show that nearly half of the First Nation communities occupy the lower half of the scale while only 3 per cent of other Canadian communities fall within this range.

Subjective Indicators of Health

Self-rated health is *subjective*, an individual's perception of their overall health on a scale from 'excellent' to 'poor' (Health Canada, 2006). The Aboriginal Peoples Survey 2006 shows that a lower percentage of First Nations people on-reserve report 'excellent' health than does the general Canadian population. For example, less than 80 per cent of First Nations on-reserve reported 'good to excellent' health compared to nearly 90 per cent of the general Canadian population. This subjective measure does not indicate an *objective* assessment of the excellence of health of Aboriginal people, but it does give us a fair impression of the overall health of the population. One might argue that the differences are not great, and if the two populations were comparable in age structure this argument would be valid. However, as noted earlier, the First Nations population is much younger than the general population and skews the data towards the relatively good health of youth, despite the fact that (for the general population) the last 13 years of life are generally those when health is not good. For First Nations people we find that health is not good from the day they are born. Second, we know that poor self-rated health is correlated with subsequent morbidity (e.g., sickness, hospitalization) and mortality (Kennedy et al., 2001).

Nevertheless, 70 per cent of First Nations people feel that they are 'in balance' with regard to their physical, mental, emotional, and spiritual well-being. At the same time, this means that nearly one-third of First Nations people feel their lives are not balanced in the four dimensions, which denotes poor health. For example, over 13 per cent of First Nations respondents noted that they had contemplated suicide compared with just over 3 per cent of the general Canadian population. Suicide and self-inflicted injuries for First

Nation youth (15–24) are six times higher than the Canadian rate. For the past decade, over one-third of all First Nation deaths have resulted from accidents and violence, compared to 8 per cent for non–First Nations deaths.

Objective Indicators of Health

We now turn to the objective indicators of health of First Nation individuals with regard to specific diseases as compared with the Canadian population. Figure 7.3 identifies the incidences of various diseases and compares them to the Canadian population.

With few exceptions, First Nations adults have a higher incidence of almost any disease than non–First Nation adults. While there are small differences for such diseases as asthma and high blood pressure, the differences are substantial for other diseases such as diabetes. Most of the diabetes suffered by First Nations people is type 2, which occurs after a person reaches adulthood. Nevertheless, young First Nation individuals are being diagnosed increasingly with type 1 diabetes. Both types of diabetes are considered to be a result of lifestyle choices and poor nutrition. For example, lack of exercise, smoking, and foods low in nutritional value contribute to both forms of diabetes. However, it also has been hypothesized (Morgan and Swann, 2000) that First Nations people suffer from diabetes because of 'hefty fetal

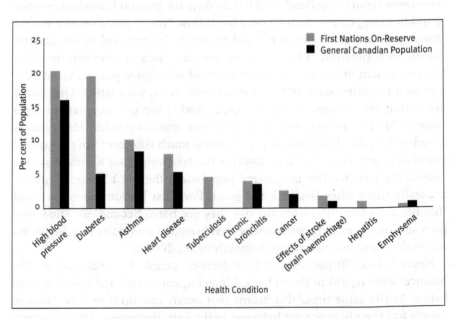

FIGURE 7.3 Age-Standardized Prevalence of Selected Health Conditions, First Nations On-Reserve (2002–3) and General Canadian Population (2003), Adults

Source: Health Canada, A Statistical Profile on the Health of First Nations in Canada: Self-Rated Health and Selected Conditions, 2002–2005, Ottawa, 15, at www.hc-sc.gc.ca/fniah-pnia/alt_formats/pdf/pubs/aborig-autoch/2009-stats-profil-vol3/2009-stats-profil-vol3-eng.pdf.

phenotype'. This view suggests that babies who are 'overweight' at birth (which normally ensures the baby's survival) may actually predispose the child towards contracting diabetes. When these children are exposed to unhealthy eating patterns as well as poverty, these factors will lead to the onset of diabetes.

Disease and Disability

We used to think that many diseases had been defeated in the 1940s when antibiotics were introduced and such changes to the infrastructure affecting quality of life and conducive to health were added, i.e., clean drinking water and sewage systems, or were eliminated, e.g., backyard privies, open cesspools, uncovered garbage dumps, and shallow dug wells. Improvements in socio-economic conditions meant healthier lifestyles, and greater knowledge and vigilance in primary health-care workers were supposed to eradicate many diseases. Over the past several decades, however, there has been a resurgence of some of these diseases, such as polio and tuberculosis. While the incidence of TB has been reduced over the years, First Nations people have experienced this disease much more than non-Aboriginal Canadians, although some immigrant populations also are significantly affected. In fact, in previous generations, some communities lost numbers of their people to tuberculosis, not through death but as they did to the residential schools and to orphanages and foster care—people with tuberculosis were sent to southern Canada for treatment and never given the means to return to their home communities after years of treatment. The resurgence of tuberculosis has impacted First Nations people, with a high of 0.84 cases per 1,000 people in 1980 although it has dropped to 0.62 per 1,000 today. To better appreciate these numbers, Africa's TB rate is 0.80 per 1,000. In 2005, the incidence of TB for First Nations people was six times that of the non-Aboriginal population and 31 times greater than the rate for Canadian-born non-Aboriginal people. In 2007, about 16 per cent of all tuberculosis cases were found in First Nation communities.

A third major disease, unheard of 30 years ago in First Nation communities, is the human immunodeficiency virus (HIV) and acquired immunodeficiency syndrome (AIDS). Today, First Nations people make up nearly 10 per cent of the HIV cases in Canada. Health Canada also claims that nearly 10 per cent of all new cases emerge from the First Nations population. This suggests that while the overall rate of HIV in Canada is stabilizing, in First Nation communities the incidence continues to grow. Well over half of the HIV cases for First Nation individuals result from the use of infected needles when injecting drugs; most of the rest of the cases are sexually transmitted. Other sexually transmitted diseases (STDs) are also high (and increasing) in First Nation communities. For example, about 20 per cent of all new STDs yearly (chlamydia, gonorrhea, syphilis) originate from individuals claiming to be members of First Nations. While antibiotics have been developed to deal with these infections, in many cases they go undiagnosed until it is too late for effective treatment. As a result, sexually transmitted infections are responsible for increasing costs and a significant number of deaths within the First Nations community.

A disease such as diabetes, previously unknown to First Nations, is over twice as high among the First Nations population than in the non–First Nations population—25 per cent of the First Nations people have some form of diabetes compared to 11 per cent of the general Canadian population. From having had 1 per cent of the AIDS cases in Canada, First Nation persons comprised over 10 per cent of total Canadian cases in 2003.

In regard to disability among First Nations people, the rates are almost the same for males and females, and also are little different from those of the general Canadian population. And, like the general population, First Nations people tend to take on more disabilities as they age. The conclusion is that disability is not a unique First Nations concern and it does not disproportionately contribute to the increasing number of people who claim disability.

Some identifiable groups of people live longer, healthier lives and have a greater sense of wellness than is the case for other groups of people. Epidemiologists and social scientists have noted that the health of an individual is a complex result of the interaction of social, economic, genetic, environmental, and individual behaviour. These are referred to as the **determinants of health**. While each of the above factors has its own impact on health, they also interact with each other. One can, for example, eat healthy, exercise, and have a good job, but if one lives in an area that is polluted, one's health will be negatively impacted. Generally, a combination of factors determines the overall health status of an individual or community. Some actions by individuals precipitate these interactions, such as smoking and alcohol use. We know, for example, that nearly 60 per cent of First Nation individuals smoke compared to 24 per cent in the general Canadian population. However, Health Canada has shown that the proportion of First Nations people consuming alcohol is considerably less than is the case for the general Canadian population. On the other hand, the proportion of those reporting heavy drinking among First Nations people is nearly double of that in the general Canadian population. Excessive use of drugs or alcohol can have a number of effects on the physiology and social aspects of an individual and her/his community. Changes in nutrition within First Nation communities—i.e., shifts from country food to store-bought food caused by settlement, development, and ease of access—have resulted in high levels of obesity, which can contribute to diseases such as hypertension, coronary heart disease, diabetes, and certain cancers. At the same time, the determinants of health may be outside the scope and control of the individual. If the nearby river or lake is polluted, catching fish from such an area will have a detrimental impact on the health of an individual. In other cases, First Nation communities have been warned about eating too much wild game that may be contaminated by having ingested a variety of pollutants. This is especially true of larger and predatory animals and fish, which are at the top of food webs where the bioaccumulation of pollutants is greatest. However, for those who are poor, the number of foods that can be substituted is limited.

Conclusion

The federal government has taken some responsibility for providing health-care to First Nation individuals and communities. A complex structure has been put in place that sees the federal, provincial/territorial, and private sectors involved in the provision of health-care services for First Nations people. The bureaucracy involves thousands of individuals within the federal government and in First Nation communities, and millions of dollars to support these people and their programs. Yet these efforts have not closed the health gap between First Nations people and non–First Nations people.

One explanation for this failure is that the federal per capita expenditure for First Nations health is much less than for the general Canadian public. A second answer lurks in the policy and programs developed for a unique cultural group—there is little evidence the health policies or programs take into account the unique cultural aspects of First Nations people. In short, a foreign system has been imposed with no consideration that culture has anything to do with its lack of effectiveness. Finally, we should note that one's health is embedded in the economic structure of society. We know that the introduction of running water and waste water management have dramatically increased the life span of Canadians and enhanced their wellness. Having more CT scans and MRIs has only a marginal impact on quality of life and wellness. Yet we know that over 80 per cent of the First Nation communities do not have safe water supplies; over 30 per cent do not have a proper waste disposal system; and nearly 50 per cent lack basic sanitary facilities.

What is more problematic is that even with a large bureaucracy and significant funding for the past 50 years, no one has yet been able to propose a health-care system that would alleviate the low level of wellness of First Nation individuals and their communities. A crisis continues.

Questions for Critical Thought

1. Why can't the federal and provincial governments come to some agreement with regard to health provisions for First Nations people?

2. How could the federal government establish a health program linked to the culture of First Nations?

3. Why do the health concerns of First Nations differ from those of mainstream Canada?

Suggested Readings

Green, A. 2006. 'Telling 1922's Story of a National Crime: Canada's First Chief Medical Officer and the Aborted Fight for Aboriginal Health Care', *Canadian Journal of Native Studies* 26: 211–26. The author reviews the history of how the federal government refused to act with regard to Aboriginal health issues in the second decade of the twentieth century. He points to a powerful set of cultural assumptions that continue to underlie federal policy.

Waldram, J., A. Herring, and T. Young. 1995. *Aboriginal Health in Canada: Historical, Cultural and Epidemiological Perspectives.* Toronto: University of Toronto Press. This is a seminal work on the health of Aboriginal peoples that also investigates the social determinants of health.

White, J., D. Beavon, and N. Spence. 2007. *Aboriginal Well-Being.* Toronto: Thompson Educational Publishing. This is just one of a series of monographs that addresses the issue of health of First Nations people. The authors attempt to formulate indicators of health for comparative purposes.

Suggested Websites

Central Mortgage and Housing Canada
www.cmhc.schl.gc.ca
CMHC deals with pan-Canadian housing issues but has several publications related to Aboriginal housing.

First Nations and Inuit Health
www.hc-sc.gc.ca
The First Nations and Inuit Health site can be found through the Health Canada site, and you will want to look at both sites for various information about First Nations health and well-being.

National Aboriginal Health Organization
www.naho.ca
The National Aboriginal Health Organization produces papers and provides information on various health-related topics and also publishes the *Journal of Aboriginal Health*, subscriptions to which are available at no cost.

8 The Duty of Government and Fiduciary Responsibility

Learning Objectives

⊛ To understand the duty of the Crown towards First Nations people.
⊛ To learn about fiduciary responsibility.
⊛ To see how the courts of Canada have dealt with the Crown's duty towards First Nations people.
⊛ To discover why First Nations people rejected the First Nations Governance Act.
⊛ To understand courts rulings with regard to 'the duty to consult'.
⊛ To appreciate the historical and contemporary context in which the courts have made their decisions.

Introduction

This chapter focuses on issues related to the federal government's response to claims by First Nations people on a variety of issues such as land, treaties, money, education, and health. It also addresses what responsibility the federal government has with regard to First Nations people. Finally, we will look at how this responsibility emerged.

Slattery (1987: 167–8) puts it best when he states that 'the Crown has a general duty toward First Nation people to protect them in the enjoyment of their Aboriginal rights.' He adds that the 'source of the duty of the Crown was a necessary condition in persuading First Nations people that their rights would be better protected by the Crown than any other source.' In other words, First Nations and their leaders, at different times and in different places, did have options. They could fight, and some did, but especially in the West during the latter half of the nineteenth century they were well aware of the brutal Indian Wars to the south, across the white man's boundary line. Flight was another option, and again, some did flee, moving westward and northward, ahead of European settlement. But one can flee only so far, and it is always a difficult choice to migrate from one's homeland. A third option, until the early nineteenth century, had been to form strategic alliances with the Europeans for peace and warfare, but this option had been foreclosed by political changes and demographic shifts. Finally, and in hindsight perhaps inevitably, they accepted in good faith the option put forth by the Crown's representatives, whereby the Crown accepted a duty to protect the First Nations. The subsequent treaties were seen by Canada's First Nations as reciprocal agreements between nations.

The Crown's duty, then, has its origins in the historical commitment to protect the First Nations from the actions of British settlers in return for First Nations agreeing to live in a peaceful manner. Given the level of prejudice and discrimination that First Nations people have endured over the past 200 years, it is safe to say they have lived up to their side of the bargain. Whether non–First Nations people and their governments have met this commitment is another question.

History of Government Duty

The genesis of this duty can be traced to the Royal Proclamation of 1763, which stated that:

> it is just and reasonable, and essential to our Interest, and the security of our Colonies, that the several Nations or Tribes of Indians with whom We are connected, and who live under our protection, should not be molested or disturbed in the Possession of such Parts of Our Dominions and Territories as, not having been ceded to or purchased by Us, are reserved to them or any of them, as their Hunting Grounds . . . .

Clearly, this overarching statement of Crown responsibility was not based on moral considerations, but was an attempt to bring about peace with various First Nations so that the threat of their engaging in conflict with the settlers would be reduced. It demarcated the vast territory beyond the Appalachian Mountains as Indian lands and stipulated that none of these lands could be alienated except by purchase of the Crown—settlers could not cut deals with local tribes to purchase land. In brief, law relating to Aboriginal people in Canada began in the eighteenth century and although it remained somewhat constant for many years, more recently it has undergone an amazing set of changes. These changes emerged with the *Calder v. Attorney General for British Columbia* (1973) case. This case, which had been before the courts for more than 60 years, deserves close consideration. The Nisga'a people claimed Aboriginal title to their traditional lands in the Nass River Valley of British Columbia even though they had never signed a treaty with the federal government. Three of the judges on the Supreme Court of Canada said that the Nisga'a had a legally recognized title that had not been extinguished by the British Crown or legislation. Three other judges agreed that the Nisga'a originally had some sort of Aboriginal right to their traditional territory but then concluded that those rights had been extinguished by British Columbia legislation before Confederation. The seventh judge did not side with either position but rejected the claim on a procedural point. In the end, the Nisga'a case was dismissed by the Supreme Court. However, it provided considerable concern to the federal government that six of the seven Supreme Court justices who heard the case *did* think that something called 'Aboriginal rights' existed. This troubling decision by the highest court reverberated through the Department of Indian Affairs, the Department of Justice, and other federal agencies. Legal experts began to discuss the issue and legal scholars began to research this issue systematically. Moreover, Scholtz (2009) has noted that the influence of what he calls 'judicial uncertainty' on executive support for negotiations in Canadian land claims policy now has to be taken seriously. The end result has been that the research carried out by scholars has had an impact on how the courts have dealt with the issue of Aboriginal rights.

The *Calder* decision, though technically it went against the First Nation claimant (the Nisga'a eventually achieved a comprehensive land claim agreement in 2000), forced the legal system, the bureaucracy, and politicians to rethink their views about Aboriginal rights and what duties and responsibilities they have when dealing with First Nations people. It also marked a major turning point in First Nation–government relations when Prime Minister Pierre Trudeau noted that 'perhaps Indians do have some Aboriginal rights', and it sparked a new federal policy of negotiating land claims and other 'rights'. In addition, the decision spurred First Nations to press for greater legal protection of their rights, a move that came to fruition in section 35(1) of the Constitution Act, 1982, which recognizes and affirms the 'existing aboriginal and treaty rights of the aboriginal peoples of Canada'.

Fiduciary Duty

The concept of fiduciary duty has a long history in English common law that is now integrated and embedded into the terminology of our legal system with a specific meaning. In early days, the term 'trust' was used to characterize a relationship between two parties, but the term 'trust' began to evolve into a specific, formal term in corporate and property law. A new term, 'fiduciary', was coined to refer to relationships that in some respects are 'trust-like' but not in the legal sense of trusts (Reynolds, 2005). Today the concept of 'fiduciary' means that a trustee has an obligation, when he/she acts, to engage in a selfless manner for the benefit of the beneficiary of the trust. This can refer to a person or to a company, to parents or to any stakeholder who is a 'trustee'. In this kind of relationship, the law holds the entity to a high degree of loyalty and good faith in order to protect the beneficiary. Supreme Court Justice La Forest points out the social justification of a 'fiduciary' principle by noting that law has recognized the importance of ensuring that our social institutions understand that not all relationships are of equal power or what he calls 'a dynamic of mutual autonomy'. He also notes that the marketplace cannot always set the rules and, thus, that some relationships will be bound by a fiduciary principle.

After Confederation, the federal government acted in a fashion to indicate that it did not have (or accept) a trust relationship or any other obligation towards First Nations people other than what was stated in the treaties. The weight of the government and the legal system simply moved forward and dealt with First Nations people as though they did not have any trust or fiduciary relationship. However, by the twentieth century, the federal government agreed that it was a 'trustee' of First Nations people and their land. Early attempts by First Nations people to challenge this view were stopped when the government made it illegal for any 'third party' to act on behalf of a First Nation.

Nevertheless, First Nations, as they understood their treaties and other pieces of legislation, were convinced that the government had some type of duty towards them. The government had shown some recognition that it was holding land 'in trust' for Indians. For example, the British Columbia terms of union in 1871 stated that the Dominion government would have charge of the Indians and be the trustee of Indian lands. The issue was whether this trust was a legal relationship between the Crown and First Nations people or simply was political rhetoric that gave some general overview of how government related to First Nations. In other words, the question was whether 'trust' was a concept that could be used in court against the Crown or if it was just a moral obligation. In various cases before the courts the government argued it did not have any fiduciary or trust relationship with First Nations and used a **political trust** argument. This stance was successful and a number of legal cases were decided on the basis that the relationship between the government and First Nations was nothing more than a political trust relationship. This is not to say that in some cases the courts did not rule in favour of a First Nation claim, for they did, but such favourable decisions were not based on a fiduciary relationship but on some other evidence and some other point of law. Over the years, the courts seemed to be saying that rights could not be considered a 'trust' property and the relationship was one of a 'political trust doctrine'. These political trusts were conceptualized at two levels: higher and lower. 'Higher trusts' are trust relationships imposed on public officers but are not legally enforceable. For example, if an elected politician were to make a decision based on his political status that led to harm, he/she could not be taken to court over the decision. On the other hand, 'lower trusts' could be enforced by the courts. For example, if a judge were to be found accepting a bribe in a legal case, he/she could be held accountable by the courts. In both cases, however, the relationship to the public is based on 'trust'.

Green (1973) was an early advocate of a very different interpretation and, on the basis of his analysis of treaties and international law, pointed out that the relationship between First Nations people and the government is not based on trusteeship. He shows that when terms such as 'ward' and 'guardian' are used in the documents relating to First Nations people and government, the relationship is fiduciary. This idea was put to the test in *Guerin* (1984). In that trial (see Chapter 1), which culminated in a Supreme Court decision in favour of the Musqueam band, it was finally established that the Crown was in breach of its fiduciary duty. This decision meant that the Crown's obligations were lower trusts such that they could be enforced by the courts. The world turned upside down after the *Guerin* case for both the government and for the First Nations people! No longer could the Crown argue that it was a 'trustees' only in the 'higher sense' and thus not subject to the courts. The decision meant that the government's unique relationship with First Nations people across the country now was encumbered with a fiduciary duty, and the federal government had to bear in mind when it acted on behalf of the First Nations people that it was subject to penalties under the law if that fiduciary duty was broken or unfulfilled.

The Courts Speak and the Government Reconsiders

Immediately after the decision, the courts were not flooded with a number of 'fiduciary duty' claims by First Nation communities as it took some time before the implications of the decision were fully understood. However, a second Supreme Court decision (*Sparrow*, 1990) supporting the fiduciary duty of the federal government opened up the flood gates in terms of bringing such cases to the courts. Subsequently, the 1995 *Blueberry River* decision by the Supreme Court added to the deluge of cases brought before the courts—all involving fiduciary duty. Some judges subsequently attempted to deny that the relationship between the Crown and First Nations was fiduciary per se and limited the fiduciary obligations to specific fact situations. However, a series of Supreme Court decisions in the late 1990s struck a blow at these efforts and firmly established the fact that the role of the fiduciary relationship was a cornerstone of the law. Thus, as Reynolds (2005) points out, a majority of cases dealing with the fiduciary obligations owed to First Nation peoples were decided during the 1990s so that by the twenty-first century, the issue largely has been settled.

The fiduciary duty issue is particularly germane with regard to First Nation lands. Experts are clear that there seems little doubt that fiduciary obligations apply to almost all aspects of the Crown's role when it comes to dealing with First Nation lands (ibid.).

Extending the Concept of Fiduciary Duty

Of interest for First Nations people has been whether or not fiduciary duty can be applied to the protection of Aboriginal rights and title—and a variety

---

Box 8.1 ❊ *Blueberry River v. Canada*: Establishing Fiduciary Obligations

In the *Blueberry River* case a First Nation community in northern BC had taken treaty with the federal government in 1916, and subsequently surrendered some of its reserve lands (1940) to the Crown, which in turn leased that land to a land reclamation company for a 50-year term. While the band initially accepted the lease terms, as time went on they noted there were no increases in the lease payment. The federal government refused to provide them with a copy of the lease, and the band pressured the government to terminate the lease. When it became known that oil and gas were being extracted from these lands, the band once again requested that the land be returned to them so they could benefit from the natural resource extraction. Again, the federal government refused to return the land to the band. It was then discovered in 1948 that there was no Order-in-Council accepting the original surrender as required by the Indian Act. The land simply had been taken by the government, transferred to another government agency, and leased to a third party without due government process. However, more than 50 years passed before Indian Affairs disclosed this state of affairs to the band. The Supreme Court ruled that the government breached its fiduciary duty, and held that:

> Where a party is granted power over another's interests, and where the other party is correspondingly deprived of power over them, or is "vulnerable," then the party possessing the power is under a fiduciary obligation to exercise it in the best interests of the other. . . . The Department of Indian Affairs' duty was the usual duty of a fiduciary to act with reasonable diligence with respect to the Indians' interests. Reasonable diligence required that the Department of Indian Affairs move to correct the erroneous transfer when it came into possession of facts suggesting error. (Boyer, 2001: 123)

---

of other issues—as it is with land. This question comes about because the Constitution Act, 1982, in section 35, affirms and recognizes 'existing aboriginal and treaty rights'. However, since the rights identified in section 35 are not part of the Charter, there is no guarantee that these existing rights would be recognized by the courts, nor was there any action that could provide protection of these rights. All the Constitution said was that it recognized and affirmed those rights, but it said nothing about protecting those rights. In fact, section 25 of the Charter worked from the other end, stating that the rights and freedoms guaranteed by the Charter 'shall not be construed so as to abrogate or derogate from any aboriginal, treaty or other rights or freedoms' of Canada's Aboriginal peoples. These two sections, taken together, seemed to create a closed circle.

Legal technicalities are as much a part of law as the 'facts' and also have to be addressed by the courts. Legal authorities began to think that the Aboriginal rights of section 35 were not protected by the Charter. Rather, they appeared to be protected from the Charter. These rights could be unilaterally done away with or changed by the government. Bartlett (1983: 187) noted that, far from protecting or guaranteeing the rights of First Nation peoples, section 35 of the Constitution may actually provide for the 'diminution and abrogation of such rights without their consent'.

Fortunately for First Nations people, the issue was put to rest by the Supreme Court in *R. v. Sparrow* (1990), which dealt with the issue of fiduciary duty with regard to Aboriginal rights. In this case and others that followed, the Court held that section 35 should be interpreted in the light of the fiduciary principle and that it should be given a liberal and generous interpretation. In essence, the Court incorporated the fiduciary principle into the Constitution, a protection that had not been provided by the politicians. One must remember that prior to the Constitution Act, 1982, the federal government, on a regular basis, unilaterally extinguished Aboriginal rights.

After 1982 the government could not extinguish Aboriginal rights unless it could satisfy a series of tests. The Supreme Court (see *Blueberry River v. Canada* for a full interpretation) said that in order to extinguish or amend Aboriginal rights, the government had to meet two tests. Using the terminology of the Supreme Court decision in *Blueberry River* (1995), first, it had to be established that an infringement had occurred at first sight rather than as a result of a test of 'balance of probabilities', and if that condition was met, then it had to be determined if there was any justification for the **prima facie** infringement. To meet the first test, the courts would have to answer three questions: (1) Is the limitation unreasonable? (2) Does the regulation impose undue hardship? (3) Does the regulation deny to the holders of the Aboriginal right their preferred means of exercising that right? However, the commentary on the judgement also pointed out that the individual or group who challenges the regulation has the responsibility of proving a prima facie infringement. If a prima facie infringement is found, the courts proceed to the second test, which is to ask whether there was justification for the infringement. For the first time, the courts had concrete criteria they could follow to make decisions. Moreover, individuals or groups wishing to bring cases before the courts would know the kinds of questions that would be asked in order to make a determination.

After the *Guerin* ruling in 1984, the courts extended their coverage of fiduciary principle, which requires governments to justify any infringement of an Aboriginal right, including a treaty right. Where First Nations people and the federal government are engaged in litigation and where funding is an issue, the principles of fiduciary duty play out differently. In some cases, the courts have held that the Crown has a fiduciary relationship, while in other cases the argument that the litigation is based on a fiduciary trust has been rejected and the facts of the case determined the outcome of the case. In summary, in cases that involve litigation and issues of who pays for the court costs, the courts have taken a robust stance and the outcomes depend on the unique aspects of the case.

The Duty to Consult

More recently, a series of court decisions have focused on the issue of **duty to consult** with First Nations. Three specific cases have framed the answer to this question and, again, have forced governments to rethink their relationship with First Nations. In 2004, in *Taku River Tlingit First Nation v. British Columbia* and *Haida Nation v. British Columbia*, the courts made important decisions; these were followed by the *Mikisew Cree First Nation v. Canada* (2005). In the *Haida* case, the Supreme Court ruled that the duty of governments to consult and accommodate Aboriginal interests arises from the principle of the **honour of the Crown** rather than from a fiduciary duty (Newman, 2009). The judges noted that both the federal and provincial governments have this duty while third parties, such as corporations, do not. However, this distinction raises another question as to whether or not Crown agencies, other than quasi-judicial bodies, have a fiduciary duty to First Nations people, for example, British Columbia Hydro and Power Authority. The courts have ruled on this issue but the outcomes have been different—some saying yes, others saying no.

Another outcome of these cases is that the courts ruled that the Aboriginal group did not have to have a court order showing the existence of an Aboriginal right in order for the duty to consult and accommodate to become operative. If the existence of an Aboriginal right was in question, the principle of the honour of the Crown would become operative instead of the principle of fiduciary duty. However, either way, the duty to consult and accommodate would have to be dealt with. The courts went on to say that the duty to consult would have to take place early on in the stages of project development and this would have to be in addition to the standard public consultation process established by various regulatory agencies. For example, in the *Mikisew Cree* case, the Court observed that the meetings between Parks Canada and the Mikisew Cree took place after a decision by Parks Canada essentially had been made and the consultations were a sham. As such, if the consultation takes place without a genuine intention of taking into consideration the views of the First Nations people, the consultations are considered invalid. The consultations have to take place before an infringement of an Aboriginal right or title occurs if it is to form part of the justification for the infringement (Reynolds, 2005). These recent decisions have been contested by provincial governments and some, like Alberta, have vigorously objected to the court decisions. How this all will play out over the next few years will be of interest to First Nations and governments.

Finally, the question arises as to whether the duty to consult is owed to individual First Nations people. Previous court decisions all dealt with Indian bands or First Nation communities recognized under the Indian Act. A number of cases have come before the courts and they have considered the application of the fiduciary relationship to individuals. Thus far it would seem that an individual can bring such an action against the Crown, but as of 2010 not one has been successful. This does not mean that the court decisions have all gone against the individual but rather that the principle of fiduciary trust has not been part of the decision—rulings state that this principle is irrelevant to the facts of the case.

As we move into the second decade of the twenty-first century, the Crown is trying to realign relations with First Nations people, although the task is troublesome and awkward. Previous legislation, authority, and powers allocated to governments allowed them to act on the assumption there was no fiduciary trust relationship between them and First Nations people and they did not need to consult with them. All of this now has to be changed. Organizations and agencies of the government must abide by these principles of fiduciary duty and the honour of the Crown, and in some cases have to rethink their operations to take into consideration the court decisions. Some have resisted changing and continue to operate as they did prior to the Supreme Court decisions. Of course, these changes in the law have precipitated challenges by First Nations: one favourable decision can lead to several other similar cases coming before the courts. In other cases, the federal government is taking steps to undertake a gradual process of transferring some of the powers of the federal government to First Nations. While part of the rationale is cost reduction, another reason is the desire to limit the government's liability for breach of its fiduciary obligations (Reynolds, 2005), although it is not clear that the transfer reduces the Crown's fiduciary obligations. In that respect the answer may be that fiduciary obligation is reduced to whatever extent the Crown releases control over First Nation interests.

Section 35 of the Constitution, 1982, has allowed First Nations people to seek legal decisions with regard to many issues that previously were considered non-issues and as such were rejected by the courts, ignored by politicians, and left by bureaucrats to languish in filing cabinets. The *Calder* case, while important, still left room for the argument that Aboriginal rights did not exist. The *Guerin* decision indicated that the Supreme Court was ready for the task of interpreting section 35 and addressing the issue of Aboriginal title as well as fiduciary obligations. The decision also provided legal experts and communities with the necessary material for examining Aboriginal rights and issues that emerge from this (McNeil, 2001).

Governance

Today, the government recognizes the inherent right of self-government under section 35 of the Constitution Act, 1982. This recognition came about without change to the Constitution. The government accepts that First Nations have the right to govern themselves specific to issues that are internal to their communities and related to their unique cultures. It also agrees that the inherent right of self-governance would be confirmed by the courts although it insists there are different views about the nature and scope of those rights. Moreover, there is the feeling that the courts, after hearing a case, would send the issue back to government and ask it to negotiate a settlement. As a result, the federal government in 1995 adopted a new policy: *Canada's Approach to Implementation of the Inherent Right and the Negotiation of Aboriginal Self-government.*

In adopting this policy, the government established three levels of self-government. At one level, Ottawa is prepared to give inherent self-governance to First Nations on a selected number of issues, matters that they define as internal to the group, integral to its distinct Aboriginal culture, and essential to its operation as a government. In this list of issues we find First Nation control over such areas as education, social services, policing, membership, housing, and property rights. The second level of governance consists of areas that may go beyond matters internal to the community. At this level, the government is prepared to negotiate some degree of First Nation jurisdiction or authority but not inherent right of control (Abele and Prince, 2006). This level includes such issues as divorce, gaming, administration of justice, migratory birds, hunting and fishing regulations, the environment, and penitentiaries. Finally, a third level is not considered relevant to First Nation communities and thus federal control remains total with no jurisdiction by First Nations. Examples of the third level include international relations, national defence, and international treaty-making.

The Rejection of the First Nations Governance Act

Indian and Northern Affairs Canada defines governance as 'how a community is run and the rules that apply in its day-to-day operation' (Canada, 1995: 6). Issues such as financial accountability, chiefs' and councils' accountability to community members, and elections fall under the jurisdiction of the First Nation community (Bianchi, 2001). In an attempt to codify this, the federal government proposed a First Nations Governance Act in 2001 to amend parts of the Indian Act in order to modernize the governance of First Nation communities and make for a more effective and efficient regime. In addition, the proposed Act aimed to provide First Nation communities with tools of governance that would enable them to respond more effectively to their unique needs and aspirations. Finally, the Act sought to assist First Nations in designing and implementing ways of selecting their leaders, establishing their administrative and financial management, and creating the appropriate accountability processes. When this bill was introduced, a vociferous rejection of it erupted, similar to First Nations' rejection of the White Paper in 1969. First Nation communities and organizations formed a coalition that lobbied against the bill—on moral and legal grounds.

The first objection to the proposed Act was that, given the high level of mistrust between First Nations people and the government, the process did not meet the minimum criteria for acceptability by First Nations communities. They claimed they were not consulted in the development and preparation of Bill C-7 and, thus, this was another top-down decision rather than a proposal that had been shaped by the people themselves. They felt that they could only react to the proposed legislation and had no meaningful say in the creation and substance of the bill, let alone amendments. They argued that they, as First Nations people, would 'draw up their own governance procedures based on traditional customs and practices at the local, community, regional and national level' (Bianchi, 2001). Moreover, they felt that it 'did not deal with the First Nations' vision of governance, self-government, treaty making or treaty implementation.' First Nations people wanted a governance document that was based on a 'nation-to-nation' relationship—acknowledged in section 35 of the Constitution Act, 1982. They also sensed that the proposed legislation would make them less accountable to their own communities and more accountable to Ottawa. So adamant was their resolve against the proposal that the Native Women's Association of Canada refused to accept $1.1 million from Indian and Northern Affairs Canada to assist with consultations with First Nations with regard to the proposed Act. First Nations people argued that the government's strategy (which also included the First Nations Financial Institutions Act and the Indian Claims Commission Act) would set the stage for the eventual extinguishment of all First Nation rights and land entitlements. For example, they saw that these Acts were in essence derived from the Indian Act and thus gave credence to an administrative regime that would perceive First Nations governance as a delegated power creating a kind of municipal government. Such a regime does not recognize constitutionally entrenched inherent Aboriginal rights. In addition, it was felt that these proposed Acts would release the federal government from its responsibilities. In changing the legal status of First Nations to something comparable to municipalities—with no rights as sovereign or semi-sovereign nations—the government would be able to totally absolve itself of its fiduciary responsibilities. For example, the proposed Indian Claims Commission Act would limit federal liability for mismanaging a treaty agreement to $5 million.

The First Nations Governance Act also required that First Nations produce a set of institutions within two years. After having spent over 100 years destroying First Nation governments, Ottawa now wanted them rebuilt in less than two years. The Act would create a single 'template' that would then be applied to all First Nation communities across the country (the 'one size fits all' mentality), once again ignoring the fact that not all First Nations are the same. In the end, First Nations people argued the content of the bill was simply unacceptable.

In response, the Assembly of First Nations presented to the federal government its own First Nations governance strategy. The Assembly of First Nations plan (*First Nations–Federal Crown Accord on the Recognition and Implementation of First Nation Governance*) offered a vision and principles on which a new policy could be based (Assembly of First Nations, 2005). For example, the Assembly of First Nations insisted that First Nations governance had to be based on a number of principles: nation-to-nation negotiation, inherent rights, diversity, consent of First Nations people, the inclusion of traditional forms of government, self-determination, and respect for First Nations culture and traditions (Cornell et al., 2002). It also identified a process for implementing and recognizing First Nation governments. The government of Canada rejected the proposal and offered a second revised proposal. In the end, the Assembly of First Nations rejected this revised plan because they saw it as nothing more than a new form of the old assimilation policy.

Cornell et al. (2002) provide additional insights into the reaction of First Nations to the proposed First Nations Governance Act. They point out that the core issue in the Act was the degree to which issues of governance are not part of the First Nation community. As noted earlier, the government provided the template of acceptable areas of First Nations concern, specified the conditions for the adoption of various codes, and once again made the minister the ultimate arbiter in a variety of disputes. Ottawa wishes to limit the areas of self-governance that First Nation communities can control and First Nation communities question the extent of the government's commitment to Indigenous self-governance. Cornell et al. also note a number of issues that the First Nations Governance Act did not address. For example, the making of laws and policy, dispute resolution, and the implementation of governmental decisions are critical concerns that any government would want to control. The claim that these are not of interest to First Nations people is one that the First Nations totally rejected.

Community Governance

The variations in governance structure in First Nation communities are small, apart from one major difference. In some cases, the community continues to use hereditary processes by which chiefs/councillors are chosen to make decisions for the community. In this system, the selection of chief and band council is through an independent community body, e.g., clan mothers who select the person(s) and this position is held for life unless the individual engages in behaviour that is unacceptable to the community. When that person retires, moves, or dies, someone in his/her family replaces the individual. Historically, this hereditary process was the manner in which chiefs and members of council were selected. Today, a few First Nation communities, such as the Mohawks, still use this procedure, but others would like to return to this form of selection of a chief and band council.

During the twentieth century the federal government objected to this procedure and formally and informally pressured First Nation communities to select their chief and council members through an electoral process. As a result of this pressure and enforcement, many communities now select their leaders through periodic elections, a procedure that is the prevalent manner in which chiefs and councils are brought into power. This political process has been filtering into the First Nation communities so that elections are fiercely fought battles where factions in the community lobby for their favourite candidates. For most elections the voter turnout is considerable, and much higher than in the general Canadian electoral process. However, in the end, gender, family connections, and social class (not so unlike Canadian politics in general) trump the selection of candidates. For example, very few women are chiefs and few women are members on the band councils. Even though women, generally, are more highly educated than men, few of them find their way into the political structure of the First Nation community.

Politics in First Nation communities favours men. It is one avenue through which men can succeed in the community despite not having the educational and skills training that one might expect of political leaders. Certainly not all leaders are required to have advanced degrees, and some exceptional leaders in both First Nation communities and the larger society have little educational or skills training. However, having some area of expertise in a technological society, in addition to leadership skills, is an asset that leaders need. This is not the case in First Nation communities. Gender issues are not specific to governance but they have become political milestones in the area of First Nation politics. The *Corbiere* decision (2000) that addressed the rights of band members living off-reserve in voting in band elections is notable in this regard. The Court found that the Indian Act violated the

Charter rights of off-reserve members when elections were held. Since most of the people living off-reserve are women, this decision effectively gave all women living off-reserve who had regained their Indian status through Bill C-31 the right to vote in band elections. Prior to the *Corbiere* decision they had been denied the right to vote. Three bands challenged this decision but their case was rejected. First Nation women also argue that the First Nations Land Management Act effectively means that Indian women can't inherit or bequeath land. Moreover, if a First Nation woman gets a divorce, she does not have the same rights as other women in Canada. The disposition of on-reserve property when a divorce occurs is not governed by provincial law but by the federal Indian Act that, surprisingly, contains no provisions for how to divide marital property. And since it is a matter of historical process that males living on the reserve, under law, possess most of the reserve property, when a woman divorces a male living on the reserve she is not able to claim a half-interest in that property if her husband holds the certificate of possession. Many other sources of tension between genders within First Nation communities produce second-class citizenship for women. This tension pits the political aspirations of First Nation leaders against the rights and needs of female band members.

Those individuals who occupy high-status positions and command substantial resources usually are the ones who become chiefs and band councillors. How the incumbents muster their resources and their decision-making will determine if they will be re-elected. However, there are few checks and balances to keep the chief and council working on behalf of the community. Few communities have established workable governance structures to ensure that the goals and objectives of the community are first and foremost in the minds of decision-makers.

In the end, self-governance has been presented by the government of Canada as a top-down process and through a single template structure. Yet, as noted above, First Nation communities vary considerably in a number of historical, social, economic, and physical attributes. Imposed uniformity may not be the best solution to develop the governance capacity of a community. In fact, Oakerson (1999: 87) argues that 'uniform decentralization often results in governments that locals do not want and in which they refuse to participate.' Cornell et al. (2002: 32) argue that the form of governance should match the Indigenous political culture of the community. They claim that a 'cultural match provides a legitimacy of the governing institutions and will fit within the community's beliefs and aspirations.' The community trust that emerges will create community support for their actions, which means, in turn, that they are less likely to be abused by leaders of the community. Having the cultural match also will allow for better accountability. This means that there will be a greater sense of responsiveness by the leaders to their constituents as they make decisions and implement policies.

First Nation communities, after over a century of oppression by the Crown, want the power to run their own affairs. Self-determination has to be backed up by responsible governance if it is to enhance the well-being of First Nations people (Castro-Rea and Jimenez, 2007). But as Cairns (2005) points out, in view of slow progress to date under the Indian Act and the Indian and Northern Affairs bureaucracy, there is certainly room for improvement. Ultimately, without genuine decision-making powers, developing good governance institutions won't accomplish much. One must have both sovereign powers as well as good governance.

The federal government presented a First Nations Governance Act in an attempt to provide First Nations with certain governmental powers. However, the Act was resisted and was never implemented because it did not give First Nations people self-governance and actually consolidated decision-making more in the hands of the federal government.

Conclusion

As pointed out by Flannigan (2004), prior to the *Guerin* decision most of the decisions of the Supreme Court of Canada employed a restrictive approach to imposing liability. However, with *Guerin*, a more expansive concept of the fiduciary principle began to reshape how the courts viewed the relationship between First Nations and the government. Today, what fiduciary duty implies has become clearer, which allows the courts to apply certain criteria to make a decision. In the *Manitoba Métis Federation v. Attorney General of Canada and Manitoba* (2008) the judges stated that 'where one party, whether by statute, agreement or even by unilateral decision, has an obligation to act for the benefit of another and that obligation carries with it a discretionary power, the party with the power takes on a fiduciary duty.' Moreover, that fiduciary duty defines the nature of the relationship; the nature or type of stakeholder is not what gives one party a fiduciary duty.

The courts have ruled that the fiduciary relationship is incorporated into the Constitution and that the relationship can be extinguished only with the consent of the First Nations people involved or through a formal constitutional amendment. Fiduciary obligations are owed by all federal departments and not just by the Indian Affairs ministry, although there seem to be some contradictory court decisions on this issue. Nevertheless, it would seem prudent for both provincial and federal departments to make decisions based on the duty to consult and accommodate when dealing with First Nations.

The implications of this new understanding of the law as it applies to First Nations people have important economic and legal dimensions. Governments will now have to rethink what 'consulting' and 'accommodation' mean in terms of the economic issues, as will private corporations.

Indeed, the first modern land claim treaty, the James Bay and Northern Quebec Agreement of 1975, was a direct result of the failure of governments to properly consult and accommodate the people whose lands were to be hugely affected by the massive James Bay hydroelectric project. The extent to which First Nation communities have the right to share in the profits that accrue to both governments and the private sector from forestry, oil and gas, and mining, as well as the spinoff benefits from such economic projects, will be determined on a case-by-case basis, as with the Innu of Labrador and the Voisey's Bay nickel mine and with the Attawapiskat First Nation and the Victor diamond mine in the James Bay region of northern Ontario.

The political aspects of this new fiduciary obligation are clear. First Nations now realize that when they are negotiating with government, they have some power in the negotiations by insisting that consultation, accommodation, and fiduciary obligations be met. Rejection of these claims can bring about litigation for which the courts now have a clear roadmap. Given these alternatives, more direct, overt conflict between First Nations and government may decrease over the next decade, particularly in the political arena as the two parties seek out a legal compromise and settlement on issues.

In the *Haida* case the Supreme Court raised the question of the relationship between the honour of the Crown and the Crown's fiduciary relationship with First Nations. In the end, the Court decided in favour of the Haida, not based on fiduciary principles but rather on the issue of the honour of the Crown. Has this decision taken us into new, uncharted lands? Will this spawn new litigation over issues that were considered resolved prior to this decision? Clearly, the relationship between First Nations and the Crown is evolving, and the Supreme Court has had a major influence on this changing relationship.

As we look at the consequences of the decisions taken by the courts over the past three decades, we see that law relating to First Nations people has been rewritten. No single case rewrote the law; a patchwork of cases emerged, each new one building on the prior decisions. Some reaction by people who argue that the current state of affairs has gone too far has arisen. The federal government responded favourably to the recommendations made in the Harvard Project with regard to economic development, but again failed to give First Nation communities real jurisdictional power. First Nations people argue that if the federal government wants them to be accountable for their actions, then they have to provide those nations with genuine decision-making powers—a stance that the federal government refuses to take.

Questions for Critical Thought

1. How have the courts changed the relationship between First Nations people and the government of Canada?

2. How different would the relations be between First Nations people and the government of Canada be if less emphasis were to be placed on litigation and more on restorative justice?

3. Could the principle of fiduciary duty be replaced by another principle in order to allow different relations to emerge between the two parties?

Suggested Readings

Barsh, R. 1993. 'The Challenge of Indigenous Self-Determination', *University of Michigan Journal of Law Reform* 26: 277–312. The author addresses some of the structural and legal impediments for First Nations people in their quest to achieve self-determination.

Burrows, J. 1992. 'A Genealogy of Law: Inherent Sovereignty and First Nations Self-Government', *Osgoode Hall Law Journal* 30: 37–64. The author, a noted legal scholar, traces the development of how the concept 'inherent' has been dealt with by the courts and its linkage to self-government.

Flannigan, R. 2004. 'The Boundaries of Fiduciary Accountability', *Canadian Bar Review* 83: 30–55. The author defines the concept of fiduciary accountability and outlines the contexts in which the principle applies.

Macklem, P. 1995. 'Normative Dimensions of an Aboriginal Right of Self-Government', *Queen's Law Journal* 21: 173–219. The author looks at Canadian law and assesses how First Nations self-government might fit into it.

Reynolds, J. 2005. *A Breach of Duty.* Saskatoon: Purich. This is a case study (including the historical context) of the landmark *Guerin* case and what the implications of the Supreme Court's final decision meant for First Nations people.

Suggested Websites

National Centre for First Nations Governance
www.fngovernance.org
  The website of this service and research organization on Aboriginal governance issues includes some videos, as well as a newsletter on current issues and various programs.

First Nations Pedagogy Online
www.firstnationspedagogy.ca/selfgovernance.html
  This site provides links to other sites that focus on First Nations governance and to practical and academic publications on the topic.

9

Self-Government, Aboriginal Rights, and the Inherent Right of First Nation Peoples

Learning Objectives

- To understand the concept of self-government.
- To learn about Aboriginal and inherent rights.
- To discover how self-government links with governance and accountability for First Nation communities.
- To understand why Canada voted against the Declaration on the Rights of Indigenous People approved by the United Nations.
- To learn how the courts have looked at the issue of self-government.

Introduction

So you read in the paper yesterday that a First Nation community in northern Saskatchewan was being investigated by Indian and Northern Affairs for misappropriation of funds. And two weeks before that you saw on TV that another reserve in Ontario was being investigated for excessive expenditures that were for the chief's salary. Sound familiar? These two events really did occur. But what you didn't know was that after investigations were completed by independent third parties, the misappropriation of funds allegation was untrue and that the expenditures for the chief's salary had been approved by the band council and the Department of Indian and Northern Affairs. The investigation results never appeared so prominently in the media. But the impression made by the first reports probably stuck for many readers and viewers: members of the First Nation communities were committing all kinds of fraud and paying themselves salaries well beyond what they deserved.

This is not to suggest that no members of First Nation communities ever engage in criminal or unethical behaviour. To be sure, there are examples of wrongdoing by First Nation individuals just as there are in the larger society. Yet, the media should be more circumspect and balanced in their treatment of the events in First Nation communities, and we should not forget that the media are in the business to make money, not to provide readers with unbiased coverage or to carry out research. Some are just more subtle than others; some are more careful than others; and some are more ethical than others.

For First Nations, self-government is a strategy by which they can regain control over their lives, manage their affairs, and actually make important decisions for their communities. As Iribacher-Fox (2010) points out, **self-determination** is necessary to First Nations survival in Canada. In 1982 the Special Parliamentary Committee on Indian Self-Government issued its report (the Penner Report, after its chairman, MP Keith Penner) recommending that First Nations should be self-governing at a level distinct from municipalities and distinct from the Indian Act. Initially, **self-government** efforts were attempted through the Indian Act. However, it became clear that this was not a workable solution because the government's idea of self-government was akin to the structure, organization, and authority of municipal government, and First Nations did not see self-government as a variant of municipal government. Municipal governments in Canada, after all, have no formal constitutional standing or authority. Consequently, alternatives had to be found. Four constitutional conferences took place from 1983 to 1987 to discuss the issue but nothing was resolved. Then, in 1993, the Liberal government publicly recognized the inherent right of self-government for First Nations people and began to implement it without opening constitutional discussions (Wherrett, 1999: 4).

Governance and Accountability

A central problem in First Nation communities is that there has been little accountability to community residents and lots of accountability to Ottawa. Moreover, much of what goes on in the governance of First Nations is not transparent and thus community residents cannot see the rationale or the logic of many of the decisions made by chief and council. To address this issue, the National Centre for First Nations Governance is working on developing strategies to ensure accountability and transparency. However, given the nature of the Indian Act and its pervasive reach, First Nation communities are constrained in terms of what they can do to ensure accountability and transparency. Nevertheless, some First Nations communities are now implementing rules for good governance.

Prior to European settlement, First Nations had developed different ways to organize their societies. As colonialization progressed, these institutions were ignored or suppressed as the federal government enforced a single, uniform political system across the country. As Wherrett (1999: 3) points out, First Nations talk about 'sovereignty and self-government as responsibilities given to them by the Creator and of a spiritual connection to the land'—powers they have held for millennia. They do not seek to be granted self-government by the Crown but want Canadians to recognize that First Nation governments existed long before the arrival of settlers, independent of the Crown.

Aboriginal Rights and the Courts

Indigenous rights were removed with Spain's initial conquest of Central America, a policy that created debate hundreds of years ago about the relationship between Indigenous people and the colonial powers. A consequence of the European assumption of rights of 'discovery' and conquest was that, for many years, Indigenous peoples were denied statehood and the right to make law. In effect, international law was European law and, depending on the European power that held control in a particular part of the New World, this law provided little if any protection or rights to the sovereign Aboriginal nations who were already here. The treatment of Indigenous people was relegated to domestic law and became a matter between the European colonizing power and the Indigenous people.

In Canada, the Iroquois from Ontario's Six Nations Reserve petitioned the League of Nations in the early 1920s to protest against Canada and Britain's refusal to acknowledge the self-governing status of their confederacy. Although their leader, Deskeheh (Levi General), journeyed to Europe where he spent over a year gaining the support of numerous smaller European and Middle Eastern countries, the British summarily dismissed the Iroquois appeal and Deskeheh, travelling on an Iroquois passport, was refused re-entry to Canada on his return.

For the next 50 years, the state showed little concern or interest in regard to the claims being made by First Nations for self-government. Pitty (2001) argues that a historical breakthrough in the re-emergence of Indigenous peoples' concerns about self-government came in 1975. This date reflects the decision of the International Court of Justice that 'the indigenous inhabitants of Western Sahara were entitled to self-determination instead of forced incorporation within a state.' Since this time, nearly all cases revolving around the issue of self-government have used this decision as their starting point. This case has political and legal significance for two reasons. First, the International Court refuted the assumption that nomadic tribes were too primitive to occupy land in any legal sense. Second, it upheld the idea that 'self-determination' is a basic principle of international law.

In Canada around the same time two important events—a court decision and a historic agreement—moved self-governance forward. In 1973, in *Calder*, the Nisga'a land claim case resulted with six out of seven Supreme Court of Canada justices ruling that Aboriginal land title did indeed exist in law. Then, in 1975, the James Bay and Northern Quebec Agreement was signed by the James Bay Cree and Inuit of Quebec and by the Quebec and federal governments. This agreement, often considered the first modern land claim treaty, paved the way for the huge James Bay hydroelectric project and for a new degree of autonomy for the Native peoples of northern Quebec.

The demands made by First Nations people in Canada led to the recognition and affirmation of existing Aboriginal and treaty rights in the Constitution Act, 1982. In 1995 the federal government recognized the existence of an **inherent right** of self-government for First Nations people as a right under section 35 of the Constitution Act, 1982 (see Hurley, 2009, for a full discussion of this as well as the document produced by the federal government entitled *Inherent Right of Self-Government Policy, 1995*). Section 35 acknowledges the pre-existing rights of Aboriginal people—government did not create them. Moreover, it protects these pre-existing rights from unjustifiable interference by the federal and provincial governments. The 1998 government document, *Gathering Strength*, formally recognized the right of self-government as an existing inherent Aboriginal right. The current government approach to recognizing First Nation self-government includes negotiations on comprehensive self-government agreements and incremental steps towards self-government through the transfer of authority to First Nations (Wherrett, 1999: 2). Over the past three decades, a number of self-government arrangements have been reached, including the James Bay and Northern Quebec Agreement (1975), the Sechelt Indian Band Self-Government Agreement (1986), the Yukon Umbrella Final Agreement (1993), the Nunavut Final Agreement (1993), and the Nisga'a Final Agreement (2000).

Inherent Rights and the Courts

'Inherent' means self-originating, in this instance, in a First Nations people. In other words, an inherent right is not dependent for its existence on Crown sovereignty or on the Constitution. It means that **Aboriginal rights** exist because Aboriginal peoples lived in Canada prior to European colonization and had their own societies, political systems, laws, and forms of government (McNeil, 2006). Rustand (2010), speaking for the Canadian Constitution Foundation, argues that the Constitution Act, 1982, has established two levels of government—federal and provincial—and that other governments, such as municipal governments, are established by provincial legislation that delegates jurisdiction and authority to these bodies. He suggests that while First Nation self-government may be obtained through delegating legislation, there is no room in the Constitution to acknowledge 'inherent' self-government. In fact, he argues that this would contravene the Constitution. Any recognition of inherent government powers, according to Rustand, is incompatible with the Constitution and contrary to over 125 years of jurisprudence. In addition, from this point of view, First Nations people cannot have self-regulatory powers that involve the coercive powers of government. In the end, this view claims that recognizing the inherent right of self-government to any group of people will take Canada down a slippery slope of allocating governmental powers and privileges to groups of

governments (Assembly of First Nations, 2005). The joint committee was to examine the requirements for establishing the recognition and implementation of First Nation governments. It also was to make recommendations as to how First Nations could create and sustain self-government. The joint committee was to come to a conclusion at the meetings to be attended by first ministers, the Prime Minister, Paul Martin, and First Nation leaders. The meeting took place in late 2005 at Kelowna, British Columbia, and an agreement—the Kelowna Accord—was signed, but the government of the day was defeated and the new minority Conservative government refused to implement the Accord.

Aboriginal people argue that without capable government it is difficult to address social, cultural, and economic issues within their communities. Autonomous governments must have the ability to make decisions on such issues as economic development, fiscal relations, health, education, justice, and citizenship. Some might argue that today many First Nation governments already administer their educational and health programs, but governance and administration are two separate functions. Administration does not involve authority.

Chartrand et al. (2008) point out that Aboriginal peoples never had an opportunity to participate in the creation of Canada's federal union; they now seek a right to have a say about that union. The goal is the realization for everyone in Canada of the principles upon which the Constitution and the treaties both rest, that is, a genuinely participatory and democratic society made up of peoples who have chosen freely to confederate. Aboriginal people are now considering the nature and scope of their own public institutions to provide the security for their individual and collective identities that Canada has failed to furnish. Today, Aboriginal people are rapidly gaining greater political consciousness and asserting their rights not only to achieve better living conditions but to achieve greater autonomy.

First Nations people have tried to distinguish between external and internal self-determination and have focused their efforts on the latter. This, as they see it, will accommodate the collective survival of First Nations people within the territorial integrity of Canada. The government, however, has taken the position that if it accedes to this form of self-determination, it will lead to the development of new constitutional frameworks based on First Nations consent, and that such an arrangement is unacceptable. That the two parties have not chosen to sit down and address the long-standing issues confronting the future of First Nations people and of Canada is problematical, but perhaps the real problem is that Canada, as a weak federal state with identifiable regions and strong regional identities, has difficulty acting in a unified manner—the consent of the provinces is often at issue. Likewise, to speak of the First Nations as a 'party' is equally misleading: there are various regional and provincial organizations, national organizations for First

Nations, non-status Indians, Métis, and Inuit, a strong women's organization, and several hundred bands or First Nations. Their issues of principal
concern do not necessarily coalesce, even in regard to self-determination. To
expect all of these voices—and the constituencies they represent—to achieve
consensus is simply asking too much.

The Royal Commission on Aboriginal Peoples and Self-Government

The recommendations of the RCAP were focused on strategies to develop
more positive relationships between the two groups and to establish a restorative justice approach in approaching reconciliation so that some form of
self-government could be established. It should be remembered that First
Nations people have never argued for secession from Canada in their bid
for self-government or self-determination. Their position is quite different
from that taken by the Parti Québécois in Quebec. First Nations people are
content to operate within the confines of Canada and its Constitution while
at the same time having the right to self-government (Belanger, 2008).

In its report, the Royal Commission on Aboriginal Peoples began by
articulating four assumptions as a basis for First Nations governance—
mutual recognition, mutual respect, sharing, and mutual responsibility.
The Commission articulated three models of self-government (see Table
9.2), discussed how each would be financed, and identified specific steps
necessary to restructure the relationship between First Nations people and
Canada. The process was described as a 'two-way street' in which both
Canada and First Nations would have to change in order to accommodate
the new models. Of these models, the nation model is essentially an extension of the reserve system and is reflected by the Nisga'a and their land
claim agreement and in the claims and actions of the Six Nations Iroquois
of Ontario over the past 100 years. The public model is best represented

TABLE 9.2 Models of Aboriginal Government

	Territory	Citizenship	Jurisdiction	Internal Government Organization
Nation Model	Land and territory base	Dual	Full core, multi-level	Will vary according to the requirements of each First Nation
Public Model	Land and territory base/ some land co-jurisdiction	Non-Aboriginal	Co-jurisdiction Aboriginal rights and culture	Centralized or federal form
Community of Interest Model	Not land-based	Voluntary Aboriginal exclusive	Limited jurisdiction to programs and services relevant to members	One level, sector-specific Specific institutions and agencies

by the territory of Nunavut, the Inuit homeland, and by Nunavik, the homeland of Quebec Inuit. In this model, ethnicity per se does not determine community membership. The community of interest model is designed for First Nations people living off-reserve in urban areas. Although there are numerous special-purpose urban organizations and drop-in centres for urban Aboriginal people in Canada's larger cities, no truly self-governing urban First Nation structure, which would provide a wide range of citizen needs and with an elective or hereditary form of leadership selection, has been developed to date—if, indeed, such would be possible.

The Government Response to the Royal Commission on Aboriginal Peoples

In response to the Royal Commission, the government argued it was in support of self-government and while not offering any specific policy changes, it outlined the long-term goal of the government to allow some form of self-government for First Nations. Moreover, the response acknowledged that First Nations people are in a disadvantaged position compared to other groups and that certain historical factors have produced this unfortunate state.

However, the government did not share the four assumptions made by the Commission, nor did it see the changes as a 'two-way' process—it was only open to discuss a 'one-way' process focused on how First Nations people could change their perspective and how they could fit into the existing Canadian legal/governance system. The government made it clear that there were limits to First Nation self-government; while some issues were negotiable, others were not. Moreover, the matter of what issues would be negotiable was strictly within the purview of the federal government.

Sovereignty is viewed by First Nations as 'inherent' and not conferred to First Nations people by some temporal power as envisaged by the federal and provincial governments. First Nations people reject any thought that there was some delegation of federal/provincial jurisdictions to First Nations governments (Doerr, 1997). The 1995 federal policy guide agreed that some 'core powers' were unique to First Nations culture and people, but beyond that, the government was not prepared to acquiesce to the demands of First Nations. A difference of opinion between what was and was not 'core' emerged, and the parties could not agree on this, on what powers were negotiable and on what remained outside the scope of First Nations authority. There also were differences between the government and First Nations with regard to how jurisdictions might be applied, once given to First Nations, e.g., the Charter of Rights and Freedoms. Land acquisition issues also could not be resolved among the three parties. In addition, financing and institution-building became points of contention and neither side was prepared to accept a compromise. Finally, First Nations viewed themselves as engaging in government-to-government relationships and the federal and provincial governments were not prepared to take that step (Wherrett, 1999: Russell, 2000; Cairns, 2000; Frideres, 2008; Coates and Morrison, 2008).

Today, most First Nation communities operate within a legal and political environment that is somewhat similar to that of a municipal government. A quarter of a century ago, the federal government tried to introduce a community-based self-government policy but it was found unworkable and generally resisted by First Nation communities. This approach lasted less than 10 years. First Nation governments, as articulated by spokespersons, are not 'mini' nation-states but rather governments that would hold a distinct jurisdictional authority within the framework of a federal state; they would be a kind of third-order government.

Opponents of this conceptualization have several arguments about why this third order of governance would be politically divisive, institutionally unwieldy, expensive, and damaging to the larger Canadian state (Flanagan, 2000; Cairns, 2000). Most arguments against First Nation self-government begin with hypothetical 'results' and then work backward. For example, they claim that waste and corruption are problems in First Nation communities, where patronage and nepotism flourish. Therefore, any other form of self-government for First Nations will just continue the waste, at taxpayers' expense. Thus, the solution to the 'problem' is to do away with reserves, assimilate the First Nations people, and tax them as ordinary citizens once they lose their Indian status. There is no recognition that First Nations have a constitutional right to exist and have signed treaties affirming other rights and responsibilities. This kind of mentality supports the rejection of any reconceptualization of Canadian politics that would allow First Nations to take on authority and power but allows the status quo to continue.

Such a view reflects an ideology of paternalism that implies First Nations people are not able to manage their own collective affairs (Warry, 2007) and, indeed, are no more collectivities in twenty-first-century Canada than are Icelanders in Manitoba or Acadians in New Brunswick. In addition, there is an underlying belief by critics of First Nation politics that they do not have any interest in achieving good governance in their communities. Evidence demonstrates the contrary, and community members have concerns just as other Canadians with regard to waste, theft, and nepotism. Finally, the position that First Nations people are no different— and no more privileged!—than other Canadians suggests that when the social and economic conditions of a people are not producing surplus revenues and generally positive social results, any previously signed agreements should be dismissed, constitutional arrangements made in the past should be ignored or overturned, and people should be expected to assimilate to a philosophy and ideology that is to the advantage of those in power (Jorgenson, 2007).

Conservative critics of present arrangements, and of attempts to improve those arrangements for the future, seem not to notice that unethical behaviour, greed, and illegal transactions are not culture-bound. Nepotism is also evident in the private sector, yet it is tolerated because *direct* taxpayer monies are not involved. Yet, taxpayers *indirectly* support the private sector far more than they do First Nations people. Nor do critics of First Nation politics seem to be aware of the fact that First Nations are accountable to the federal government and that the Auditor General, for years, has noted the poor business practices of the Indian Affairs department and the department's waste and lack of accountability. Yet, when First Nation councils carry out the mandate of Indian and Northern Affairs, they often are the ones identified by critics as engaging in waste, greed, or unaccountability. There is no suggestion that alternative constitutional arrangements might be needed. On the other hand, some moderates in this debate (Cockerill and Gibbins, 1997) suggest that First Nations self-government need not be a threat to the Canadian political system and could be integrated into a revised parliamentary system.

Over the past quarter-century, the federal government has considered its definition of self-government to be one major solution to achieving sound governance in First Nation communities. However, this process takes a long time, and in some instances there is no political will, on the part of government or of First Nations constituencies, to see the process through to a successful conclusion. As the Auditor General noted, in one instance a land claim and self-governance negotiation under the BC Treaty Process took 12 years and cost $426 million (and the First Nation leadership had borrowed $300 million), yet an agreement was never concluded. Other claims, such as those of the United Annishnaabeg Councils, the Meadow Lake Tribal Council, and the Montagnais and Attikamek, have followed similar time frames, resulting in fruitless results and high expenditures. It would seem, then, that the federal government is not prepared to deviate from its 'one-sided' approach to self-government.

Conclusion

Graham (2007) has suggested that since negotiations between the two parties seem fruitless, alternative strategies and outcomes should be considered. Moreover, he notes that the process of obtaining self-government is a long-term goal. There is no magical panacea that will bring about First Nations self-government. It has taken hundreds of years of colonial domination to produce what we now have, so there is no reason to suggest that change will happen overnight. Moreover, the experience of colonialization has permanently changed First Nations people's concept of governance. As Bruhn (2009) points out, the imposition of the Indian Act not only brought an abrupt closure to First Nations governance forms but also, as noted by Helin (2006), erased their underlying principles for many years. In short, a void was created between the past and the present.

It is foolhardy to expect people to accept outsiders' plans for their self-government. The imposition of a municipal-type government onto First Nation communities has little meaning to them. Canada's 'first-past-the-post' electoral system simply is not how many First Nations did or would choose their leaders, and it has undermined traditional forms of leadership selection. When the Canadian government, in 1869, began to impose elected band councils on the First Nations—a policy that became widespread in the twentieth century—it sought to undo earlier tribal forms of government based on tradition, heredity, and consensus (Dickason with McNab, 2009: 229). The government wanted its 'wards' to conform to the governance structures of the ruling majority. At the same time, this imposition divided communities between those who supported the new elective system and the traditionalists. In short, the current system of government in place has produced an unbalanced structure compared to the prior web of relationships that made up the political order of traditional First Nation political systems. Outsiders cannot impose good governance. Individual members of the society must develop their own style of government and make a strong political commitment to develop and sustain good governance.

The development of good governance does not have a 'blueprint' that each community can adopt, as was discovered over 100 years ago when the government imposed an elective system. Given the uniqueness of each First Nation community, they will have to look at existing models as nothing more than 'guidelines' to follow over the years. Finally, there is no doubt that today some of the past is gone. First Nations people have blended traditional approaches of their lives with contemporary ones. They have accepted modern technology, the written word, a money economy, and diversity as part of their everyday lives. The question remains as to whether or not good governance can blend the old and the new.

Questions for Critical Thought

1. How will giving First Nations people the right to self-government affect their integration into Canadian society?

2. Why didn't the federal government take the advice of the Royal Commission on Aboriginal people with regard to restructuring the relationships between First Nations people and the existing political structure?

3. How can the Canadian government say that it is in support of self-government for First Nations people and then refuse to sign the UN Declaration on the Rights of Indigenous Peoples?

4. Why are some people upset with the government agreeing to the 'inherent' rights of self-government for First Nations people?

Suggested Readings

Flanagan, T. 2000. *First Nations? Second Thoughts*. Montreal and Kingston: McGill-Queen's University Press. Flanagan, a political scientist and former mentor and adviser to Prime Minister Stephen Harper, argues for assimilation and not self-government.

Graham, J. 2007. *Rethinking Self-Government: Developing a More Balanced, Evolutionary Approach*. Ottawa: Institute on Governance. The author provides a thoughtful analysis with regard to what self-government means and how it might be implemented in Canada.

Slattery, B. 1987. 'Understanding Aboriginal Rights', *Canadian Bar Review* 66: 697–739. The author, a legal scholar, presents a clear statement of what Aboriginal rights are, how they came about, and the courts' determination of their content.

Suggested Websites

There are many websites of various First Nation organizations, and a lot of First Nations maintain their own sites with a variety of news, announcements, and information on economic development and governance. Simply enter the name of a nation/tribe/band/organization into the search engine on your computer and see what is available. For example, the Nisga'a (www.nisgalisims.ca) in northern BC have a lot to say on self-governance. Also, see the following sites that are specific to governance.

Institute on Governance
www.iog.ca
　　Partially funded by the federal government, the Institute on Governance produces papers and opinion pieces on the issue of Aboriginal governance.

National Centre for First Nations Governance
www.fngovernance/org
　　This organization produces papers, from an Indigenous perspective, on the issue of Aboriginal governance. It is partially funded by the federal government.

10 The Political Economy of First Nations

Learning Objectives

⚜ To understand the historical and contemporary causes of First Nation poverty.
⚜ To be able to evaluate proposals (e.g., the Harvard Project) to enhance First Nation economic involvement.
⚜ To learn about one First Nation's strategy to break the poverty cycle.
⚜ To discover the current strategies of chiefs and councils to deal with community economic development.

Introduction

First Nations people are the poorest in the nation and, on average, have incomes well below the poverty line. Unemployment in First Nation communities runs as high as 60 per cent and most of their income comes from social services, pensions, disability payments, and children's benefits, not from involvement in the labour force. A question asked over and over is why. Many people argue that First Nation individuals do not wish to enter the labour force, are not interested in working, or are simply lazy and interested in other, non-productive activities. Others suggest an ethos of 'dependency' characterizes First Nation communities. And still others claim that the lack of education and skills prevents them from entering the labour market. To address this issue, we need to have an understanding of history and geography.

The Genesis of the Problem

From the time European settlers entered Canada, they felt the country was theirs, citing the fact that in many regions of the country there were no people (invoking the concept of *terra nullius*). And, where there were people (First Nations), they were not defined as 'real persons', just as the Canadian government did not define women as 'real persons' until well into the twentieth century. Moreover, if these people were to become 'real persons', they would have to be assimilated and take on the ways of life of the European settlers.

Canadian governments tried many different strategies to assimilate First Nations people and to make them just like themselves. The creation of the reserves was one way to place them in 'holding pens' until they could take on the ways of the European settlers. With the government not wanting to spend a lot of money on this assimilationist strategy, religious groups were given the task of providing education as well as religious instruction, which, it was believed, was necessary for the assimilation of First Nations people. To do this, the residential schools were created. These schools were based on widely accepted social science theory that says if you want to change a culture, then you first need to change the beliefs, values, and language of the young generation. While the older generations—the parents and grandparents—might hang on to their traditional culture, the new generation could be trained to take on the new. And when the young generation grew up, they would be just like the settlers. The residential schools began to isolate the children from their parents, their grandparents, and their communities. For one or two months during the summer the children were allowed to return to their communities, only to find that they no longer quite fit in. As time went on, they knew and understood less of the culture of the community, and their ability to speak and even understand their native language faded. The children were caught between two very different worlds, with a firm foothold in neither, and gaps between the generations of First Nations people developed as the younger generation began to take on the culture of the dominant society—so far so good for the government and interventionists.

But then things went wrong. In addition to the schools isolating the children from their communities and culture, the children became prey to pedophiles, sexual objects for adults, and targets for physical and psychological abuse. And, central to this grand assimilation project, what were they being educated for? Girls were taught to cook and sew with the goal of working as domestic servants and, possibly, marrying at some future time when they matured. Literacy generally was limited to the Bible, and this did differentiate the training received by First Nations and non–First Nations young females. For boys, little literacy training was provided and most activities focused on menial agricultural activities and chores for the school, such as feeding the chickens, milking the cows, and tending gardens. Little if any trades training was provided for these young men so that they might enter the mainstream economy as anything other than agricultural labourers. The government did not want its young wards to return to the First Nation communities where, it was felt, they would 'regress' into the culture of their elders and thus remain 'Indians'. Consequently, the education focused on religious training, on understanding their need to acquiesce to authority, and on learning English/French. In short, the education was at least as much about taking away language, culture, spirituality, and traditional values as it was about giving new lessons to prepare students for a different but presumably better future.

When these young people left the residential schools, their options were limited. They did not have funds to enter the agricultural enterprise—and were denied access to government programs or the banks that might have provided start-up financing to purchase equipment and seed in order to farm. Nor, for that matter, did they have the land for farming, in most cases being on reserves that, at best, had been established at the agricultural fringe or beyond. Moreover, they were not skilled enough to actually farm. For girls, the options were limited to day labour, working for a family as a servant or in other menial, part-time jobs. If their thoughts turned to marriage, young First Nation women were quickly reminded that they were not 'white' and thus not appropriate marriageable spouses for settler men. Young men found that their options were to work as farm or ranch hands (usually for room and board) or in other non-skilled activities. If these young people tried to return to the reserve, their options were equally limited.

In some respects, those who returned to their reserves found the social aspect of their lives a bit easier, but since many of them, in the earlier years of the residential schools, no longer spoke the language of the community, life on the reserve was difficult if not impossible. Moreover, if they went back to the reserve to engage in agricultural pursuits, they would find their expectations thwarted. Even though the government's stated intent was to 'help' First Nation communities, little actual help was provided for those on reserves. As we saw in Chapter 1, historical data document how even though First Nation leaders requested farm animals and implements so they could pursue farming, the federal government rejected those requests (Carter, 1990). And when neighbouring farmers lobbied the federal government to stop providing support for Indians because they saw it as unfair competition, the government acquiesced and denied support. So, a group of people had lost their traditional way of life and were denied any support to develop a new way of life. They could not magically involve themselves in the economy of the day. Members of the dominant society only wished to involve these untrained, unskilled individuals to the extent that they could be exploited to their own advantage. To add to this condition, many Canadians were sure that First Nations people were not real persons—they were not even 'second-class' citizens, for they had no rights of citizenship. Although they might have converted to Christianity, they were not considered the equal to settler Canadians. The level of racism and discrimination against First Nations people has decreased over the years, but a recent survey indicates that of all ethnic groups in Canada, First Nations still are the least desired in terms of marriage, work partners, and neighbours (Environics, 2010).

If the lack of economic opportunity were not enough, starvation, high rates of disease (tuberculosis), and housing stock that would lead to disease and other ailments were tolerated in the name of cost savings and collateral costs of assimilation. In addition, health-care often was difficult to access on remote reserves and environmental damage from resource projects in some cases intensified the inability to live off the land or to maintain a minimum quality of life. All of these factors led to extremely high death rates, which in turn led to assumptions, on the part of bureaucrats and elected politicians, about the 'vanishing Indian'.

By the late nineteenth century a pattern had been set, but the First Nations people did not vanish, even though they had been forcibly excluded from the agricultural economy that was the mainstay of Canada at that time. The Indian Act, as amended in 1881, prohibited First Nations persons in the West from selling wheat on the open market because this competed with non–First Nation farmers. Besides the unavailability of financing for economic enterprise, lack of training, and their sequestration on marginal lands, First Nations people were kept from obtaining government support by the continuous squabbling between the provinces and Ottawa as to who was responsible for them. Lengthy federal–provincial discussions and arguments allowed governments to do nothing as they continued to disagree as to whose responsibility took precedence, which would be the lead partner in any assistance, and who was responsible for developing policy and paying for its administration.

Since the extreme **poverty** of First Nations people did not impact Euro-Canadians, most members of the dominant society could care less. White Canadians could go about their lives blissfully ignorant and unencumbered by the plight of these people. When Canadians and their governments are inconvenienced, then they will begin to mount campaigns against First Nation communities, as occurred in regard to the misappropriation of land at Oka, Quebec, in 1990, at Ipperwash, Ontario, in 1995, and at Caledonia, Ontario, in 2006 (see Chapter 11).

Labour Markets and Canada's First Nations

Following World War I and especially after World War II, Canada increasingly became industrialized, and this meant that, as new technologies were introduced, new skills would have to be learned. First Nations people, once again, were left on the sidelines, a result of their isolation, lack of education and training, and rejection by the larger society for the previous three generations. As Levitte (2004: 45) points out, most of the policies advanced by the federal government to encourage economic development in First Nation communities have been geared towards individual **entrepreneurship**, as the philosophy of capitalism assumes that 'individual economic success will strengthen the community by generating jobs and wealth. . . . Moreover, the individual is defined as the key in providing jobs for other individuals and at the same time, generating investment opportunities for the community as well as for social and economic programming.' As First Nations people were not allowed to participate in the educational processes that would have provided them with a head start in the entrance to the increasing technological demands, few were able to participate in the new technological economy.

By the 1950s the First Nations population was uneducated, unskilled, traumatized, and isolated from the rest of Canada. Their ability to compete in the new economy was non-existent. Their involvement in new technology was marginal at best, and those who did participate in the labour market held jobs that did not require skills or education. Seasonal wage labour, at minimal wage and with no benefits, was their 'gateway' into the new economy. It was more like a closed door. As it was, many people who were involved in the wage economy had to leave their First Nation communities and take up residence in urban centres since Indian Affairs refused to support economic development projects on the reserves. Initial forays into the cities were widespread, although as the people quickly discovered, entering the wage economy was difficult and, even if successful, the work they could find did not provide enough cash to live in the city except in substandard housing in poor inner-city neighbourhoods. In the end, there has been considerable migration in and out of the urban areas as First Nations people tried to integrate into the capital economy. Today, many First Nations people yet again find themselves marginalized and largely unable to participate in the new **knowledge economy**.

In the early days, the explanations as to why First Nations have remained outside the labour market and are the poorest of Canada's minorities focused on their lack of religion, motivation, and 'repugnant' cultural activities (e.g., potlatches or giveaway ceremonies; thirst dances). The residential schools and the assimilation project were to take care of these shortcomings. When the schools seemed not to have done the job, then the explanation shifted to their 'innate' lack of ability to understand the complexities of settler society and their inability to integrate. The First Nations people had not 'assimilated' themselves well enough! Others were sure that First Nations people were simply lazy and preferred not to enter the labour market, especially since they relied on government handouts, which created a level of dependency and shiftlessness. First Nations people, for example, were said to be lacking an awareness of time, and thus they did not understand the necessity of showing up for work 'on time'. Arguments also were put forward that their culture was detrimental to economic development. Mythical features of the First Nations culture were invented to support these claims, e.g., First Nations were said not to be able to understand the concept of 'private property'. In fact, they understood it perfectly well; however, from their more communalistic view, they simply didn't believe this was the best way, or the Creator's way, to pursue social and economic life. Property was a gift to be shared, not a possession to be kept to oneself.

Early research attempts at identifying the cause of the economic failure of First Nation communities looked at the First Nations people themselves, at their physical and human capital (or lack thereof). The attendance records of workers, for example, might tell a lot about their character, just as how much land the community had and whether it was any good for agriculture or had valuable resources on it could indicate their chances of economic success. Demographic attributes also suggested what might need amelioration within communities: age structure, linguistic abilities, levels of education, skill level, and other such individual factors might explain their lack of involvement in the labour market and lack of economic development. As these incomplete explanations have faded because of their inability to explain, other explanations have come forward.

These explanations have focused on the structure of society and how it impacts specific groups within it. For example, 'world systems' theory, as proposed by Wallerstein (1979), has tried to show how 'core' (highly developed) societies have stunted 'peripheral' (less developed) nations and their economic development to ensure that core societies remain highly advantaged, developed, and wealthy, but to the detriment of peripheral societies. These structural explanations reveal how the structure of society protects and enhances the interests of those in power—core centres versus peripheral areas. This argument claims that it has always been in the interest of the developed countries or the industrial core within a particular country to maintain the periphery, such as First Nations people, in a dependency state and to use it as a resource hinterland. Thus, for example, if First Nations people were able to succeed economically, then scarce resources in the society would have to be shared with them. And as these people gained power, they would have to be consulted with regard to how resource allocations were handled. It means that power would have to be shared, and the dominant group would have to allow those kept in a state of dependency a say in how the country was run, how the laws were formulated, and what institutions were put in place. This explanatory paradigm has been partially taken up by those involved in the Harvard Project that carried out research on First Nation communities and their level of economic development.

The Harvard Model

Cornell and Kalt (2000) have most systematically sought to find what institutional arrangements would promote economic development for First Nation communities. They began to look at the types of institutions and the links between them to see if they held the clue to what makes an economically successful First Nation community. Their research on over 1,000

First Nation communities in the United States revealed that institutional structure, type, and linkage do indeed matter. They also found that natural, human, social, and financial capital are important factors in economic success, but that the institutional structure of a First Nation community is the most important.

In brief, they discovered that if First Nation communities are unable to make collective decisions and sustain those decisions, and if they lack the institutions necessary to develop and maintain an environment for investments, they will not be able to engage in viable economic development. Anderson and Parker (2006) agree that economic development in First Nation communities will depend on the nature and type of institutions that exist and the extent to which they create a stable environment. On the basis of their research they conclude that the wealth and income of First Nations will remain low as long as economic development policies continue to focus on cultural differences, endowments, and welfare payments and do not emphasize the institutions within the First Nation community and links to institutions beyond the community.

The results of this longitudinal study reveal that both the institutional environment in which resource allocation decisions are made and **natural and human capital** provide the best explanation (Anderson and Parker, 2006) for the success or failure of economic development. The Harvard Project indicates that viable economic development in First Nation communities depends on three conditions:

1) practical sovereignty which includes genuine decision-making power over internal affairs such as governance, resources and institutions, 2) capable governing institutions which means that institutions in the community are capable of exercising power effectively, responsibly and reliably, and 3) cultural match which consists of a fit between the formal institutions of government and First Nations conceptions of how authority should be organized and exercised. (Cornell and Kalt, 2000: 159)

Cornell et al. (2002) reiterate that these three social/organizational factors are most important in predicting economic success in a First Nation community. Only if these factors are present can other factors, such as natural resources, size of reserve, or demographic attributes, have any lasting impact. They also indicate that the extent of 'strategic orientation' held by the First Nation community is related to economic success. This means that when a community moves away from being 'reactive' to being 'proactive' with regard to development dilemmas, success follows. Finally, as Salee (2006) argues, with strong and innovative leadership, an articulation of a new vision for the community will contribute to its development. This new vision will require basic 'foundational' changes to the community organization if lasting change

FIGURE 10.1 The Development Pyramid

Source: Cornell, S., M. Jorgensen, and J. Kalt. 2002. The First Nations Governance Act: Implications of Research Findings from the United States and Canada, Phoenix, Udall Center for Studies in Public Policy and Native Nations Institute, 6.

is to be achieved. In sum, researchers find these core elements are much more important than factors such as geographic location, natural resources, level of education, and financial capital in predicting the economic success of a First Nation community. Cornell et al. (2002) refer to the implementation of these core factors as 'nation-building' and point out that they are crucial in creating effective self-rule and self-government. Their model is illustrated by a development pyramid (Figure 10.1).

Management and Control

Historical evidence shows that when contact with settlers and colonial governments took place, First Nation communities had developed sophisticated institutional orders that enabled them to produce goods using the resources they had at the time. However, once reserves were established, institutional autonomy for First Nation communities was destroyed as the colonial powers (and later the government of Canada) began to create a new institutional order and operate it in the First Nation communities. This began through the control of how much land would be available for establishing reserves and what the land would be used for. The implementation of the Indian Act gave total control over the affairs of First Nations people to the government.

This discussion leads us to change our sole focus from the attributes of individuals, e.g., human capital, or the physical attributes of the community, e.g., size of the reserve and its resource base. The extent of economic development may be limited as a result of such factors, but economic development is not dependent upon these factors. A different perspective shows that structural variables, such as the type and nature of the institutions in the community, the extent of autonomy, and the removal of constraints imposed by government legislation, are crucial in the emergence of sound and sustainable economic development (Flanagan et al., 2010). Once development begins, then the human capital and resources of the First Nation community need to be addressed in order to build upon the initial development. In other words, the federal and provincial governments need to fundamentally change their relationship with First Nation communities. The process of 'devolution' of the *management* of their own affairs to First Nations that began in the 1970s was the government's attempt to move decision-making from the Department of Indian Affairs to the First Nation communities. Band schools and First Nation health facilities were established and managed by First Nation members. However, the policy of devolution did not allow First Nation communities to take *control*. Indian Affairs still sets priorities, still allocates funds to specific programs, and still demands accountability from First Nation communities. If there is disagreement in fund allocation, Ottawa holds the trump card. In short, devolution was a strategy to cut costs and to allow First Nation administrators to bear the brunt of any dissatisfaction on the part of community members.

First Nations in the Canadian Economy

Within the larger economic structure of Canada, employment levels for First Nations people hover around 50–60 per cent while in mainstream Canada the level approaches 90 per cent. In mainstream society, any time the unemployment rate nears 10 per cent, the government becomes concerned and policies and programs are put in place to ensure so-called 'full employment'. For First Nations people, this is not the case. Moreover, much of their involvement in the wage economy is in marginal, part-time positions—those jobs that require low levels of education and skill training and are seasonal or episodic. Incomes for First Nations people are about half of the average for Canada as a whole. In 2005 the median total income for non-Aboriginal people was $33,400; for First Nations people it was $19,100, with much of that income from non-wage sources, e.g., social programs, pensions. At the same time, First Nations people do pay taxes for any income generated off the reserve. The Supreme Court has defined narrow conditions when a First Nations person can avoid paying federal/provincial taxes. Only if the individual can demonstrate that she/he lives on the reserve and generates her/his income from a business residing on the reserve can a tax exemption be claimed. At present the tax relief provisions for First Nations people impact relatively few individuals.

The state of economic involvement by First Nations people has changed over time. Aboriginal Business Canada carried out a recent survey regarding the number of Aboriginal entrepreneurs in Canada. In 1950, there were an estimated 200 First Nation-owned/run businesses; 25 years later this number had increased to nearly 1,000. Today, well in excess of 30,000

First Nation businesses are operating throughout the country (Sawchuk and Christie, 2004). This is projected to increase to over 50,000 by 2020. However, while these businesses range in size from small one-person operations to major national enterprises with more than 500 employees, most are small enterprises with fewer than five employees. Over two-thirds of businesses operate under a sole proprietorship structure and more than three-quarters are home-based. Most businesses are in the primary/construction sector and in wholesale and retail trade, although some First Nation businesses are involved in the 'knowledge' and technology sectors. Aboriginal businesses focus primarily on local markets to sell their goods, although about 10 per cent of them export a portion of their goods and services to other countries. While half of the Aboriginal businesses did not borrow funds to set up operations, almost one-third borrowed 50 per cent or more of their start-up funds. About 20 per cent of these funds came from government or Aboriginal organizations (ibid.). These data confirm that one of the most serious barriers to First Nation business development is access to start-up and growth financing.

Even for those reserves near urban centres, non–First Nation businesses are not enticed to establish on the reserves because of negative tax implications and the uncertainty of land title: it would cost a non-Aboriginal company more in taxes on a reserve than it would if it chose to locate on non-reserve lands. In brief, since a company cannot buy reserve land, it must lease land on a reserve, and the overall tax base is higher because, in contrast to the leasing of fee simple land, the cost of leasing cannot be written off as a business expense. Other issues, too, such as the gap between federal and provincial laws, have kept the private sector out of the reserves. However, in 2010 the federal government passed the First Nations Certainty of Land Title Act, which resolves the gaps between federal and provincial legislation so that industrial and commercial development projects on reserve lands can now take place. This is a step in the right direction, but it is interesting that the government had known about this problem for more than 50 years and did nothing. The result of such inaction meant that little commercial or industrial development took place on reserves. The tax issue remains unresolved and is still a barrier to economic development on reserves.

The simple fact of Aboriginal entrepreneurialism, as suggested by the figures discussed above, should alert you to the fact that there are some very wealthy people living in First Nation communities. There is a 'class' hierarchy within any First Nation community, with a few wealthy people, a small emerging middle class, and a lot of poor people (Liodakis, 2009). As the rest of Canada, each community includes some families who have benefited from political power, access to resources, and investments they have made over the years. Others have found alternative means, such as borrowing from Asian companies or signing leases for casinos, for accumulating financial resources and have become among the rich and powerful in the community. Thus, one should not think of a First Nation community as being a homogeneous collectivity of poor people.

First Nations people living in the cities also have problems in participating in the labour market. Zietsma (2010) finds that off-reserve First Nations people have an unemployment rate of 14 per cent, double that of non-Aboriginal city-dwellers. Any First Nations person trying to obtain financing will find that because of low income (and discrimination), the banks are reluctant to provide loans or start-up funds for business. Consequently, many First Nations people are forced to approach 'fringe' banking institutions such as pawn shops, cheque-cashing instant loan companies that charge exorbitant interest, and rent-to-own establishments in order to obtain goods and services. Across the board, this alternative banking system charges usurious fees and there is little regulation with regard to this activity. In the end, many of the individuals using these fringe banks will lose all their assets and continue in the downward spiral of economic insolvency (Martin et al., 2006).

Because this population has high unemployment and low incomes, few people are able to accumulate savings for business investments. Moreover, lending agencies see First Nation businesses as risky since land and most buildings owned by the band cannot be used as loan collateral. As well, many First Nation businesses lack a sizable trained labour force and are located far from areas that could produce skilled labour. For example, only 5 per cent of the employees in the oil and gas industry are Aboriginal, but Aboriginal peoples make up over 40 per cent of the population in the North where oil/gas activities are the greatest.

Nevertheless, the businesses First Nations people are involved in today include more than traditional primary/extractive activities, e.g., farming and logging, and range from personnel services to finance and banking (Peace Hills Trust), resource development in the oil and gas sector (Lakota Drilling), and transportation (Hobbema Trucking). First Nations people have entered into other ventures and been successful. The First Nations Bank, for example, is a federally chartered bank begun in the late 1990s by the Saskatchewan Federation of Indian Nations with start-up and infrastructure assistance from Toronto-Dominion Bank (now TD Canada Trust). The bank now has regional offices in Saskatchewan, Ontario, Manitoba, Quebec, and Yukon. It was created to provide service for the Aboriginal market and today offers a full range of banking services.

Another example in the financial services industry is the Peace Hills Trust, which was funded by Indian Affairs by accident in 1980. It was funded from the Indian monies fund held by Ottawa that can only be used for projects that have a tangible 'delivery', e.g., a building, a road. The money to start the Peace Hills Trust was allocated contrary to Indian Affairs policy and was not noted by bureaucrats until after the minister signed for the allocation. Part of the answer as to how this happened is that the department, as we shall see in the next chapter, has one of the highest turnovers of personnel and they simply did not know the 'rules'. As it turned out, the minister did not change his mind but bureaucrats made it clear such an accident would not occur again—and it hasn't. Today, Peace Hills Trust serves the financial needs of First Nations people and corporations, both on- and off-reserve, as well as non-Native clientele. With a head office in Edmonton, it is looking to expand its regional base. Both Peace Hills Trust and the First Nations Bank reflect the interest and capacity of First Nations to enter the economic institutional world and succeed.

One important source of income for some First Nations has been the gambling industry. Numerous Amerindian communities in the US reap millions of dollars each year from casino gambling—indeed, in Arizona alone the Arizona Indian Gaming Association has 19 member communities—and in Arizona and other states some of these communities have developed elaborate casino/resort/entertainment/golf destinations, such as Turning Stone Resort near Syracuse, New York, owned and operated by the Oneida Indian Nation.

There are few such major enterprises in Canada, although Casino Rama at Orillia, Ontario, owned by the Chippewas of Rama, is a large operation with headline entertainers, managed by an American-based company. Generally, however, the population base in Canada is simply too small to generate large amounts of revenue. Moreover, since First Nations do not have the funds or skills to set up a casino, they must look to outside companies to provide the start-up funds and to teach the skills necessary to run a casino—everything from accounting to card-dealing. In these agreements, the third parties pay for the infrastructure, equipment, and training in return for long leases, e.g., 25 years, at which time the business will be turned over totally to the First Nation community. Although a number of First Nations operate casinos—most often 'charity' casinos with no infrastructure besides a building to house the gaming activity—and make money in this way, much of the profit is taken by the companies that invested into the sunken costs of infrastructure and equipment. In addition, there has been some concern that casinos do not provide a necessary skill for people—card-dealing will not lead to a better job in the outside world. There also is some concern that First Nations people themselves will become addicted to gambling. Finally, some argue that the gaming business will attract criminal elements and lead to an increase in crime. An analysis of First Nations gaming (Belanger, 2006), however, reveals that these gaming operations have provided meaningful jobs for a number of people, and have not attracted a criminal element or sparked an increase in gambling by First Nations people.

Finally, the First Nations Fiscal and Statistical Management Act, which became law in 2005, was designed to enable economic development activity and represents the first time that First Nations have a legislative base for their economies. This amendment to the Indian Act gave First Nation governments new power to tax the people and their companies within reserves. By 2007, 115 First Nations were collecting over $55 million per year in property taxes.

The following case study reveals the actual implementation of the strategies outlined in the Harvard Project with regard to economic development on a reserve. While there are other examples, the Membertou Reserve in Nova Scotia exemplifies how economic development emerges and what is required of the chief, band council, and community.

A Case Study: Membertou Reserve

In 2000, the Membertou band, an urban First Nation community located in Sydney, Nova Scotia, and with a population of just over 1,000, began to reorganize its institutions as well as take control over the funding they received from the Department of Indian Affairs. Nine departments (different from the First Nations institutional structures that mirror Indian Affairs institutional structure) were created. These include education services, corporate division, health services, and finance and administration. The band leaders agreed that each department would develop a strategic plan with a vision and a mission (goal) so that the organization would have direction as to where it was going and would know when it achieved its objectives. These strategic plans also allowed the departments to determine if their goals were not being met and to intervene with mitigating actions, if necessary, to achieve those goals.

In short, the band began to move away from its 'standard model' of economic planning. This standard model (used by many of the bands today) focuses on short-term gains and on creating income and jobs while allowing others to set the development agenda (Scott, 2006). In choosing this type of economic model, the community sees development simply in terms of jobs and dealing with 'Aboriginal culture', which is assumed to be a mediating effect against economic development. As Cornell (1999) points out, this standard model has six steps:

1. Identify potential business ideas and funding sources.
2. Apply for outside funds and/or respond to external initiatives.
3. Start whatever can be funded.
4. Appoint family/friends to run the project.
5. Micro-manage.
6. Pray for success.

The end result of this short-term model has resulted in 'politics of spoils' in which those individuals/families in the community who have power or influence make decisions that will allow them to reap the short-term benefits. They focus on obtaining the greatest benefits for themselves and their families, disregarding the goals of the project or the good of the community. As a result, perceptions of incompetence and chaos result, and in some instances those perceptions perhaps are grounded in truth. Decisions about specific projects are not business decisions but rather result from a faction within the community deciding that it can incur benefits from the project, regardless of whether it continues or benefits the community. The singular goal is to skim profit from the project for those who hold power at the time. In the end, these types of projects generally fail within a short time and continue the life of poverty of most band members.

The alternative approach taken by the Membertou band is referred to as the 'nation-building' model. This approach uses de facto sovereignty and self-governance to gain control of and authority over band resources. It then creates a set of institutions in order to establish and achieve goals, and allocates resources to achieve those goals within the context of a long-term strategic orientation (Scott, 2006). At the same time, it pursues those goals commensurate with the local First Nation culture so that the community will support the band leaders and their actions.

For the Membertou community, steps had to be taken before economic development could occur. First, they began by asserting their sovereignty over their resources and social capital. Second, they created institutions that promoted stability and separated organizational decisions from bureaucratic and political decisions. For example, if the health organization was to sustain itself, it had to develop both short- and long-term goals as to what the community wanted. Then, decisions were made on the basis of how those structures and processes would achieve the goals of the community with regard to health-care. In short, business decisions were separated from political decisions. The hiring of a family member or friend was superseded by the aim of achieving the goals of the organization. If family members or friends had the qualifications to fit into a job, so be it. But if not, such people would be passed over and those with the needed skills would be hired. In short, patronage politics had no part in business decisions.

A third strategy employed by the band leaders was to use First Nation cultural standards by which the institutions and their processes would be carried out. In other words, community elders are an integral part of the decision-making process. Finally, the band moved from short-term to long-term goals, from reactive to proactive decisions and from opportunistic to systemic thinking. All of this was within a communitarian perspective—for the good of the community rather than for the good of an individual—although individuals would certainly benefit from the economic development taking place in the community.

Once this structural and organizational template has been established, initial economic development can occur. As development proceeds and people see it as sustainable and successful, they then can turn their efforts to building their human and social capital in order to support the economic development. As individuals in the community see the value of obtaining an education, skills, and technological competence, they will begin to support the institutions that provide those skills. For example, if parents see that the end result of a good education is a job that will better the individual and the community, there will be some reason for them to ensure that their children go to school, study, and take advantage of the opportunities that emerge when they complete their education. The Membertou example also demonstrates that leadership is an important component in development. Where leadership is strong and consistent, development occurs and is sustainable.

The Harvard Project has shown that if a community has control over decision-making and over the benefits that accrue from such decision-making, those involved likely will make better decisions than if they had no control. When people are sure they can have some effect on an economic proposal, and that the results of their decisions are going to have some long-term effect on their community, then they will get better information about it, carry out a more intense analysis of the proposal, and make a more unbiased decision (Sullivan, 2007). Conversely, when people are asked to make decisions without any real control or accountability, they more likely will make irresponsible decisions because of the lack of repercussions on the decision-maker. In Canada, when the federal and provincial governments claim they 'consulted' with the First Nation communities about economic development, they fail to recognize that the 'consulted' community has no idea or say as to what the final outcome will be. If I ask you for your opinion/advice about an action, and you give it but then I do what I want to do, the consultation is hollow. I will have to engage in this only two or three times and you will quickly understand that the process is meaningless. If I pay your travel costs, a per diem, and a set fee of $400 for the day, you will attend the consultations about a proposal—not because you have prepared for the meeting or because you care about the proposal, but because you will make $400 a day plus travel and per diem. Moreover, the person giving the advice/opinion will not really care the next time he/she is asked to provide input on a possible decision. It points out that the process of consultation is meaningless since those affected have no real control over the course of the project or its outcomes.

Conclusion

Scott (2004) suggests that economic development, sustainability, and new First Nation economies are emerging. Projects involving **co-management** strategies are allowing First Nation communities to access capital and technological expertise as well as develop projects for the long term. The question is when First Nations self-government will be provided so that communities can develop **firewalls** between politics and business. Many bands have resisted government attempts to push projects into their community. They have seen the folly of such short-term projects that do not allow any actual development in the community but rather provide monies for a small segment of the community. Now, with the information from the Harvard Project to guide them, they can begin to pursue better development plans. There is no reason that First Nations people cannot remain on the land and continue traditional land-based economic activities while participating as employers, employees, entrepreneurs, and decision-makers in modern industries (Warry, 2007). The idea that First Nation economies can never be integrated with mainstream economic interests is just one more myth perpetuated by those in power who would wish to keep First Nations people in a state of dependency. This false dichotomy between First Nation economies and 'modern' economies continues to influence government policy and is still used in funding and promoting programs in First Nation communities.

The key to successful economic development is to reduce risk by enacting good governance rules and to attract both external and internal investments to First Nations land. To achieve this, the process will need to ensure transparency and accountability of all actions taken by officials in the community. Moreover, it means that the community must have the ability to replace or redirect the leaders and ensure that there is good record-keeping for all transactions that take place. This is why the involvement of elders is so important. Notable, too, is that research has indicated that commercially exploitable natural resources within a First Nations community—oil and gas, diamonds, stands of timber, fisheries—are at best secondary, and possibly irrelevant in the long term, to the sustainable economic development of the community.

Questions for Critical Thought

1. Why are First Nations people not involved in the labour market?

2. Why are First Nations people not more active in economic issues in Canada?

3. What has the Harvard Project told Canadians and why is it not more widely used by First Nations people?

Suggested Readings

Carter, S. 1990. *Lost Harvests: Prairie Indian Reserve Farmers and Government Policy*. Montreal and Kingston: McGill-Queen's University Press. The author provides detailed evidence on how Aboriginal people were kept out of the labour market through government policy and how this had a lasting impact.

Cornell, S. 1999. *Keys to Nation-Building in Indian Country*. Tucson: Udall Center for Studies in Public Policy, University of Arizona. The author, a key researcher in the Harvard Project, reveals the structural factors related to economic success on reserves in the United States.

Levitte, Y. 2004. 'Bonding Social Capital in Entrepreneurial Developing Communities—Survival Networks or Barriers?', *Journal of the Community Development Society* 35: 44–64. The author analyzes the success and failures of economic development on reserves and synthesizes the factors related to success and failure.

Pendakur, K., and R. Pendakur. 2008. *Aboriginal Income Disparity in Canada*, No. 08–15. Vancouver: Metropolis British Columbia. The authors analyze census data and provide a longitudinal analysis of the income gap between Aboriginal and non-Aboriginal people.

Suggested Website

The Harvard Project
www.hunap.harvard.edu/alumni/connect
   The Project lists all of its publications and provides the reader with its history as well as information about the principal researchers.

11 The Bureaucracy: Indian and Northern Affairs Canada

Learning Objectives

- To explore the historical importance of the federal agency.
- To understand the actions of Indian and Northern Affairs Canada (INAC) with regard to First Nations people.
- To be able to critically evaluate policies and programs implemented by INAC.
- To learn about the organizational structure and mandate of INAC.
- To discover some of the strategies employed by INAC in dealing with First Nations people.
- To see how INAC is evaluated by the Auditor General.

Introduction

No book about First Nations people would be complete without considering Indian and Northern Affairs Canada, the most recent of several names for the administrative bureaucracy that has controlled the lives of First Nations people for more than 150 years. Prior to 1830, the military had full responsibility to deal with First Nation peoples, and First Nation warriors and their leaders, such as Tecumseh and Major John Norton, fought alongside the British, as in the War of 1812. Since that time, 'Indian Affairs' has been the responsibility of many different federal departments; it would not be until the 1960s that the current system was put in place. From the outset, the basic role of Indian Affairs has been to fulfill the conditions of the Indian Act. Inuit, historically, were not dealt with under the Indian Act, although in 1939 the Supreme Court ruled that, administratively, they were to be considered Indians and therefore a federal responsibility (Dickason with McNab, 2009: 367).

The Indian Affairs Mandate

Over time the Indian Act has been amended (about 700 times) and employees in the department frequently have been busied dealing with the implications of these changes. Bill C-31, discussed in Chapter 2, is just one of many examples of how changes to the Act precipitate additional changes that in turn precipitate still more changes. Unanticipated consequences lead to further changes and reflect the inability of the policy-makers to correctly predict how policy will impact people's lives.

The department also deals with treaties and other agreements made with First Nations and Inuit, and has various special sections for focusing on particular issues and policy areas, such as oil and gas. Moreover, new legislation created by Indian and Northern Affairs Canada and passed by Parliament with regard to First Nations, such as the First Nations Fiscal and Statistical Management Act, requires that people who work for Indian and Northern Affairs look after implementing and monitoring the new legislation. Just as the government continues to change its policies, Indian Affairs and its civil servants also must respond to court decisions that deal with First Nations people, and programs must be harmonized and dealt with in terms of other federal and provincial legislation. Since the department has **devolved** some of its functions to First Nation organizations, these also must be dealt with by officials from Indian Affairs.

The department also deals with land claims. These are of two quite different types. A specific claim is related to the terms of a previous treaty agreement and the claim of a First Nation that the government in some manner has not met its fiduciary responsibility, for example, by misappropriating First Nation land. This has been the case in several recent conflicts where specific claims had not been addressed in a timely fashion so that First Nations felt they had no recourse but to take action themselves: at Oka, Quebec, in 1990 with the Mohawks of Kanesatake, when the town began to extend a golf course onto reserve land; at Ipperwash, Ontario, in 1995 with the Chippewas of Kettle and Stoney Point First Nation, when a former military base on First Nation land was later turned into a provincial park rather than being cleaned up and returned to the Native people; and at Caledonia, Ontario, in 2006 with the Six Nations Iroquois, when a land developer began to build a subdivision on disputed land. Comprehensive agreements, on the other hand, are sought in areas of the country not covered by treaty, and besides settlements in the Far North (e.g., Inuvialuit, Nunavut, Nunatsiavut, Nunavik) finalized claims have been reached in Yukon, parts of the Northwest Territories, and, to much lesser extent, in British Columbia.

Finally, the federal Minister of Indian and Northern Affairs also is the interlocutor for Métis and non-status Indians and Inuit, is responsible for the three northern territories and, to some extent, for northern resource development, and is responsible for the Canadian Polar Commission, the lead government agency in polar research. This means that the Indian Affairs minister attempts to use his/her influence with other government departments to raise awareness of the circumstances of First Nations people and to increase their opportunity to participate in the larger society. In short, Indian and Northern Affairs Canada is the lead federal department for nearly half of the land mass of Canada, has a leading role in the development of the North, and has considerable responsibilities for land and environmental management across the country. It also has been, in the past few years, involved in international Indigenous and circumpolar activities. We might assume it must be an important department in the federal bureaucracy. We would be wrong.

In terms of a 'pecking order' among federal government departments, it ranks near the bottom. Civil servants prefer not to work for Indian Affairs and most will move to another department with a higher ranking if given the opportunity. This fact has three implications. First of all, newcomers to the civil service often will be offered jobs at Indian Affairs as an entry point, which means they come to the job with little experience in the civil service or in First Nation affairs. Second, there is little continuity in the departmental bureaucracy as the turnover in this department is extremely high. Thus, a collective memory in the department is minimal. Third, since there are few old-timers, these individuals will tend to hold a disproportionate amount of power in providing information, advice, and evidence to the revolving ministers that take up this portfolio. These three factors have important implications in terms of how the department is run. Those few who have been there a long time hold sway over initiatives, decisions, and interpretations of legislation and thus the status quo is maintained. Those new to the department are not about to challenge the old guard and prefer simply to do their jobs and then, when the opportunity comes along, move to another department with greater prestige and more clout inside and outside government.

On a day-to-day basis, the department deals with mundane issues— community bylaws (e.g., should dogs and cats be licensed?); the installation or upgrading of local sewage systems; where a person should be buried and recording the death—and somewhat more important issues such as whether a person should be registered as an Indian. In most cases, the decisions made public by Indian Affairs really are made behind the scenes after consultation and direction from the Treasury Board and the Department of Justice. For example, no comprehensive land claim or even specific claim would be undertaken by Indian and Northern Affairs Canada unless the Department of Justice approved it. No policy with regard to scholarships for students to go to post-secondary educational institutions would be approved unless Treasury Board first approved the funding. Even data collection beyond the registry would involve other departments or agencies, such as Statistics Canada, which in turn would set the parameters for who can use the data and what data will be released to the public. Moreover, Indian Affairs is only one of 34 federal departments and agencies that participate in Aboriginal and northern programming—dealing with First Nations people involves a complex web of departments, agencies, organizations, and sectors. This also indicates that Indian and Northern Affairs Canada is not a very powerful or influential department in the government of Canada.

On the other hand, it has a massive 'reach': the current estimate is that about 4,500 full-time equivalent employees work for the department and they have a hefty budget—well in excess of $10 billion—to work with. The bureaucratic structure of the department is not very different from other departments in that it has a minister, deputy ministers, assistant deputy ministers, headquarters, regional offices, and a variety of other managers. Because its primary constituency—First Nations people—is scattered across the country, it is rather more decentralized in some respects than many other government departments, although its program activity architecture is not any more complex. Figures 11.1 and 11.2 show the department's organizational structure and its strategic outcomes and program activities, which suggest something of the departmental priorities for the year 2009–10. Of course, these priorities change over time and in fact some of them might not have existed three years ago and others may be deleted the following year. Canada's shifting social, political, and economic landscape strongly influences Indian Affairs' priorities, performance, and programs. In addition, as Scholtz (2009) reports, the influence of the courts has a disproportionate impact on the policies developed by the department. Policy-makers take into consideration the overall changing policy environment and they view judicial decisions as an important context of uncertainty. Moreover, policies and priorities are impacted by the demography of Canada and First Nations people, the skill/leadership level of the First Nation organizations and communities, and the different levels of economic integration of First Nation communities across the country.

Policy Initiatives and the Budget

For the 2009–10 year, five strategic outcomes are identified. Within these program themes there are 17 specific programs (Figure 11.2). The seven-. teenth activity is the Office of the Federal Interlocutor, which deals with urban Aboriginal strategy as well as Métis and non-status Indian concerns. The department decides how important each of these specific programs is, determines projected budgets for each, and then allocates funding to each program. Overall, nearly two-thirds of the budget is allocated for education, social development, and community infrastructure. An additional 12 per cent is set aside for claims settlements and 19 per cent is allocated to nine other program activities. The remaining 5 per cent is dedicated for northern projects. Specifically, under the theme 'People', nearly $2 billion is allocated to education, $1.5 billion for social development, and $22 million for managing individual affairs.

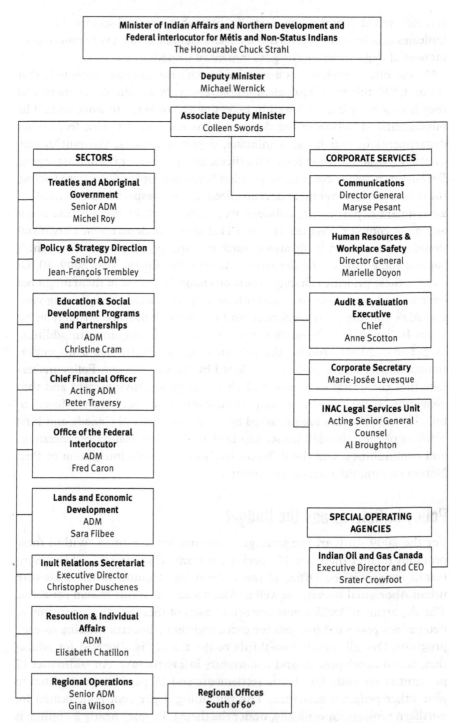

FIGURE 11.1 Organizational and Governance Structure of Indian and Northern Affairs Canada

Source: Indian and Northern Affairs Canada www.ainc-inac.gc.ca/ai/scr/index-eng.asp.

Strategic Outcomes				
The Government *Good governance, effective institutions, and co-operative relationships for First Nations Inuit and Northerners*	**The People** *Individual and family well-being for First Nations and Inuit*	**The Land** *Sustainable management of lands, resources and environment by First Nations and Inuit*	**The Economy** *Economic well-being and prosperity of First Nations, Inuit, and Métis people*	**The North** *The people of the North are self-reliant, healthy, skilled, and live in prosperous communities*

Program Activities				
Governance and Institutions of Government Sub-activities: • Supporting Governments • Institutions of Government • Fiscal relations	**Education** Sub-activities: • Elementary and Secondary Education • Special Education • Post-secondary education • Cultural Education Centres	**Clarity of Title to Land and Resources** Sub-activities: • Clarification of Reserve Title • Comprehensive Claims Land Transfers • Additions to reserve	**Individual and Community Business Development** Sub-activities: • Viable Businesses • Business Financing Institutions	**Northern Governance** Sub-activities: • Political Development and Government Relations • Circumpolar Liaison
Co-operative Relationships Sub-activities: • Negotiations of Claims and Self-Government • Treaty Commissions • Treaty Tables • Inuit Relations • Consultations and Accommodation	**Social Development** Sub-activities: • Income Assistance • First Nations Child and Family Services • Assisted Living • Family Violence Prevention • National Child Benefit Re-investment • Family Capacity Initiatives	**Responsible Federal Stewardship** Sub-activities: • Land and Resources Management • Oil and Gas Management • Environmental Management	**Community Investment** Sub-activities: • Community Economic Strategies • Community Economic Institutional Capacity	**Healthy Northern Communities** Sub-activities: • Hospital and Physician Services • Food Mail • Knowledge and Adaptation
Claims Settlements Sub-activities: • Specific Claims • Special Claims • Comprehensive Claims • Residential Schools Agreement	**Managing Individual Affairs** Sub-activities: • Registration and Membership • Management of Band and Individual Monies • Estate Management • Treaty Annuities	**First Nations Governance over Land, Resources, and the Environment** Sub-activities: • First Nations Land Management • First Nations Oil and Gas Management	**Community Infrastructure** Sub-activities: • Infrastructure Facilities • Education Facilities • Housing • Community Management of Infrastructure	**Northern Land and Resources** Sub-activities: • Contaminated Sites • Management of Lands and Resources • Arctic Science **Northern Economy** Sub-activities: • Regional Economic Development • Innovation and Partnerships

Strategic Outcomes	Office of the Federal Interlocutor		
	Improved socio-economic conditions of Métis, Non-Status Indians, and urban Aboriginal people		
Program Activities	**Urban Aboriginal**	**Métis and Non-Status Indian Organizational Capacity Development**	**Métis Rights Management**

Internal Services
An effective and responsibly managed and operated department positioned to achieve its strategic outcomes
• Governance and Management Support • Resource Management Services • Asset Management Services •

FIGURE 11.2 Indian and Northern Affairs Canada Program Architecture, 2009–10

Source: Indian and Northern Affairs Canada and Canadian Polar Commission, *2009–2010 Estimates, Report on Plans and Priorities*, 5.

A comparison of the present Indian and Northern Affairs Canada budget with that from the late twentieth century shows major budget increases not experienced by other departments. These increases are a result of the increasing funding required to meet the high demand for ongoing First Nations services, the increasing liability the department is exposed to, and the costs associated with various court decisions. For example, the responsibility for dealing with the $2+ billion payout for the Indian Residential Schools Settlement Agreement, payments to the Quebec Cree (emerging from the James Bay and Northern Quebec Agreement) and other major comprehensive settlements, payments for cleaning up contaminated sites, and increases in funding for a new framework for economic development all are cumulative expenses. In 2010, $200 million will be added to the departmental budget to support the disbursement of the Indian Residential Schools Settlement Agreement funds, nearly $300 million will be invested in the Aboriginal Diabetes Initiative and the Youth Suicide Prevention Initiative, and over $300 million will be invested in the First Nations Water and Wastewater Action Plan to improve access to safe drinking water on reserves. Some claim that projections into the near future indicate that many of the above expenses will have been paid out by 2011 and thus the budget could decrease (Canada, 2010, *Main Estimates*). However, it is likely that costs associated with recent court rulings will once again bring additional costs to the department.

The total allocation for Indian and Northern Affairs Canada based on the budget passed by Parliament is about $7 billion (*Main Estimates*; see Table 11.1). However, this hides the fact that other 'line item' costs, such as operating expenditures of $1 billion and benefits of $61 million, must be met. In addition, numerous 'supplementary' requests are made to Parliament

TABLE 11.1 **Selected Program Activity Structure and Budget for INAC, 2009–10** (*Main Estimates*)

	Program Activity			
Government	People	Land	Economy	North
Governance and institutions of governance	Education	Title of land and resources	Individual and community business development	Northern governance
Co-operative relationships	Social development	Responsible federal stewardship	Community infrastructure	Healthy northern communities
Claims settlements	Managing individual affairs	First Nations governance over land, resources, and the environment	Community investment	Northern land and resources
		Budget estimates		Northern economy
$1.54 billion	$3.3 billion	$82 million	$1.2 billion	$197 million

Source: Indian and Northern Affairs Canada and Canadian Polar Commission, *2009–10: Report on Plans and Priorities*, at: www.tbs-sct.gc.ca/rpp/2009-2010/inst/ian/ian02-eng.asp.

by Indian Affairs during the year to deal with unexpected needs, and thus the total budget will likely increase to over $10 billion. Finally, it should be remembered that more than 30 other departments and agencies contribute to the total Aboriginal portfolio, such as Health Canada, Industry, Justice, and Heritage Canada, as well as provincial contributions. When all of these are combined, they offer more than 350 different programs to First Nation communities across the country. Adding the expenditures of these departments to the total reveals a total budget exceeding $10 billion that is directed towards First Nations people across Canada. That seems like a lot, but it works out to an annual expenditure of about $10,000 per First Nation person per year.

Changing Priorities

Each year Indian and Northern Affairs identifies strategic outcomes and then proceeds to develop a plan to implement those outcomes. Over the years there have been changes in the relative importance of various policies as well as shifts within individual programs; all reflecting changing social and economic conditions. However, for the most part, the main philosophy underpinning the policies continues to be clearly evident in public welfare provisions (Boychuk, 2004). The establishment of the priorities is based on the department's assessment of issues that need to be addressed to ensure a minimum quality of life for First Nations people and help them integrate into the larger social and economic structure of Canada. Each year elaborate plans for each of the themes identified are presented to Parliament. For example, for 2009–10, Indian Affairs noted that it would be working with public- and private-sector partners to increase First Nation participation in the Canadian economy. The department provided funds and other technical support to ensure proposals brought forward by First Nation entrepreneurs and communities would succeed. A new 'whole of government' policy approach was implemented for this year with the goal of fostering First Nation economic development.

The structural nature of these outcomes, however, means that even if they were correctly and fully implemented, changes in the lives of First Nations people would not be evident for several years. In other words, if massive infusions of money are directed to education, for example, it will take several years for students to receive that upgraded education, graduate from school, and then move into the labour market or post-secondary educational institutions. It will take even more years for those attending post-secondary educational institutions to complete their education/training and enter the labour market with their expertise and skills. Since there is a **time lag** in considering the impact of policy and programs, and the process of policy development remains removed from First Nations people and is secretive in nature, it is almost impossible to assess the value of Indian and Northern Affairs programs or to see how they have bettered the lives of First Nations people.

Accountability and Goal Achievement

The current structure of policy development allows Indian Affairs to enact almost any action, with any goal, and with complete immunity, and then to bring forward anecdotal and statistical data to support a claim that the goals/objectives were achieved. For example, the department states that it wants to improve the educational attainment of members of First Nation communities and introduces two new programs to attain its goal. Unfortunately, benchmarks for success or lack of success are not offered to determine if the policies and programs achieve the vague goals, and consequently it becomes difficult to know if these two new programs are effective. Again, the department says it will ensure that its post-secondary education program is co-ordinated with other programs to provide the support that students need in order to stay in school and complete their education. We can all agree that this is a good objective, but at the same time we already know that the demand for post-secondary education support far exceeds the current funds set aside. This means that many First Nation students who wish to attend post-secondary educational institutions will not be able to do so. And what does 'co-ordinated with other programs' mean?

Generally, the stated goals of department programs are couched in vague terms. For example, it would not be claimed that 'Through increasing funding to post-secondary education training by $14.7 million each year for the next five years for First Nation students, post-secondary educational completions will increase by 2 per cent' or that 'The number of graduating students will increase by 1,300 students for each of the next five years.' Rather, the claim is 'Graduation rates of First Nation students will increase by 2013' or 'The goal is for First Nations learners to complete post-secondary education at a rate comparable to their provincial average.' In the first case, an increase of one student would mean the goal had been met. In the second instance, nothing is said about when the comparable rate will be achieved. Until concrete benchmarks are presented, no policy or program can be evaluated in terms of its impact. To be fair, in some cases the department has made such pronouncements. In the area of social development, for example, the department has declared that it will reduce the gap between First Nations and provincial rates of the proportion of on-reserve children in the care of child and family services agencies by 2.5 per cent. Evidence thus far reveals that this target has been achieved. And what are the consequences for not meeting a target? If the department does not meet its stated goals, no one begins an investigation and no one will lose a job—even if the objectives are not met over several years.

In this manner, Indian Affairs has been able to operate for a century and a half, always arguing that it works in the interest of First Nations people. For example, the department's mandate is to:

- promote improved education for First Nations people;
- help empower First Nation citizens, and protect those who are most vulnerable;
- ensure that the department's programs change so they deal with the many facets of First Nation peoples' lives;
- effectively implement past initiatives and agreements;
- build and sustain partnerships necessary to achieve defined outcomes.

These are all admirable goals, but little is said about how Indian Affairs operationalizes them or to demonstrate how they have resulted in a better life for First Nations people. Moreover, even success, in Indian Affairs terms, in some instances can be seen as a step backward in relative terms. Thus, the level of educational attainment for First Nation students has increased in the past 20 years, so that today the secondary school graduation rate is about 40 per cent while for non–First Nation students it is nearly 80 per cent. At the same time, however, the data show that the gap between First Nation and non–First Nation students has increased over this 20-year period. In addition, the quality of education in many reserve secondary schools is substandard in providing students with the necessary skills to move into post-secondary educational institutions. Most First Nation students are deficient in science, math, and English and when they attempt to enrol in colleges and universities they often are rejected; or, if allowed to enter through special Aboriginal entrance policies, many will fail because they do not have the requisite skills and don't have access to the mentoring and tutoring that would be required for them to make up their skill shortfall.

Primary and secondary school success of students is only partially due to what goes on in the school. The other important element in student success is family and community support. Indian and Northern Affairs has done little to address these issues. This demonstrates the lack of a 'holistic' perspective taken by the department in dealing with issues confronting First Nations people. The tendency is to deal with a specific issue, more than likely by funnelling money in that direction, without taking a broader view that addresses the problems and potentialities surrounding the specific issue. Why is there a lack of parental support for education in some families and communities? That gets into the issues of health, poverty, substance abuse, housing, and domestic violence. These issues have to be dealt with simultaneously if there is any chance that the level of community or parental support will be increased. Unfortunately, the department is not in the business of trying to provide an integrated solution to the issues facing a First Nation community. These are all well-known conditions and have been documented over the years (Corrado and Cohen, 2003; Chansonneuve, 2007; Kirmayer et al., 2007; Richards, 2009; Richards et al., 2008).

Over the past four decades, Indian and Northern Affairs has repeatedly acknowledged that it needs to develop a new relationship with First Nations people in order to correct long-standing problems. And the department has undertaken a number of actions to deal with these long-term problems and issues. In other words, the government seems to be good at starting something for First Nations people, but it has great difficulty in following through. A case in point is the Royal Commission on Aboriginal Peoples. The Commission was created in 1991, in the aftermath of and, in part, as a response to the 'Indian summer' of 1990, which included the events at Oka, Quebec, and clearly indicated that something was badly amiss in the government–First Nations relationship. Five years later, after assessing the current conditions of Canada's Aboriginal peoples, the Royal Commission's massive five-volume report included well over 400 recommendations. Some few of the recommendations were acted upon; most were not (see Dickason with McNab, 2009: 417–23). The Canada–Aboriginal Peoples Roundtable was created in 2004, a First Ministers' meeting on Aboriginal issues was held in 2005 (and the watershed agreement that came from this meeting—the Kelowna Accord—was scrapped by a new government early the next year), and the residential schools settlement was reached in 2007, with an official apology from the Prime Minister presented in 2008. Ostensibly these efforts were undertaken to understand the issues and to develop new relationships with First Nations people. The input from these efforts certainly made it clear what the 'problems' are, and such meetings and actions are not short on ideas as to how the new relationship can be implemented to enhance the quality of life of First Nations people. But then, the RCAP was not short on ideas either. Despite these efforts, long-standing problems remain because there has been little follow-through on the actions undertaken or planned to occur in the future.

Indian and Northern Affairs has argued that you can't fix everything at once, and that may well be true. The department has tried to identify priority issues that need the most attention over the next few years, such as education, economic issues, health, and land claims. But we need to insist that the department focus on these issues and involve the First Nation communities in finding solutions. We also must expect the Truth and Reconciliation Commission (see Chapter 4) to become something more than what the government might have intended it to be. Rather than simply being another 'Indian' commission for 'Indians', it must find ways to grasp the imagination of non–First Nation Canadians and to engage the larger public in dialogue, discovery, and reconciliation.

Like many other departments, Indian and Northern Affairs is a big proponent of 'pilot' or 'experimental' projects and programs. These are short-term investments of one or two years, and then funding is dropped. In addition, the department, like others, seeks 'new, innovative' projects. However, these also are limited in terms of time and funding. Generally, a new idea comes to the attention of INAC and it looks worthy of support because it has not been tried before—it is innovative. Thus, the department will agree to fund the project for up to three years. At the end of the allotted time period, the program/project funding will be dropped, even if it turns out to have a positive impact on the issue it was dealing with. At that point, the department is more interested in funding another 'new' project. In 2008, the First Nations Student Success Program and the Education Partnerships Program were touted as the programs that would solve some of the problems with First Nation students staying in school and graduating from secondary school. Yet, these programs only have a shelf life of three years and then they will be abandoned. The assumptions are that they have achieved their stated goal, that the community will now have to pick up the costs of the programs on their own, and/or that, because of their success, other communities will implement the same or similar programs with their own funding. This creates a revolving door with regard to sustainable programming, and individuals involved with such programs dealing with First Nations are aware of the limited life of the programs. Not only does this lead to poor management, potential fraud, and limited impact on people, but it also keeps funds from projects that actually work.

The Auditor General and Indian and Northern Affairs Canada

The Auditor General of Canada, a position held by Sheila Fraser since 2001, has had quite a lot to say about the department on specific issues. In Chapter 5 of her 2006 report, for example, where the management of First Nations programs is examined, the Auditor General (2006: 145) follows up on earlier assessments made in 2000 and 2003:

> The progress in addressing our 37 recommendations on First Nations issues has been unsatisfactory. While the issues are extremely complex, federal organizations had agreed with most of our recommendations and had committed to taking action. We found their progress on 15 of our recommendations to have been unsatisfactory. These are generally the recommendations that are the most important to the lives and well-being of First Nations people. We found that little had been done to deal with the serious problems.

Thus, over a period of six years, action was not taken to address nearly half of the concerns expressed by the Auditor General.

The report recognizes that in recent years funding to various programs for First Nations people has increased, but emphasizes that population growth has far outstripped this increase. For example, she notes that the population growth rate of First Nations people increased by over 11 per cent between 1999 and 2004 but their funding increased by less than 2 per cent. The report also notes that the extreme level of close supervision of First Nation communities reflects the departmental ethos of controlling First Nations people. In examining this problem, Fraser found that four federal departments (including Indian Affairs) required nearly 170 reports annually from each First Nation community. Indian Affairs alone obtains more than 60,000 reports a year from over 600 First Nation communities. This represents a report from each community almost every three days of the year. The Auditor General explains that these reports are neither important nor necessary, and they are not used by Indian Affairs in correcting problems or developing new policies or programs.

In 2009 the Auditor General reviewed the land entitlement obligations of Indian and Northern Affairs Canada and found that the six most recent land settlement agreements took 29 years, on average, to finalize. She also identified other issues related to land entitlement. In Manitoba and Saskatchewan, for example, a number of treaty land entitlement agreements allowed First Nations people to select Crown land or receive funds provided as compensation to purchase private land. These agreements were legal commitments that recognized the government's failure to comply with its treaty obligations. Her analysis found that more than 315,000 acres had been purchased and made part of reserves in the two provinces. However, since the department does not monitor the length of time it takes to process land selections, it is unable to demonstrate that processing times have improved over the past decade. Moreover, Indian Affairs has never supported the First Nations people in Manitoba 'to resolve third-party interests nor has it created plans for converting these 250 land purchases to reserve status' (Auditor General, 2009). Fraser found that between 1997 and 2009 Indian and Northern Affairs Canada had converted only 12 per cent of the land selected by First Nations in Manitoba and, between 1992 and 2009, 58 per cent of the lands selected in Saskatchewan. More shocking is the fact that it had no plan in place to process the remaining selections and to fulfill commitments under the treaty land entitlement agreements.

The Auditor General also found that Indian Affairs has 'routinely failed to regulate environmental threats on reserves while regulations are strictly enforced in off-reserve areas' (ibid.). She identified nearly 5,000 contaminated sites across Canada on reserves and yet only a handful are being cleaned up. For example, the department took action on only 58 sites during the 2008–9 fiscal year and spent just under $11 million on these sites when it actually had access to a $3.5 billion fund to deal with contaminated sites. When the Attawapiskat Cree community had an Indian Affairs-funded gas line burst in 1979, which allowed oil to pool under the community school, it took them 30 years to demolish the school that the community abandoned when the contamination took place. When the school was torn down, a rash of health issues emerged in the community and yet Indian Affairs refused to look into the issue. At the time the minister noted that the entire issue was a publicity stunt by the community to get additional government money. Today the Marwell Tar Pit remediation project is being touted as an example of how Indian and Northern Affairs deals with contaminated areas. This tar pit in Whitehorse, which is highly contaminated with concentrations of hydrocarbons, was identified as toxic and fenced off in 1958. Phase one of remediation is now scheduled to begin, and the cleanup is expected to be completed by 2020. This means that neighbouring First Nations people have lived in a toxic environment for over 50 years and it will be another decade before the site is clean.

The Auditor General also found that in 60 per cent of cases, Indian Affairs has failed to meet the legal requirements to evaluate the condition of the land when reserve land is leased to non–First Nation entities. In fact, she suggests that these leases are actually illegally obtained. Indian and Northern Affairs Canada does not meet its basic 'duty to consult' or accept the 'honour of the Crown' with a First Nation community before telling a company it can use First Nation land.

David versus Goliath

Indian and Northern Affairs Canada has virtually unlimited power in terms of what it wants to do with regard to First Nations people. Moreover, its linkages with other federal departments, such as Treasury Board, Justice, Industry, and Environment, force it to incorporate the agendas of these departments into its own policy without taking into consideration the needs of First Nations people. In an attempt to deal with the authority and power of Indian Affairs, First Nations began to organize, first at local levels, then into regional organizations, and finally nationally. A history of Aboriginal organizations reveals that they have confronted the government at many junctures, although their level of success in dealing with Indian Affairs has been limited (Frideres and Gadacz, 2008). These fledgling Indigenous movements occurred within normal political channels. However, more recent actions by First Nations people have been both within and outside normal political channels, the latter consisting of demonstrations, marches, occupations, roadblocks, and seizure of land or buildings, as has occurred, for example, with several clear-cut logging operations and in regard to the misappropriation of First Nation lands, such as at Oka, Ipperwash, and Caledonia (Wilkes, 2006).

Nevertheless, their current and most ambitious efforts focus around the national Assembly of First Nations. This organization, which represents status Indians, emerged in 1982 out of the National Indian Brotherhood and has taken the role of the 'giant slayer'. Since its creation, National Chiefs of the Assembly have tried various strategies when dealing with Indian Affairs, some taking a conciliatory stance while others have chosen a more confrontational position. However, there does not seem to be any evidence that one or the other position has produced policies or programs that were more favourable for First Nations people. Nevertheless, in the past two decades the Assembly of First Nations has learned how to organize effectively, deal with the media, pool its limited resources (part of which are provided by Indian Affairs), and partner with other organizations to enhance its political power and influence. The Assembly of First Nations also has given some support to various Indigenous movements that have championed the rights of First Nations people, e.g., Oka, and has supported grassroots movements within First Nation communities. The Assembly's objections to the First Nations Governance Act proposed by Indian Affairs in 2002 and its successful strategy in preventing the legislation from being implemented attest to this organization's power. Likewise, the residential school settlement was partially due to the efforts of the Assembly.

However, like other lobbying organizations, the Assembly of First Nations needs to retain its credibility and legitimacy with both its own constituents (First Nation communities) and mainstream Canada, as First Nations people learned years ago when the government attacked the National Indian Brotherhood and was partially successful in calling its credibility into question. And there are limits to the Assembly's influence, as the government response to the recommendations of the Royal Commission on Aboriginal Peoples demonstrates. While the Assembly supported the recommendations and mounted a major public campaign to try and influence the government into implementing the recommendations, it was not largely successful.

The most salient attributes of First Nation movements identified by Hall and Fenelon (2009) are the emphasis on local community, identity politics, communal ownership, land claims, and the right to practise a variety of traditional ceremonies. These attributes challenge deeply held values of Canadians and the state. As such, First Nations' claims for autonomy are a threat to neo-liberal ideology because they challenge the argument that there is no alternative to capitalism that will result in a positive quality of life. Nevertheless, one might argue that the presence of First Nations people suggests that there is an alternative to neo-liberal capitalism. As Hall and Fenelon point out, the goal of First Nation organizations thus far is not to destroy or replace the dominant social structure but rather to carve out a social space where they can continue to exist. Why, then, are they viewed as such a serious threat? They remain a threat to neo-liberal capitalism because there is no conceptual, political, or social space within neo-liberalism that would allow the continued existence of First Nations people and their claim to autonomy (ibid.).

Conclusion

Although significant measures have been taken by Indian and Northern Affairs Canada to change the government's relations with First Nations people and to allow some decision-making on the part of First Nation representatives, the department still maintains a significant degree of control over the lives of First Nations people. In addition, though all recognize that the philosophy of implementing integrated programs and ensuring easy access to the many services being provided is necessary for the efficient and effective use of tax dollars, many Indian Affairs-funded programs remain fragmented. While many Aboriginal people have not survived the current phase of 'domination', those who have are products of a complex and intense process that has allowed them to preserve some cultural attributes while adopting and adapting others. In the end, Indian and Northern Affairs Canada has a broad mandate that has not been fulfilled for over a century. Moreover, this department seems to lack the vision and mission that are necessary to meet the goals and objectives that most Canadians would expect a government department to achieve. Part of the problem can be attributed to the relatively low status of Indian and Northern Affairs Canada within the federal government and, consequently, the lack of continuity and longevity within the department bureaucracy. Part of the problem, too, is a broader view in society—a legacy from the past—that 'Indians', de facto, are a problem to be solved, not a valuable resource and a central component of the Canadian heritage and society. The singular focus of Indian and Northern Affairs Canada on control, which stems from these issues, has led it to fail in the provision of an opportunity for a positive quality of life for many First Nations people.

Struggles over sovereignty and autonomy are conflict points for First Nations people whereby they try to work out their relationship with the dominant society. Over the past two centuries, Aboriginal people have had to deal with the dominant society: first, in the profiteering mode aimed at economic exploitation; second, during a long period that focused on assimilation and on the obliteration of Aboriginal cultures; and currently, through a phase of control and domination.

Questions for Critical Thought

1. Is a government department such as Indian and Northern Affairs Canada really necessary?

2. Could INAC be reorganized so that it might play a more appropriate role in facilitating the needs and aspirations of First Nations people? What would it look like?

3. What actions should INAC take to deal with the concerns, needs, and aspirations of First Nations people?

4. Was Pierre Trudeau correct when his government introduced the 1969 White Paper that proposed to do away with the Indian Affairs department, with the concept of 'Indians' and reserves, as a strategy for allowing First Nations people to integrate into Canadian society?

Suggested Readings

Frideres, J., and R. Gadacz. 2008. *Aboriginal Peoples in Canada*, 8th edn. Toronto: Pearson Prentice-Hall. The authors provide an in-depth discussion of the structure and organization of INAC.

Ponting, J.R., and R. Gibbins. 1980. *Out of Irrelevance: A Socio-Political Introduction to Indian Affairs of Canada*. Toronto: Butterworths. Although dated, this book provides a good outline of the structure of Indian Affairs 30 years ago so the reader can compare its mandate and accomplishments with the present situation in regard to INAC.

Suggested Websites

Department of Indian and Northern Affairs Canada
www.ainc-inac.gc.ca
    The Indian and Northern Affairs Canada website includes a wealth of information with regard to Aboriginal issues and is linked with several other websites.

Assembly of First Nations
www.afn.ca
    The Assembly of First Nations provides information on current events, position papers, and proposals for policies and programs. It is linked to many other regional Aboriginal associations.

12 Surviving in the Contemporary World: The Future of First Nations People in Canada

Learning Objectives

- ⊛ To gain an overview of changing First Nation demographic trends.
- ⊛ To understand the components that produce demographic changes.
- ⊛ To learn about the implications of the changing socio-demographic profile for First Nations people.
- ⊛ To consider some projections about demographic trends for First Nations people.

Introduction

Where you have been in the past is sometimes a good predictor as to where you might go in the future. At other times, the future brings the unexpected—surprises that have no basis in the past. Trying to meld the past, current, and future produces many unknowns, and predictions for the future based on the past may be difficult. However, to understand the behaviour of a people, one has to understand their history, their current status, and their aspirations for the future. Consequently, we need to look carefully at the past and current characteristics of First Nations people in order to create a vision of the future. Moreover, the demography of Canada's First Nations may be looked upon as part of a phenomenon happening in the wider community of Indigenous minorities across North and South America and, indeed, the world. The history of First Nations population reveals that for many years they existed in a stable demographic state, periodically impacted by natural disasters and inter-tribal conflicts (Romaniuc, 2003). However, by the eighteenth century, the First Nations population began a three-century-long decrease, a result of European-introduced diseases, changes in lifestyle, and in some instances the genocidal actions of settler populations. This long period of population decline was followed by stabilization and slow recovery, culminating in a dramatic increase after the 1950s that will continue for some time into the future before the population stabilizes (Ubelaker, 1985; see Table 12.1). In brief, the population of First Nations people has vacillated dramatically from near extinction to impressive recovery (Romaniuc, 2003).

In this chapter, we will begin by considering the linkage of space to demography and look at the residential patterns of the First Nations people. Next

TABLE 12.1 Aboriginal Population and First Nations Population, 1500–2021

Year	Total Aboriginal Population (ooos)	First Nations Population (ooos)
1550	300	290
1871	123	112
1901	107	99
1931	133	123
1951	166	156
1971	313	295
1991	632	461
2001	916*	690
2021	1,191*	940

*Totals are based on multiple responses.
Sources: Historical records and *Census of Canada*, 1871 to present.

we will examine some of the determinants of population size and composition, e.g., **fertility**, **mortality**, and migration of First Nations. Following this, we explore past and projected future population growth, and identify some salient demographic attributes of First Nations people. The chapter concludes by showing how these factors will impact the future of First Nations and Canada.

How Many First Nations People?

In Canada, from 1876 until 1982, from a government perspective, only Indians constituted a formal, legal minority group and the Indian Act was created to deal with them. There were, however, a couple of exceptions. Alberta, in 1938, passed the Métis Population Betterment Act, which led to the formal creation of and support for several Métis settlements in the northern part of the province. And, as noted in the previous chapter, a 1939 Supreme Court ruling meant that Inuit were a federal responsibility. However, with the Constitution Act, 1982, these three groups all were formally recognized: Inuit, with a current population of about 50,000; Métis, with an estimated population of 200,000+; and the Indians (First Nations), consisting of approximately 800,000+. As discussed in Chapter 2, the legal definition as to who is to be classified as Indian has changed considerably over the years, with the most notable recent change taking place in 1985 when Bill C-31 was passed, which fundamentally changed the definition of who is an Indian person today as well as tomorrow (Canada, 2005).

Residence

The Royal Proclamation of 1763 confirmed First Nation rights to lands and established the groundwork for later negotiations between First Nations people and Canada. Currently they reside on approximately 2,700 reserves spread across the country. The largest reserve is the Six Nations of the Grand River in Ontario with over 22,000 people. In terms of physical space, the Blood reserve (Alberta) remains the largest, at over 800 square hectares, while others are just a few hectares in size. In the early twentieth century, a vast majority of First Nations people resided on the rural reserves (over 90 per cent) with only a few venturing into the large metropolitan areas, but over time there has been a major movement to the cities. By the beginning of the twenty-first century, just over half of all First Nations people remained on the reserves. Overall, the data show that over the past half-century there have been few shifts in the residential distribution throughout Canada, although the percentage of First Nations people residing in the Prairie provinces has increased slightly. Regionally, Aboriginal people make up a majority of the population in northern regions of Canada, e.g., Nunavut and the Northwest Territories, and in Yukon they are a sizable minority. In the provinces, they comprise from less than 1 per cent of the total population in the Atlantic provinces to nearly 10 per cent in Saskatchewan and Manitoba. In many smaller towns in Canada the First Nation population makes up more than a third of the total population, and larger and mid-sized cities in western Canada have significant Aboriginal populations. For example, today, just over 50,000 reside in Edmonton, nearly 70,000 Aboriginal people, or 10 per cent of the total population, live in Winnipeg, and Regina and Saskatoon have Aboriginal populations that comprise 9 per cent of their total populations. Other western Canadian cities, such as Calgary, Vancouver, and Prince Albert, have substantial numbers of First Nations residents.

Nearly a quarter of Canada's First Nations people reside in Ontario, where they comprise only 1.4 per cent of the total population, and 20 per cent live in British Columbia. Around 14 per cent are in each of the Prairie provinces and less than 10 per cent are in Quebec. The remainder of First Nations people are spread throughout the territories and the Atlantic provinces (Gionet, 2009).

Treaties

Apart from the Haldimand Grant of 1784, which awarded a large tract of land in southern Ontario to the Six Nations Iroquois, who had fought alongside the British as allies during the American Revolutionary War, it was not until the nineteenth century that the British government and later the Canadian government began to negotiate specific land treaties with First Nations. Earlier 'friendship' treaties were established in the Atlantic region of Canada but these did not involve land transfers and usually did not include any payments besides gift distributions. With the signing of the Robinson treaties of 1850 in Ontario and the completion of the 11 numbered treaties spanning a 50-year period in the late nineteenth and early twentieth centuries (see Chapter 1), much of western Canada and parts of central and northern Canada were covered by treaty. It would be another half-century before any further treaties would be signed with First Nations. Since the establishment of a federal policy for the settlement of modern First Nation land claims in 1973, 15 major comprehensive land claim agreements (modern-day treaties) and many other lesser land settlements have come into effect in Canada, e.g., Yukon Indian Nations, Nisga'a, Tli Cho, James Bay Cree, and many more are in the process of being negotiated. These negotiations focus on land, compensation, and governance. It is currently estimated that about $59 billion and thousands of hectares of land are part of outstanding claims waiting for the politicians and courts to decide.

Treaty lands are part of the **homelands** of First Nations people and serve as protected areas that developers and land settlement supposedly could not intrude upon. They were normally in rural areas and on land that was not desired by settlers at the time. However, as history reveals, as towns grew in size and the lands of some First Nations held valuable natural resources, intrusion onto reserves was widespread and much of the First Nation lands initially allocated to them were lost.

Population Growth and Size: Fertility, Mortality, and Migration

At the time the Europeans first arrived in northern North America, the population of the First Nations in what is today Canada is estimated to have been about 500,000. With the introduction, at different times in different places across the continent, of a variety of diseases, such as smallpox, measles, and typhoid fever, the First Nations population decreased rapidly. By the beginning of the twentieth century, just over 100,000 First Nations people were residing in Canada, but by the early twenty-first century this population had increased nearly eightfold from the nadir of 100 years earlier and is expected to continue to increase in the coming decades (Figure 12.1). Today, First Nations people make up about 3 per cent of the total Canadian population (Department of Indian Affairs and Northern Development, 2004).

This dramatic increase in First Nations population is a result of three demographic factors: a high fertility rate, relatively low mortality, and a high 'migration' rate by people from non-Indian to Indian status as a result of new legislation and changes in government definitions. Together these factors have resulted in a population explosion. In addition, Guimond et al. (2009) point out that 'being Aboriginal' has achieved some 'cache' over the past decade and more and more people are declaring their 'Aboriginal' status in the census and in other social/political contexts. They point out that these **ethnic drifters** are markedly different from those of the base

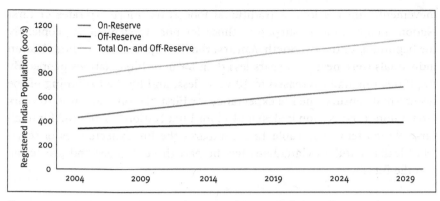

FIGURE 12.1 Registered Indian Population, Medium-Growth Scenario, Canada, 2004–2029

Source: Indian and Northern Affairs Canada, Registered Indian Demography—Population, Household, and Family Projections, 2004–2029, at: www.ainc-inac.gc.ca/ai/rs/pubs/re/rgd/rgd-eng.asp.

population and need to be taken into consideration when policy is created. It is estimated that by the third decade of the twenty-first century there will be about one million First Nations people in Canada. However, as the First Nations population begins to age, their fertility rates will decrease and the overall growth rate will slow down.

Fertility

In 1921, the crude birth rate for First Nations was over 50/1,000 population. Fifty years later, this rate had decreased to 35/1,000 (Loh and George, 2003). Since that time, the rate has continued to decrease—by 2001, the rate was just under 12.2/1,000. Nonetheless, this rate is over twice the national Canadian rate. In regard to fertility rates for First Nations women (15–39), in 1950 the average was 5.6 children for each First Nations woman. This has subsequently decreased to 2.7 children, but still is nearly twice the number of children of non–First Nations women (1.53) (Ram, 2004) and well above the replacement rate of 2.1 children. Of particular note is that young First Nations women (teenagers) have the largest contribution to First Nations fertility with 100 births per 1,000, while for the general Canadian population the 25–29 age group makes the largest contribution, 11.2 per 1,000 (Belanger, 2003; Hull, 2001).

Mortality

The second factor in determining the growth and growth rate of a population is mortality. Data from the nineteenth century suggest that First Nations had a lower mortality rate than European immigrants settling in Canada. However, with the introduction of disease, constricted geographical movement, and the loss of traditional foodstuffs, mortality rates of First Nations people quickly surpassed those for non–First Nations people. By the beginning of the twentieth century, the life expectancies of First Nation individuals were nearly 20 years less than for non–First Nations people. By the 1960s this had decreased to 10 years less, and by the beginning of the twenty-first century, the life expectancy for First Nation males was 70 years (76 for non–First Nation males) and 76 for First Nation females (82 for non–First Nation females). Table 12.2 compares the life expectancies of registered Indians and all Canadians for the past three decades and projecting into the future.

TABLE 12.2 Life Expectancy for Registered Indians and All Canadians, by Sex, 1975–2021

Year	Male		Female	
	First Nations	Total Canadian	First Nations	Total Canadian
1975	59.2	70.3	65.9	77.6
1980	60.9	71.8	68.0	79.0
1985	63.9	73.1	71.0	80.0
1990	66.9	74.3	74.0	80.8
1995	68.0	75.2	75.7	81.4
2000	68.9	76.3	76.6	81.8
2005	69.8	77.3	77.5	82.4
2016	71.6	78.8	79.5	83.3
2021	74.1	79.3	79.8	83.6

Sources: INAC, *Basic Departmental Data*, 1999, 2000, 2001, 2002, 2005, 2006; INAC, Registered Indian Population by Sex and Residence, 2008; INAC, Registered Indian Demography—Population, Household and Family Projections, 2004–2029, at: www.ainc-inac.gc.ca/ai/rs/pubs/sts/ni/rip/rip07/rip07-eng.pdf.

In 2005, the infant mortality rate for First Nations people was 3.5 times higher than the national rate, with the neonatal death rate 2 times higher and the post-neonatal mortality rate 5 times as high as the national rate. An overall standardized death rate for First Nations people is currently 9.4 per 1,000, while for non–First Nations people it is 5.4. The eradication of specific diseases such as smallpox and tuberculosis that killed thousands of First Nations' individuals during the first half of the twentieth century and the concomitant establishment of basic infrastructure in the communities, e.g., running water and septic systems, has resulted in an increase in life expectancy. In addition, First Nations have access to state-supported health-care facilities to enhance their quality of life.

Despite these improvements, other factors work against the health of First Nations people. The increased reliance on store-bought processed foods, high unemployment, and poverty have led to new forms of illness that have increased the mortality rate. Smoking, obesity, drug use, lack of physical activity, and lack of adequate and properly serviced housing have brought about a major crisis. Today, suicide, hypertension, diabetes, and arthritis/ rheumatism are major health issues on practically all reserves. Other health issues, such as AIDS, cancer, and heart and liver disease, previously unheard of in the First Nations population, are now major causes of death. A resurgence of tuberculosis and the number of accidents, likewise, have impacted the mortality rates of First Nations. Even in remote areas where traditional lifestyles continue to be practised, the extensive pollution from mining and other forms of development has had a negative impact on the health of First Nations people. The people of the Athabasca Chipewyan First Nation at Fort Chipewyan, Alberta, downstream from the huge tar sands projects in northern Alberta, are only the most recent community to make headline news because their health and fisheries have been severely compromised by industry. Over 40 years ago, for example, the Ojibwa at Grassy Narrows and Whitedog reserves in northwestern Ontario gained public attention after years of suffering the effects of mercury poisoning from pollution in the English–Wabigoon River system caused by a large pulp mill nearly 200 kilometres upstream (Dickason with McNab, 2009: 389).

Finally, for most Canadians, major, life-threatening illnesses generally are limited to the final 13 years of life. However, for First Nations people, illness and health issues impact all age groups, thereby reducing their well-being throughout life and not just as they enter old age. In summary, if mortality rates were decreased for younger First Nations individuals, the growth rate would increase even more than it currently is.

Migration

Migration traditionally refers to the number of individuals coming into or going out of a country or location within the country. While Canada is experiencing about a 1 per cent population growth rate per year, nearly 60 per cent of this is a result of international migration and this will increase in the next three decades. In the case of First Nations people, a different form of migration has taken place—defining who is an Indian. As we saw in Chapter 2, the government, over the years, has unilaterally defined who is a First Nations person and who is not and there has been little anyone could do about the final decision. This process of enfranchisement—becoming a voting citizen—was carried out for nearly 100 years and the basis for such change was both voluntary and involuntary. The creation of the Indian Act in 1876 provided the legal basis for the extraordinary control that the federal government exhibited with regard to defining who is and is not a First Nations person, and some people, because they had earned a higher education or served in the armed forces, for example, were enfranchised and lost their Indian status as a consequence. An estimated 80,000 individuals were enfranchised or otherwise lost their Indian status over the past century through government redefinition. While this number is small, it means that for the past five generations, the descendants of these enfranchised individuals were not defined as status Indians. Consequently, demographers have estimated that over one million people, across several generations, lost their status through enfranchisement.

With Bill C-31 in 1985, the government again redefined 'Indian' (Clatworthy, 2004), and nearly 150,000 people were added to the Indian register. In 2010 the federal government proposed necessary revisions to Bill C-31 (based on the *McIvor* case) and the implications of these changes are now being analyzed. At present it is estimated that 40,000 more people will be added to the Indian registry as 'Indians' and another 60,000 already listed on the Indian registry will be able to change their status from section 6(2) to section 6(1) Indians (see Chapter 2). It is expected that further revisions will take place in the future and will further impact the official number of First Nations people in Canada.

Demographic Profile of Indian People

Age distributions, education, dependency ratios, and labour force participation are perhaps the most telling demographic attributes in understanding the integration of First Nations people into the larger society and their economic success, as well as the social cohesion and future of Canadian society (Mueller, 2004).

Age

The First Nations population is much younger than the total Canadian population. At the beginning of the twentieth century, their median age was similar to that of the Canadian population. However, over time, the high birth rates and lower death rates, especially lower infant mortality, resulted in a very different **population pyramid**. Figure 12.2 reveals the age distribution of First Nations for 2004 and a medium-growth scenario for 2029. Today, the median age of First Nations is 24.7 while that of the Canadian population is 37.1 years. By 2017, the median ages are estimated to be 27.8 and 41.3 years, respectively. At the same time, the number of First Nations people over 65 will increase from 4 per cent to 6 per cent of the total First Nations population in the next decade while for the Canadian population the increase is expected to be from 13 to nearly 17 per cent. It is predicted that by 2025, over 25 per cent of the Canadian population will be over the age of 65.

The high growth rate of the First Nations population also has resulted in a young population. Currently, those under 15 years old make up one-third of the total population while those under 29 comprise over half of the total

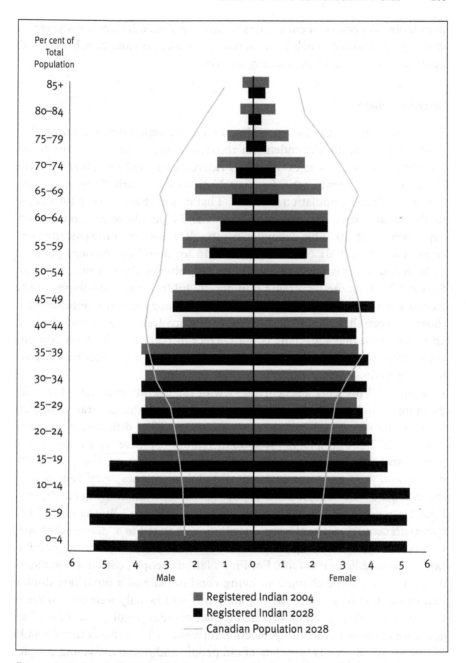

FIGURE 12.2 Population Pyramids for Registered Indian and Canadian Populations, Medium-Growth Scenario, 2004 and 2029

Source: INAC, Registered Indian Demography—Population, Household and Family Projections, 2004–2029, at: www.ainc-inac. gc.ca/ai/rs/pubs/re/rgd/rgd-eng.asp.

population. As can be seen, a series of demographic dilemmas, with significant repercussions on such social services as education and health-care, will confront Canadians in the coming decades.

Dependency Ratios

The dependency ratio for First Nations people represents the number of people economically dependent on those individuals in the labour force, usually designated as ages 20–62 (Frideres and Gadacz, 2009). In the 1970s, the dependency ratio for First Nations was nearly 74 while for the non–First Nation population it was 40. That means that for every 100 people in the labour force age group, for Indians 74 people were economically dependent on them. This dependency ratio decreased over the past quarter-century to 58 in 2001 (but increased to 46 for non–First Nations people). In both cases, this is due to the increasing number of older people, although for First Nations the increasing number of children also contributes to the changes in the dependency ratio. The dependency ratio also assumes that those between the ages of 20 and 62 are fully involved in the labour market, an assumption that especially is not correct in regard to the First Nations population. Hence, the real dependency ratio for First Nations people may be closer to 65.

Figure 12.3 presents a schematic view of the overall structure of the age groupings for both the Aboriginal population and the general Canadian population over time. When we compare the two, the differences are quite remarkable. For example, in the 1950 distributions, there were many young people and relatively few old people in Canada. Among the Aboriginal population, however, a truncated distribution shows very few people reached old age. Through disease, poor health, and harsh living conditions, First Nations people died before reaching an 'old age'. By the end of the twentieth century, Canada's age distribution changed to a 'diamond' shape, with relatively fewer young people and very elderly and most of the population in the middle years of life. For First Nations people, with improvements in health-care, some changes in living conditions, and a birth rate double that of the Canadian rate, the population is still heavily weighted towards the young but there is an increasing number of older people, i.e., those of an age to be in the workforce. A projection forward to 2030 shows that Canada will be an aging society with lots of old people and not many young people. The Aboriginal population, on the other hand, will have reached the type of age distribution that Canada as a whole demonstrated 80 years earlier, in 1950. The implications are clear. For example, today Canadians and their governments are gearing up for a 'grey' society with many elderly people who require additional health-care, public pension support, and, in many instances, different kinds of housing and infrastructure. At the same time,

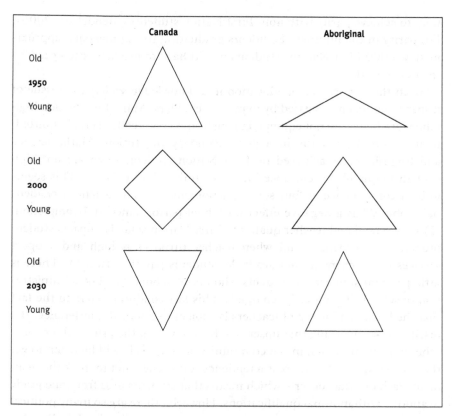

FIGURE 12.3 Population Distributions, Canadian and Aboriginal Canadian, 1950–2030

First Nation populations are and will continue to be focused on providing education and jobs for young people. Currently and for the future, the divergent demographic facts of the two populations call for rather different policy emphases.

Education

The First Nations population is not as well educated as the general Canadian population. Over 40 per cent of the adult First Nations population do not have a high school certificate (more than twice the rate for the Canadian general population). The index of dissimilarity shows that over one-quarter of the Indian population would have to increase their educational attainments if this population were to have a similar profile to the general Canadian population. First Nation students complete high school at a rate less than half that of the general population. Looking at the post-secondary numbers, 23,000 First Nations people would have to enter post-secondary educational institutions over the next 10 years if they were to achieve parity with non–First Nation students (Mendelson, 2006). For parity in the number of students graduating from university, approximately 5,000 First Nations students would have to graduate each year for the next decade.

Given the importance of education in a 'knowledge society', the issue of disparity has been discussed by many stakeholders. Many First Nation high school graduates are not equipped to enter university/college or, if admitted, to maintain their status in a post-secondary institution. Math, science and English scores achieved by First Nation students often are not high enough to qualify for entrance into most universities/colleges. This seems to be a consequence of four social phenomena. (1) The extent of residential mobility has a negative effect on school performance and completion. (2) Low school and teacher quality in First Nation schools impacts student progress and learning, and when teacher turnover is high and support services for teachers are not available, students pay the price. (3) There is little parental support for students who are in school. (4) The administration of schools is politically 'charged'. This last condition refers to the fact that the hiring and firing of teachers is subject to political interference. If a teacher says something that upsets the band council, the principal, or some other important faction in the community, action likely will be taken to get the teacher fired. Thus there is a tendency for teachers not to 'rock the boat' in any fashion whatsoever—which means that students pass from one grade to another with minimal qualifications. However, there are so many political issues within a First Nation community—many stemming from Indian Act and bureaucratic control over the lives of the people—that over time practically any teacher is likely to be perceived as a problem and thus get fired. Little opportunity exists to appeal the firing and, consequently, very high turnover rates are the norm.

Another major difference in the First Nation student education profile is the major gap between men and women going to university and/or obtaining a university or college degree/certificate. First Nations women are more likely to attend university and obtain a degree than First Nations men. Finally, First Nations education (at all levels) reveals a lack of linkage between the school and the community (Aman, 2009). Today, generally, there is little support for education from First Nations parents. The end result is that students are not guided by their parents (and the community) in order to ensure that they successfully complete primary and secondary education.

It is important to realize that dropping out of school or not continuing one's education is not a single act. The social determinants are many and they begin to impact such an act within the first three years of a students' educational career. Furthermore, we know that factors such as family and household attributes, housing conditions, nutrition, mobility, language, community support, and whether or not the student's parents attended residential school all are powerful determinants for the student's decision regarding his/her education. Unfortunately, many of these 'non-educational' factors are generally ignored by federal policy that seeks to enhance First Nation students' completion rates.

As Mendelson (2009) argues, the proportion of First Nation students finishing high school has not changed over the past decade. More importantly, the disparity between First Nation students and the general population completing high school is getting larger. He suggests that the creation of a First Nations Education Act needs to be developed by the federal government after decision-making has been given to First Nation communities. The end result would be an Act of national scope to allow First Nations to exercise control over their education, ensure that both government and the community are accountable for their actions, and provide long-term (and sufficient) funding for First Nation schools.

The creation in 1999 of the Mi'kmaw Kina'maatnewey in Nova Scotia, established under the terms of the province's Mi'kmaq Education Act, is a good example of how this would work and could serve as a general model for federal legislation. It defines the nature and scope of power transferred to the Mi'kmaq in their taking control of elementary and secondary education. The agreement identifies the duties and functions of participating schools, such as developing a fair, open, and transparent process when they exercise their power. It also established a Mi'kmaq liaison office that bridges activities between the provincial Department of Education and the First Nation communities, and allows band schools to access provincial services for teachers and administrators through professional and curriculum development. Under this agreement, the Indian Act, with regard to education, ceased to apply to participating communities. To date, this new arrangement has produced positive outcomes for learning by First Nation students in Nova Scotia.

Labour Force Participation and Income

Research by Pendakur and Pendakur (2008) show that, on average, First Nation individuals have incomes about 60 per cent lower than those of mainstream Canadians. They also indicate that even highly educated First Nations people face substantial income disparity. In 2008, the average total income of Canadians was just under $36,000, while for on-reserve First Nations people the average income was less than half that. Martin and Guimond (2009) note that while the per capita income of First Nations men rose from $7,850 to $8,870 between 1980 and 2000, it jumped to $10,460 in 2005. However, the average income of other Canadian men rose from $16,000 in 1980 to over $28,000 in 2005; in other words, the gap increased significantly over a 25-year period.

In addition, unemployment among First Nations people is more than three times that of the general population. Involvement in the labour force shows that First Nations people continue to be at the margins. They are more likely to hold part-time or seasonal jobs that do not include pension or other benefits.

Implications of Demographic Changes

In the late nineteenth and early twentieth centuries, Canadian politicians and bureaucrats were convinced that First Nations people, as a distinct cultural group, would soon cease to exist. Through disease, cultural disruption, intermarriage, and a variety of other social and political forces, the physical and cultural existence of First Nations people was expected soon to become a memory, to be revisited through pictures, museums, and scholarly works. The demise of First Nations people was predicted as late as the 1930s. The consequence of such predictions was that, from the government's perspective, there was no need to develop policies or programs to ensure the integration of First Nations people into the social and economic fabric of Canadian society. In other words, there was neither a vision nor a plan for integrating First Nations people into the structure and organization of society. The imagined success of the assimilation project, centred on the ill-conceived residential schools, made the question of integration moot. What little planning existed was premised on the assumption that the 'Indians' as a group would soon disappear. This, of course, did not happen, and the impact of the First Nations on the politics and economics of Canada has been significant. Table 12.3 shows the on-reserve and off-reserve populations of First Nations people in Canada, by region, for 2000 and the projected populations for 2021.

Table 12.3 Total Population of Registered Indians in Canada by Region, On- and Off-Reserve, 2000 and 2021

Region	2000			2021		
	Total	On-Reserve	Off-Reserve	Total	On-Reserve	Off-Reserve
Atlantic	27,000	17,000	10,000	34,000	26,000	8,000
Quebec	64,000	45,000	19,000	82,000	65,000	16,000
Ontario	159,000	82,000	77,000	206,000	136,000	71,000
Manitoba	109,000	72,000	38,000	161,000	127,000	34,000
Sask.	108,000	56,000	53,000	159,000	116,000	43,000
Alberta	87,000	58,000	30,000	128,000	102,000	26,000
BC	112,000	58,000	55,000	141,000	105,000	36,000
Territories	15,000	15,000	0	20,000	20,000	0

Source: INAC, *Basic Departmental Data*, 1990, 1996, 2000, 2003, 2007; Population Projections of Registered Indians, 1990, Registered Indian Demography—Population, Household and Family Projections, 2004–2029, at: www.ainc-inac.gc.ca/ai/rs/pubs/sts/ni/rip/rip07/rip07-eng.pdf.

While First Nation communities continue to expand in population, the size of the reserves has not increased at a commensurate rate. Moreover, mobility of First Nations people suggests that in the past decade there has been a 'return to community' movement and more First Nation individuals are moving back to the reserves than are moving to the cities (Clatworthy, 2007). This movement is reflected in the 2021 projections in Table 12.3, which show that while population in each region is expected to increase considerably, at the same time the off-reserve populations are expected to decrease. This movement has precipitated a number of land claims as First Nations attempt to regain lost land and to build larger protected areas for growing populations. As in the past, these reserves remain largely invisible to non–First Nations people; they do not significantly touch the lives of other Canadians and are not regarded as a policy priority by the government except in times of crisis. As a result, many First Nations find themselves living in communities with little economic viability, poor infrastructure and services, and inadequate housing. In short, they are not 'creative communities' that will become economically viable and sustainable under existing circumstances (Florida, 2002).

Equally important is the fact that Canada is becoming increasingly urbanized, with over 80 percent of the Canadian population now living in urban centres across the country. Consequently, more government policies are developed to focus on urban Canada, and both industry and governments have progressively devoted their efforts to supporting the urbanization of Canada. Except at election time, rural residents and rural needs are seen as peripheral and unimportant to the country's future, in contrast to cities and the new 'knowledge network' that thrives in the urban environment. First Nations people who move to the city choose to live in census metropolitan areas of at least 100,000, where, because of their relatively small numbers, their impact is greatly diminished and their presence is too often ignored—except by the controlling powers of the state. At the same time, as suggested in Table 12.3, Indian and Northern Affairs Canada estimates that the proportion of registered Indians living on reserves could increase from 60 per cent in 2005 to over 75 per cent in 2021. The disjuncture between policies and programs for rural and urban people, it appears, will continue, yet, according to Clatworthy (2001), the First Nation on-reserve population will increase for the next two and a half generations (about 50 years) before beginning to decline.

These data clearly reveal that the population distributions are different and thus reflect different needs. In the total Canadian population, more old people, fewer children, and earlier retirement add up to growing demands on the health-care and pension systems, as well as a significant reduction in labour force growth. Annual labour force growth is expected to stabilize below 1 per cent over the next two decades. If present trends continue, by 2050 there will be 65 pensioners for every 100 workers. On the other hand, First Nations will be focusing on very different issues: support for young people to attend primary, secondary, and post-secondary educational institutions; development of 'wellness' programs focused on health issues relevant to their needs, especially those of youth and working-age individuals; the necessary skills for and access to the labour force.

The different demographic profiles of the two groups inevitably lead to a divergence of interests that can result in increased tension between the two groups. Notwithstanding the fact that the federal government spends over $10 billion per year to govern the lives of First Nations people as well as to provide for their basic health, social, and educational services, the people, relative to other Canadians, remain poor, unhealthy, uneducated, and un-integrated into the larger economy. Canadian governments have shown more interest in dealing with the economic issues (employment, productivity) by increasing immigration and extending the retirement age. There has been no interest in focusing on the unemployed or underemployed groups already in Canada, such as First Nations people, who represent a potential internal resource of manpower and expertise to meet the growing demands of the country.

Finally, it should be noted that the demographic impact of Bill C-31 will begin to have its secondary impact by 2035 unless it is changed once again. At that time, offspring of individuals who have been defined as 'Indian' will begin to lose their Indian status and the rights that go along with that status. The total population of survivors and descendants of status Indians is projected to increase throughout the twenty-first century from the current level of about 800,000 to 2.1 million by the end of the century. At the same time, intermarriage between pre- and post-Bill C-31 individuals will grow over this century from the current 15,000 marriages to well in excess of 210,000. The number of registered Indians will increase until 2049, and then a continuous decline will occur so that by the end of the century there will be just over 700,000 officially registered Indians in Canada. In other words, by the end of this century, there could be about the same number as or even fewer registered Indians than there are today (Clatworthy, 2001, 2007).

Conclusion

First Nations people are attempting to deal with their changing demography. Under pressure to allow First Nations people to engage in some form of self-government, the federal government embarked on a policy of devolution of governance in the 1970s. This allowed First Nation communities to take on more responsibility with regard to management on a variety of issues (Belanger and Newhouse, 2004). Thus far only education and some aspects of health-care have been 'transferred' to First Nation communities. Although *management* of almost all areas of Indian life is carried out by local political organizations, *control* over these activities is lacking. Nevertheless, in their quest to achieve self-government, First Nation communities are using their social capital, land base, and increasing knowledge base to enter the financial, educational, and commercial world and achieve de facto self-government.

Canadians are being forced to deal with First Nation issues, not because they are concerned about the First Nations people, though many are, but because their governments see their own self-interests are at stake (Siggner, 2003). Canadians are responding because First Nations people are engaging in activities that are impacting their lives. Some of the impact is direct, such as litigation by survivors of residential schools that cost the government $2 billion to settle. In other cases, the impact is indirect, such as the increasing number of social welfare cases, increasing costs of incarceration, and the number of young First Nations people who are under the care of provincial social services. However, there is no overarching plan for integrating First Nation people into the larger economy. For example, while everyone agrees that labour shortages exist in some sectors of the economy, there has been no sustained effort to ensure that young First Nations people are being prepared to enter the labour market. Divergent thinking among politicians as to how to resolve First Nations poverty and the inability to integrate has resulted in a hopeless morass of indecision. Others have no interest in providing skills for this population as they represent the secondary labour resource pool that the private sector has exploited for over a century. Finally, others suggest that a single focus on issues such as increasing educational attainment or economic involvement will serve as the engine of sustainable development, while others argue that a more holistic approach is necessary for development to take place in First Nation communities.

Canadians need to see that diversity can contribute to learning and innovation, both of which are required for building a knowledge-based economy. Lenihan and Kaufman (2001) point out that government and the private sector need to transform Canada from an 'educated' to a 'learning' society. In an educated society, achievement (usually within the first 30 years of life) is the key factor. However, in a learning society, the institutional orders foster learning as a 'way of life' that continues from birth to death. To achieve such a goal will require formal education and training and extensive opportunities for personal growth.

Community and political leaders will need to consult with the First Nations to ensure that everyone is onside with whatever strategy is chosen. They also will need to make a decision soon as to how they propose to address the issue of integrating First Nations into the larger political economy (ibid.). At minimum, they must create and implement a development plan, in partnership with First Nation communities, and then stay the course for many years if any measurable changes are to take place. Given that we know that the Indian population will increase substantially in the years to come and numerous young people will be of the age to enter the labour market, new policies and programs need to be created to meet that challenge.

Questions for Critical Thought

1. What will happen when the demography of the two groups (First Nations and non–First Nations) present opposite demographic pyramid forms?

2. What are the major factors in changing the population distribution for both First Nations and non–First Nations peoples?

3. Given the projections about the social demographic attributes of First Nations people, what will be the social issues of 2035?

Suggested Readings

Frideres, J., and R. Gadacz. 2009. *Aboriginal Peoples in Canada*. Toronto: Pearson Prentice-Hall. The authors provide a detailed description of Canada's Aboriginal peoples in the twenty-first century, focusing on such political and social issues as land claims, demography, and crime.

Indian Affairs and Northern Development Canada. 2004. *Basic Departmental Data*. Ottawa, Minister of Public Works and Government Services Canada. Each year Indian and Northern Affairs Canada prepares a profile of First Nations people in Canada. Topics include residential distribution, health, education, labour force involvement, and other socio-demographic factors.

Romaniuc, A. 2003. 'Aboriginal Population of Canada: Growth Dynamics under Conditions of Encounter of Civilizations', *Canadian Studies in Population* 30: 75–113. The author presents a detailed demographic profile of the Aboriginal population for the past 300 years.

Suggested Website

Statistics Canada
www.statcan.gc.ca
Statistics Canada collects and analyzes vast amounts of statistical information on all ethnic groups in Canada, including First Nations people. Whatever topic you would like, you will probably find it here. Also check out *The Daily*, which is a publication on a specific demographic topic each day. This is where the radio and TV stations go to get the 'hot topic' of the day for their newscasts.

Conclusion

During the first half of the twentieth century, First Nations people were ignored, protected, and oppressed but never fully treated as members of Canadian society. A continual contradictory relationship emerged between settlers and First Nations people. On the one hand, settlers wanted First Nations people to be like them. On the other hand, there was a clear recognition that even if they integrated into mainstream Canadian society, they would never be accepted as equals by the settlers. Hence, the relations between First Nations and non–First Nations people have tried to deal with this inherent tension between the two groups. The creation of the Indian Act by settlers was the strategy undertaken to deal with this bifurcated view of First Nations people.

The result is that the social organization of First Nations people has been held together with Band-aids and is in need of major renovations (Flanagan et al., 2010). The continual fixes to the Indian Act over the years make the document a mixture of new and old, resulting in a frequent discontinuity between the Act and current political policies and court decisions. Indeed, the ruling document for Canada's First Nations is so complex and outdated that its contents defy logical analysis (Boychuk, 2004), although the government continues to tinker with it. Nevertheless, today there is agreement by scholars, First Nation leaders, workers in the field, and policy-makers that the time has come to rethink the relationship between First Nations and the state. As reconciliation now is a central component of the policy agenda, we need to look at the social architecture of Canada, make the necessary revisions, and create a more acceptable place within it for First Nations people. Abele (2004: 48) has identified four policy challenges that Canada must address quickly and decisively if we are to integrate First Nations people and reconcile with them for our past actions.

- Deal with the growing First Nation population.
- Address the needs of First Nation children in such areas as education and health.
- Ensure that First Nations youth are able to obtain an education.
- Bring First Nations youth into the labour market as potential contributors to Canadian society.

She suggests that two changes in Canadian society make it possible to bring about social change that would integrate First Nations people into mainstream society without their having to assimilate. First, the political ideology in Ottawa over the past quarter-century has emphasized the decentralization of responsibilities to lesser levels of government. Second, First Nations and other Aboriginal organizations continue to pressure government to allow them to take control of their lives through self-government and inherent self-governance. First Nations people are demanding that they have a say in the future of Canada, and a liberal democracy has to take these concerns into account if it is to build a cohesive society. Numerous First Nations regional and pan-Canadian organizations represent their political and social interests in virtually every area of social provision, and have contributed to fundamental change in Canada's political and social landscape, creating new jurisdictions and new forms of government. But except in some instances at the local community or band level, they have not been able to develop economic organizations that would allow for First Nations people to more fully develop their institutional completeness.

At present, many mainstream institutions in Canada are trying to integrate the legal and constitutional transformations that have taken place in the last 35 years with regard to First Nations people. Such integration will bring about an increase in their economic and social well-being as well as a greater capacity to build self-sustaining and self-directed community organizations. At the same time, however, the dominant mainstream institutions will need to address the issue of poverty, and child poverty in particular. Canadians and their governments also must come to understand the tension between universality and uniqueness with regard to the provision of social and economic goods. This is the point on which the government's 1969 White Paper on Indian Policy foundered: it proposed an individualistic, liberal view of society wherein one group cannot or should not be in a position to make treaty with the rest of the society. In brief, it failed to recognize the legitimacy or the possibility of communitarian rights existing alongside and in some instances trumping individual rights. Numerous court decisions and political incidents in Canada over the ensuing decades have shown such an exclusively individualistic view to be untenable. Respect for the particular needs and qualities of First Nation cultures will need to be integrated into the institutional orders of Canadian society, and can be in a fashion that was inconceivable over 40 years ago.

The Royal Commission on Aboriginal Peoples completed its mandate in 1996 and presented the government with a number of recommendations to integrate First Nations people into Canadian society. As we know, the government of the day rejected most of those recommendations and developed its own guidelines and principles as to how it would embark on a process of integrating First Nations people into the social fabric. It now has been nearly 20 years since the government began implementation of its 'plan' to settle land claims and other issues involving First Nations, and the results have been underwhelming. The recent failure by government to implement the First Nations Governance Act reminds us that change must fully involve the First Nations people. This is a two-sided process, and unilateral methods to invoke social change, whether imposed from the top down or welling up from the grassroots, are doomed to failure. At present, neither First Nation communities nor their organizations have a central role in the development of policy or its execution. New models of representing First Nations people in the policy development process need to be established so that their aspirations can be included in the development of Canada. As Abele (2004) points out, we cannot afford to ignore the growing role of First Nation governments and their organizations in the development of social policy and the cohesion of Canada without risking subverting the small progress that has been made. We need to go back to the recommendations made by the Royal Commission on Aboriginal Peoples and begin the long process of implementing the recommendations made with a commitment by both the federal government and First Nations to bring about that change. These recommendations—well over 400 in total—are far too extensive to be elucidated here, but a few of the more significant ones as they relate to the present discussion include:

- Self-determination for Aboriginal nations rather than for small local communities, so that the nearly 1,000 First Nation communities would be combined to create something in the neighbourhood of 60 or 80 self-governing First Nations.
- The creation of a third order of government at the federal level—an Aboriginal parliament—that would have an advisory role in decisions affecting Aboriginal people.
- Extension of the land base of the First Nations—i.e., an increase in the size of many reserves—so that they might be in a better position to become economically self-reliant.
- First Nations development of their taxation system.
- The abolishment of Indian Affairs and its replacement by two new federal departments: Aboriginal Relations (a senior-level cabinet portfolio) and Indian and Inuit Services.
- In the short term, $1.5 to $2 billion additional annual funds for Indian Affairs over a 15-year period to reduce poverty and increase self-sufficiency. (Dickason with McNab, 2009: 417–19)

Clearly, these recommendations alone are a tall order, but the quickly scrapped Kelowna Accord of 2005 was a beginning in this direction. As noted by others, the vision put forth by the Royal Commission was underlined by the four principles of mutual respect, mutual recognition, sharing, and mutual responsibility. A new architecture regarding how Canada might integrate First Nations people into society was provided by the Royal Commission and this model now needs to be implemented. It is time to begin again.

One would think that after more than 400 years of European settlement in this country, the issue of land claims would be settled. However, evidence suggests that over $50 billion of outstanding claims against the government are currently on the table and more claims are being introduced every year. Over time the government has tried to implement a variety of strategies to resolve these claims (comprehensive and specific) but the results have not been encouraging. In 1996, over 700 specific claims had been received by the federal government, and in the meantime some of these have been resolved, yet by 2008 there were 800 specific claims before the federal government (Canada, 2008).

Urbanization of First Nations people is an issue that looms large in the next decade (Peters, 2002). Data show that an increasing number of First Nations people have established permanent residence in urban centres. The large size of First Nation populations in cities like Vancouver, Calgary, Winnipeg, Toronto, Saskatoon, and Regina poses major challenges to city officials, to non–First Nation populations, and, especially, to social service agencies (Hanselmann, 2001; Graham and Peters, 2003). More recent events reveal moves to create reserves within the boundaries of urban centres. Saskatchewan and Manitoba now have these and their operation and linkage to the municipal centres has provoked considerable debate. How this will unfold over the next decade as the number of First Nations people living in urban centres increases, before a levelling off or slow decline (Table 12.3), will be an important process.

Helin and Snow (2010) point out the importance of education and its funding, its structure, and the provisions for ensuring that teachers are qualified and students are provided an appropriate K–12 education. The policies and programs that help First Nation students complete their secondary education and move into post-secondary educational institutions are of great importance as Canada continues to embrace the knowledge economy. An issue of less pressing interest for many Canadians but of crucial importance to this country as well as to First Nations people relates to water. As development takes place and populations increase in Canada and the United States, the question of who has rights to water will become extremely significant. In the midst of this is the question of how First Nations people fit into this discussion. First Nations claim water rights under the broad rubric of Aboriginal title, Aboriginal rights, treaty rights, or even riparian rights. Yet, there has never been a court ruling in Canada that has unequivocally established or denied First Nation rights to water (Laidlaw and Passelac-Ross, 2010). A number of other issues that demand recognition as having an impact on First Nations people and on Canadians as a whole have not been dealt with in this book. For example, gender issues need to be more fully addressed in many dimensions within First Nation communities as well as by government (Voyageur, 2007; Tiedemann, 2009; Mann, 2009). Justice issues related to the disproportionate number of First Nations people in Canada's jails and prisons will need to be more concretely addressed (beyond the *Gladue* decision) over the next decade. All of these issues will have important implications for how First Nations people fit into the Canadian social fabric. Our task will be to develop the strategies to deal with these and other issues that we have brought upon ourselves and to make sure that this time we get it right.

Glossary

Aboriginal rights Those rights that First Nations people retain as a result of their original possession of the land. They are property rights that date from time immemorial.

Assimilation A process by which the dominant group imposes its institutions and culture onto another group through which the subordinate group is absorbed into the dominant group.

Blood quantum A measure of 'ethnic' identity that places you within a group depending on the amount of 'ethnic blood' you have, e.g., if you are a non-Indian and marry an Indian person, the children from that partnership would then have 'half' blood.

Cartesian theory The belief (typical of Western ways of knowing) that there is a distinction and a separation between mind and body (in contrast to 'monism', which posits that mind and body comprise a unified, inseparable whole).

Charlottetown Accord An attempt in 1992 to revise the Constitution by recognizing Quebec's 'distinct character' that included a proposal to recognize self-government for Aboriginal people, the creation of a Triple-E Senate, and a broad decentralization of federal power to the provinces. It was rejected in a national referendum.

Colour bar The informal norm that there are different rights and responsibilities for people of different skin 'colour'. Dark skin means few rights and privileges while lighter skin means more. Primary interaction between the two groups is circumscribed.

Co-management The process by which a project or policy (development, environmental protection, hunting/fishing) is administered and managed by both a First Nation community and government or the private sector.

Constructivism A belief that social reality and its meaning are produced by actors as they relate to their social and physical environment. Reality is a process of negotiation and revision.

Corrective justice Another word for 'litigation'; a process by which the courts decide if harm has been committed and what the compensation will be. A return to the status quo as it existed prior to the harm is the goal.

Cultural genocide When the culture of a people is destroyed but the people themselves are not killed.

Dependency The reliance of one group of people in a society on another group in all aspects of life.

Determinants of health Social, economic, genetic, environmental, and individual factors that have an impact on the level of well-being of an individual or community.

Devolved (devolution) A process by which the federal government has given up some of its management activities and allowed First Nation communities to carry them out.

Duty to consult In reference to land and development projects, the requirement that if government intends to take action that may impact First Nations, it must stop and consult with the First Nations before proceeding.

Entrepreneurship The process by which an individual creates a business.

Epistemology The study of the foundations of knowledge, i.e., how we come to know what we know.

Ethnic ancestry Identifying one's ethnic group using the male lineage. An objective measure of identity.

Ethnic drifters Those individuals who might not be considered 'true' First Nations people because of their more integrated, assimilated, mainstream lifestyle, but who have been given an opportunity to self-declare as such.

Ethnic identity Subjective measure of identity by which an individual selects his/her most important ethnic group to which he/she identifies.

Exogamy The process by which members of one language group marry someone from another language group.

Fertility The average number of children born to a woman. Usually expressed as a rate of births per year per 1,000 women of child-bearing age (ages 15–44).

Fiduciary The legal concept that one person or group is responsible for the affairs of another group. Generally, it focuses on economic issues but can extend to other areas of social behaviour.

Firewall The placement of a barrier between activities. This means that decisions about one activity, e.g., health, should not impinge on decisions in other political realms.

Friendship treaty An agreement between First Nations people and a colonial power in which each agreed to maintain peace between them.

Governance How a community is organized and governed—politically, financially, and socially. There is an assumption that the leaders will be accountable to the people.

Grounded theory The process by which one makes observations and then tries to develop a theory on the basis of those observations.

Group vitality The extent to which a community carries out activities that support their language use in the community.

Hawthorn Report A federally sponsored study, conducted by anthropologist Harry Hawthorn, to examine the socio-economic status of Indian people in the early 1960s. It was the first time the government had undertaken a pan-Canadian study of Indian people.

Homeland A land area considered by First Nations people to be their 'home', which generally refers to a reserve as well as to a wider area (usually Crown lands) where the people have traditionally pursued hunting, fishing, and other activities.

Honour of the Crown The principle that government has a responsibility to honour its commitments to its people.

Human capital Attributes of an individual that are important to economic success in society, such as education, age, sex.

Index of continuity A mathematical prediction about how long a language will continue to be used by a people.

Inherent rights Rights of a people that emerged out of their culture. They are not dependent on the Crown bestowing them to First Nations or even approving them.

Instrumental language use The use of a language to obtain a functional goal, e.g., to get a job.

Integrative language use The use of a language for expressive or symbolic reasons.

Intergenerational trauma The process by which the effects of trauma are passed from one generation to the next.

Inuit One of three groups (along with First Nations and Métis) of constitutionally recognized Aboriginal peoples in Canada. The Inuit are descended from the Thule, people of the Far North who migrated about 1,000 years ago from Alaska into the Canadian Arctic.

Knowledge economy The new types of economic activities based on knowledge rather than on the manufacture of material goods.

Language shift The extent to which a group of people changes languages over time.

Language viability The prediction of whether or not a language will survive over the next generation.

Linear The belief that things happen in a 'straight line'.

Main Estimates The budget estimates submitted each year by all federal departments, which must include justifications for projected expenditures. The budgets are then reviewed and voted on in Parliament, at which point, upon passage, they make up the government's initial budget for the forthcoming year.

Manifest Destiny A nineteenth-century American political/ideological belief that the US was destined by God to extend to the Pacific coast and, in the view of some, to control all of North America or even a wider territory. This essentially religious belief was similarly held by early settlers in Canada, who believed it was their God-given right to control and rule over the northern half of North America and the Aboriginal peoples who happened to be here when they arrived.

Meech Lake Accord A 1987 agreement between Ottawa and the provinces—but without any First Nations input—to change the Constitution and, most significantly, recognize Quebec as a 'distinct society' within Canada. It had to be ratified within three years by all the provincial legislatures, but Manitoba and Newfoundland failed to do so. Elijah Harper, a Cree chief and Manitoba MLA, famously refused, on procedural grounds, to cast a vote on the ratification of the Accord, which led to its defeat.

Metaphysics The study of what you cannot empirically demonstrate.

Métis Originally, a distinct group of people of mixed European (French-Canadian and Scots) and Indian (chiefly Cree and Ojibwa) heritage who were born of relationships between Indian women and European fur traders and trappers and who subsequently developed a unique culture based around the Red River Settlement in Manitoba; sometimes, in earlier times, referred to as 'halfbreeds'. Today, the term is more broadly applied to other identifiable groups in Canada of mixed Indian–European heritage.

Mortality The incidence of death for a group of people, usually expressed as a rate per 1,000 people.

Mother tongue The language of an individual that was learned during infancy and is still spoken and understood.

Natural capital Attributes of the environment that will help to create economic benefit and lead to successful businesses.

Ontology Beliefs about how reality is constructed; a philosophy of reality.

Pass system An informally instituted system whereby First Nations people had to have a signed document from the local Indian agent saying they could leave the confines of the reserve, where they were going, and for how long.

Patriarchal Pertaining to patriarchy, a social system wherein descent is traced through the male lineage; also, a system of male dominance of the institutions of society.

Participatory action research A research methodology that involves the community in developing the questions to be asked, selecting the sample, asking the questions, and determining how the data will be analyzed. The results are then sent back to the community for commentary.

Patrilineal Tracing lineage through the male line.

Phenotypes Biological markers such as skin pigmentation, hair texture, stature, and eye colour that are distinguishable among people.

Political trust The responsibility that people with authority have when dealing with people without authority. The courts have ruled that this type of trust is not legally enforceable unless a law has been broken.

Population pyramid The age distribution of a people, as shown graphically with the youngest cohorts at the bottom of the pyramid and the oldest at the top.

Positivism The belief that reality is objective and can be measured.

Poverty A term used to identify a point where people do not have enough income to provide them with the necessities of life such as adequate housing, food, and health.

Prima facie In law, 'on the face of it' or 'at first look', so that if a first look reveals something problematical, then action can be taken.

Relative deprivation The process by which one compares his/her own situation with someone else's as a way of determining how poorly off the individual or group is. The assessment is based on the position of someone else.

Residential schools Schools funded by government and operated by church organizations that were generally built in the rural countryside and intended to assimilate First Nations children to the majority society. The students were removed from their families and communities and resided in these isolated schools for 10 months a year.

Resiliency The ability of an individual to deal with traumatic events and resist their negative impacts.

Restorative justice Justice that seeks to restore a relationship to a balance that may have existed before a harm was done by one party to the other party. Compensation is only secondary, but the harmed party wants the other to know that harm was caused and balance and equity need to be restored.

Royal Commission on Aboriginal Peoples A Royal Commission set up by the federal government to investigate the state of Aboriginal–government affairs. It started in 1991 and submitted its final five-volume report in 1996. Hundreds of studies were undertaken by researchers for the Commission.

Royal Proclamation of 1763 A pronouncement of the British Crown that if lands were to be taken from Aboriginal people, they had to give their approval. Land cessions had to be freely made by the First Nations and purchase of these lands could be done only by the Crown. Private parties or government representatives acting without explicit Crown approval could not alienate Indian lands. It is still considered a legal document.

Self-determination The right to participate in the democratic process and to influence one's future—political, cultural, and social.

Self-government Arrangements by which First Nations people govern their affairs and have full responsibility and control over decision-making.

Self-rated health A subjective measure of how an individual rates his/her health status.

Social capital The extent to which people are embedded within their family relationships, social networks, and communities, and therefore have a sense of belonging and civic identity and opportunities for economic betterment.

Soul wound A metaphor for historical trauma.

Terra nullius The concept that a geographical land area is not occupied by people.

Time lag The gap of time between something done (cause) and its consequent effect, as in the time between when a policy is implemented and when its effect(s) can be determined and measured. Generally, with changes in social policy, there is a considerable period of time between when the change is operative and when the effect(s) can be noticed.

Tipping point A hypothetical point in a group's life where the use of a language, for example, is not sufficient to maintain its existence.

Tort law Litigation law. A person says you have harmed him/her and wants compensation for that harm. You make your case, the defendant argues against your position, and in the end the judge or jury makes a decision.

Trauma The direct result of an extreme event that injures a person physically and/or emotionally so that the capacity to deal with reality is impaired.

Wardship The belief that First Nations people were to be under the control of the federal government because they were thought to be unable to manage their own affairs.

Well-being The level of the quality of life of an individual or group.

Wellness Measure of the extent to which an individual or community is free from illness.

White man's burden A central belief of colonialism and empire-building that 'white' Europeans, the colonizers, had the responsibility to 'civilize' Indigenous peoples, from Rudyard Kipling's poem, 'The White Man's Burden'.

Bibliography

Abele, F. 2004. *Urgent Need, Serious Opportunity: Towards a New Social Model for Canada's Aboriginal Peoples*. Ottawa: Canadian Policy Research Networks.

——— and M. Prince. 2006. 'All Four Pathways to Aboriginal Self-Government in Canada', *American Review of Canadian Studies* 36: 568–95.

Aboriginal Healing Foundation. 2006. *Final Report of the Aboriginal Healing Foundation*, vol. 3. Ottawa.

Adams, H. 1975. *Prison of Grass: Canada from the Native Point of View*. Toronto: New Press.

Ahenakew, E. 1929. 'Cree Trickster Tales', *Journal of American Folklore* 42: 309–53.

Aikenhead, G., and M. Ogawa. 2007. 'Indigenous Knowledge and Science Revisited', *Cultural Studies of Science and Education* 2: 539–620.

Albanese, P. 2009. *Children in Canada Today*, Toronto: Oxford University Press.

Alfred, Taiaiake. 2009. *Peace, Power, and Rightness: An Indigenous Manifesto*, 2nd edn. Toronto: Oxford University Press.

Ali, M., and K. Kilbride. 2004. *Forging New Ties: Improving Parenting and Family Support Services for New Canadians with Young Children*. Ottawa: Human Resources and Skill Development Canada.

Allec, R. 2005. *First Nations Health and Wellness in Manitoba: Overview of Gaps in Service and Issues Associated with Jurisdiction* At: www.manitobachiefs.ca.

Aman, C. 2009. 'Exploring the Influence of School and Community Relationships on the Performance of Aboriginal Students in British Columbia Public Schools', in J. White et al. eds, *Aboriginal Education: Current Crisis and Future Alternatives*. Toronto: Thompson Educational Publishing, 175–96.

Anderson, E. 2009. 'The Treaty Annuity as Livelihood Assistance and Relationship Renewal', in, J. White, E. Anderson, J.-P. Morin, and D. Beavon, eds, *Aboriginal Policy Research*, vol. 3. Toronto: Thompson Educational Publishing, 153–85.

Anderson, T., and D. Parker. 2006. 'The Wealth of Indian Nations: Economic Performance and Institutions on Reservations', in, T. Anderson, B. Benson, and T. Flanagan, eds, *Self-Determination*. Stanford, Calif.: Stanford University Press, 159–93.

Archibald, J.A. 2006. *Promising Healing Practices in Aboriginal Communities*. Ottawa: Aboriginal Healing Foundation.

Assembly of First Nations. 2000. *Royal Commission on Aboriginal Peoples at 10 Years*. Ottawa.

———, Joint Committee of Chiefs and Advisors. 2005. *Our Nations, Our Governments: Choosing Our Own Paths*. Report of the Joint Committee of Chiefs and Advisors on the Recognition and Implementation of First Nation Governments, Final Report. Ottawa.

Auditor General of Canada. 2006. *Status Report of the Auditor General of Canada to the House of Commons*, Chapter 5: 'Management of Programs for First Nations'. Ottawa.

———. 2009. *Status Report of the Auditor General of Canada to the House of Commons*, Chapter 4: 'Treaty Land Entitlement Obligations'. Ottawa.

Barman, J., Y. Hébert, and D. McCaskill, eds. 1986. *Indian Education in Canada*, 2 vols. Vancouver: University of British Columbia Press.

Barrena, A., et al. 2007. 'Does the Number of Speakers of a Language Determine Its Fate?', *International Journal of Sociology of Language* 186: 125–39.

Barsley, P. 1999. 'Native Women Pan Bill C-31', *Windspeaker* (June).

Bartlett, R. 1983. 'Survey of Canadian Law—Indian and Native Law', *Ottawa Law Review* 15: 431–500.

Baskey, J. 2002. *A Critical Analysis of Canada's Aboriginal Justice Strategy*. At: www.mediate.com.

Battiste, M. 2002. *Indigenous Knowledge and Pedagogy in First Nations Education*. Ottawa: Indian and Northern Affairs Canada.

——— and J. Henderson. 2000. *Protecting Indigenous Knowledge and Heritage*. Saskatoon: Purich.

Beaudry, D. 2000. 'I Am Canadian. I Am Anishinabek', *Anishinabek News* (Union of Ontario Indians–Anishinabek Nation) (July).

Beavon, D., and J. White. 2007. 'Aboriginal Well-being: Canada's Continuing Challenge', in J. White, D. Beavon, and N. Spence, eds, *Aboriginal Well-Being*. Toronto: Thompson Educational Publishing.

Belanger, A. 2003. *Report on the Demographic Situation in Canada, 2002*. Ottawa: Statistics Canada, Catalogue 91-209-XPE.

Belanger, Y. 2006. *Gambling with the Future: The Evolution of Aboriginal Gambling*. Saskatoon: Purich.

———, ed., 2008. *Aboriginal Self-Government in Canada: Current Issues and Trends*. Saskatoon: Purich.

——— and D. Newhouse. 2004. 'Emerging from the Shadows: The Pursuit of Aboriginal Self-Government to Promote Aboriginal Well-being', *Canadian Journal of Native Studies* 24: 129–222.

Bell, C. 1993 'Comment on Partners in Confederation, A Report on Self-Government by the Royal Commission on Aboriginal Peoples', *UBC Law Review* 27: 361–77.

Bianchi, E. 2001. 'First Nations Government Act: A New and Improved Assimilation Policy'. At: www.kairoscanada.org.

Biddle, N., J. Taylor, and M. Yap, 2008. Closing Which Gap? Demographic and Geographic Dilemmas for Indigenous Policy in Australia', paper presented at Aboriginal Population in Transitions—Demographic, Sociological and Epidemiological Dimensions conference, University of Alberta, Edmonton, 17–18 Oct.

Blackstock, C. 2007. 'Residential Schools: Did They Really Close or Just Morph into Child Welfare?', *Indigenous Law Journal* 6: 71–8.

———. 2009. 'The Occasional Evil of Angels: Learning from the Experiences of Aboriginal People and Social Workers', *First Peoples Child and Family Review* 4: 28–37.

Boermann, M. 2007. 'Language Attitudes among Minority Youth in Finland and Germany', *International Journal of Sociology of Language* 187/188: 129–60.

Borgoiakova, T., P. Gilmore, K. Lomawaima, and M. Romero. 2005. 'Indigenous Epistemologies and Education: Self-Determination, Anthropology, and Human Rights', *Anthropology and Education Quarterly* 36: 1–7.

Bougie, E., H. Tait, and E. Cloutier. 2010. *Aboriginal Language Indicators for Off-Reserve First Nations Children under the Age of Six in Canada*. Ottawa: Statistics Canada.

Boychuk, G. 2004. *The Canadian Social Model: The Logics of Policy Development*. Ottawa: Canadian Policy Research Networks.

Boyer, Y. 2001. 'First Nations, Metis and Inuit Health Care: The Crown's Fiduciary Obligation'. Saskatoon: National Aboriginal Health Organization.

Brady, H., and C. Kaplan 2009. 'Conceptualizing and Measuring Ethnic Identity', in R. Abdelal, Y. Herrera, A. Johnston, and R. McDermott, eds, *Measuring Identity*. New York: Cambridge University Press.

Brass, E. 1987. *I Walk in Two Worlds*. Calgary: Glenbow Museum.

Brownlie, R. 2005. 'First Nations Thinking in Canada', paper presented at University of Manitoba, May.

Bruhn, J. 2009. *In Search of Common Ground: Reconciling the IOG Governance Principles and First Nations Governance Traditions*. Ottawa: Institute on Governance Policy Brief No. 33.

Brunnen, B. 2003. *Achieving Potential: Towards Improved Labour Market Outcomes for Aboriginal People*. Calgary: Canada West Foundation.

Buckley, H. 1992. *From Wooden Ploughs to Welfare*. Montreal and Kingston: McGill-Queen's University Press.

Burnaby, B. 1999. 'Policy on Aboriginal Languages in Canada: Notes on Status Planning', in L. Valentine and R. Darnell, eds, *Theorizing the Americanist Tradition*. Toronto: University of Toronto Press, 299–314.

Burrows, J. 2002. *Recovering Canada: The Resurgence of Indigenous Law*. Toronto: University of Toronto Press.

———. 2006. *Indigenous Legal Traditions in Canada*. Ottawa: Law Commission of Canada.

Caduto, M., and J. Bruchac. 1989. *Keepers of the Earth: Native American Stories and Environmental Activities for Children*. Golden, Colo.: Fulcrum.

Cairns, A. 2000. *Citizens Plus: Aboriginal Peoples and the Canadian State*. Vancouver: University of British Columbia Press.

———. 2003. 'Coming to Terms with the

Past', in J. Torpey, ed., *Politics and the Past: On Repairing Historical Injustices*. Lanham, Md: Rowman & Littlefield, 63–90.

———. 2005. *First Nations and the Canadian State in Search of Co-existence*. Kingston, Ont.: Institute of Intergovernmental Relations, Queen's University.

Cajete, G. 1997. *Natural Laws of Interdependence*. Santa Fe, NM: Clear Light.

———. 2000. *Native Science: Natural Laws of Interdependence*. Santa Fe, NM: Clear Light.

———. 2004 'Philosophy of Native Science', in A. Waters, ed., *American Indian Thought*. Malden, Mass.: Blackwell, 49–57.

Canada. 1987. *Report to Parliament: Implementation of the 1985 Changes to the Indian Act*, Indian and Northern Affairs Canada. Ottawa: Queen's Printer.

———. 1995. *The Government of Canada's Approach to Implementation of the Inherent Right and the Negotiation of Aboriginal Self-Government*, Indian and Northern Affairs Canada. Ottawa: Queen's Printer.

———. 2005. *Towards a New Beginning: A Foundation Report for a Strategy to Revitalize First Nation, Inuit, and Métis Cultures*, Task Force on Aboriginal Languages and Cultures. Ottawa: Canadian Heritage, Aboriginal Affairs Branch.

———. 2005. *Projections of the Aboriginal Populations, Canada, Provinces and Territories*. Ottawa: Statistics Canada.

———. 2006. *Negotiation or Confrontation: It's Canada's Choice*. Final Report of the Standing Senate Committee on Aboriginal Peoples, Special Study on the Federal Specific Claims Process. Ottawa.

———. 2008. *Specific Claims: Justice at Last*. Ottawa: Indian and Northern Affairs Canada.

Canadian Bar Association. 2005. *The Logical Next Step: Reconciliation Payments for All Indian Residential School Survivors*. Toronto.

Canadian Institute for Health Information. 2009. *Mentally Healthy Communities: Aboriginal Perspectives*. Ottawa.

Canadian Population Health Institute. 2005. *Developing a Health Communities Index*. Ottawa: Canadian Institute for Health Information.

Cardinal, H. 1969. *The Unjust Society*. Edmonton: Hurtig.

Carter, S. 1990. *Lost Harvests: Prairie Indian Reserve Farmers and Government Policy*.

Montreal and Kingston: McGill-Queen's University Press.

———. 2004. 'Your Great Mother across the Salt Sea', *Manitoba History* 148 (Autumn): 137–64.

Castellano, M. 2006. *A Healing Journey: Reclaiming Wellness*. Ottawa: Aboriginal Healing Foundation.

———, L. Archibald, and M. DeGagne, eds. 2008. *From Truth to Reconciliation*. Ottawa: Aboriginal Healing Foundation.

Castro-Rea, J., and I. Jimenez. 2007. 'North American First Peoples: Self-Determination vs. Economic Development', in Y. Abu-Laban, R. Jhappan, and F. Rocher, eds, *Politics in North America: Redefining Continental Relations*. Peterborough, Ont.: Broadview Press.

Cech, M. 2010. >*Interventions with Children and Youth*. Toronto: Oxford University Press.

Chandler, M., and C. Lalonde. 2008. 'Cultural Continuity as a Moderator of Suicide Risk among Canada's First Nations', in L. Kirmayer and G. Valaskakis, eds, *Healing Traditions: The Mental Health of Canadian Aboriginal Peoples*. Vancouver: University of British Columbia Press.

Chansonneuve, D. 2007. *Addictive Behaviours among Aboriginal People in Canada*. Ottawa: Aboriginal Healing Foundation.

Chartrand, L., B. Feldhusen, and S. Han. 2008. 'Reconciliation and Transformation in Practice: Aboriginal Judicial Appointments to the Supreme Court', *Canadian Public Administration* 51: 143–53.

Clarke, J.N. 2008. *Health, Illness, and Medicine in Canada*, 5th edn. Toronto: Oxford University Press.

Clatworthy, S. 2001. *Re-assessing the Population Impacts of Bill C-31*. Winnipeg: Four Directions Project Consultants.

———. 2004. 'Registration and Membership: Implications for First Nations Communities', paper presented at Congress, Winnipeg, 4 June.

———. 2006. 'Indian Registration, Membership, and Population Change in First Nations Communities', in J. White, S. Wingert, D. Beavon, and P. Maxim, eds, *Aboriginal Policy Research: Moving Forward, Making a Difference*, vol. 3. Toronto: Thompson Educational Publishing, 99–120.

———. 2007. *Analysis of Select Population*

Impacts of the 1985 Amendments to the Indian Act (Bill C-31) and Select Hypothetical Amendments to the 1985 Act. Winnipeg: Four Directions Project Consultants.

———. 2009. 'Housing Needs in First Nations Communities', *Canadian Issues* (Winter): 19–24.

——— and M.J. Norris. 2007. 'Aboriginal Mobility and Migration: Trends, Recent Patterns, and Implications, 1971–2001', in J. White, S. Wingert, D. Beavon, and P. Maxim, eds, *Aboriginal Policy Research: Moving Forward, Making a Difference,* vol. III. Toronto: Thompson Educational Publishing, 123–54.

CNW Group. 2006. *First Nations Bank in Canada,* 18 Jan.

Coates, K., and W. Morrison. 2008. 'From Panacea to Reality', in Y. Belanger, ed., *Aboriginal Self-Government in Canada.* Saskatoon: Purich.

Cockerill, J., and R. Gibbins. 1997. 'Reluctant Citizens? First Nations in the Canadian Federal State', in J. Cockerill and R. Gibbins, eds, *First Nations in Canada: Perspectives on Opportunity, Empowerment and Self-Determination.* Toronto: McGraw-Hill Ryerson, 383–402.

Copway, G. 1850. *The Traditional History and Characteristic Sketches of the Ojibway Nation.* London: Gilpin.

Cornell, S. 1999. *Keys to Nation-Building in Indian Country.* Tucson: Udall Center for Studies in Public Policy, University of Arizona.

———, C. Curtis, and M. Jorgensen. 2003. *The Concepts of Governance and Its Implications for First Nations,* Report to the British Columbia Regional Vice-Chief, Assembly of First Nations, Native Nations Institute for Leadership, Management and Policy.

———, C. Goodswimmer, and M. Jorgensen. 2004. *In Pursuit of Capable Governance: A Report to the Lheidli T'enneh First Nation.* Phoenix: Native Nations Institute for Leadership, Management and Policy.

———, M. Jorgensen, and J. Kalt. 2002. *The First Nations Governance Act: Implications of Research Findings from the United States and Canada.* Phoenix: Udall Center for Studies in Public Policy and Native Nations Institute.

——— and J. Kalt. 2000. 'Where's the Glue? Institutional and Cultural Foundations of American Indian Economic Development',

Journal of Socio-Economics 29: 443–70.

Corrado, R., and I. Cohen. 2003. *Mental Health Profiles for a Sample of British Columbia's Aboriginal Survivors of the Canadian Residential School System.* Ottawa: Aboriginal Healing Foundation.

Crystal, D. 2000. *Language Death.* Cambridge: Cambridge University Press.

Daes, E.-I. 1995. *Protection of the Heritage of Indigenous People,* Final Report of the Special Rapporteur, 21 June, UN Doc. E/CN.4/Sub.2/1995/26.

Daniel, H. 1998. *Unity of Our Grandchildren.* Ottawa: Native Women's Association of Canada.

Danieli, Y. 1988. *Intergenerational Handbook of Multigenerational Legacies of Trauma.* New York: Plenum Press.

Deiter, C., and D. Rude. 2005. *Human Security and Aboriginal Women in Canada.* Ottawa: Status of Women.

Dempsey, J. 2005. 'Status Indian: Who Defines You?', in D. Champagne, K. Torjesen, and S. Steiner, eds, *Indigenous Peoples and the Modern State.* Walnut Creek, Calif.: AltaMira Press.

Denham, A. 2008. 'Rethinking Historical Trauma: Narratives of Resilience', *Trans Cultural Psychiatry* 45: 391–414.

deVries, M. 1995. *Culture, Community, and Catastrophe: Issues in Understanding Communities under Difficult Conditions.* Dordrecht, The Netherlands: Kluwer.

Dib, K., I. Donaldson, and B. Turcotte. 2008. 'Integration and Identity in Canada: The Importance of Multicultural Common Spaces', *Canadian Ethnic Studies* 40:161–88.

Dick, C. 2006. 'The Politics of Intragroup Differences: First Nations' Women and the Sawridge Dispute', *Canadian Journal of Political Science* 39: 92–116.

Dickason, O.P. 2002. *Canada's First Nations: A History of Founding Peoples,* 3rd edn. Toronto: Oxford University Press.

——— with D.T. McNab. 2009. *Canada's First Nations: A History of Founding Peoples,* 4th edn. Toronto: Oxford University Press.

——— with William Newbigging. 2010. *A Concise History of Canada's First Nations,* 2nd edn. Toronto: Oxford University Press.

Dion, J. 1979. *My Tribe the Crees.* Calgary: Glenbow Museum.

Dion, S., M. Kipling, and G. Kipling. 2003. *Aboriginal People, Resilience and the Residential School Legacy*. Ottawa: Aboriginal Healing Foundation.

Dodds, G. 2003. 'Political Apologies and Public Discourse in America: Conversation and Community', in J. Rodin and S. Steinberg, eds, *The Twenty-First Century*. Philadelphia: University of Pennsylvania Press, 135–60.

Doerr, A. 1997. 'Building New Orders of Government—The Future of Aboriginal Self-Government', *Canadian Public Administration* 40: 274–89.

Duran, B., E. Duran, and M. Yellow Horse Brave Heart. 1998. 'Native Americans and the Trauma of History', in R. Thornton, ed., *Studying Native America*. Madison: University of Wisconsin Press, 60–76.

Duran, E., and B. Duran. 1995. *Native American Post-Colonial Psychology*. New York: New York State University Press.

———, ———, M. Yellow Horse Brave Heart, and S. Yellow Horse-Davis. 1998. 'Healing the American Indian Soul Wound', in D. Yael, ed., *International Handbook of Multigenerational Legacies of Trauma*. Albany: State University of New York Press.

Dust, T. 1997. 'The Impact of Aboriginal Land Claims and Self-Government on Canadian Municipalities', *Canadian Public Administration* 40: 481–94.

Dyck, N. 1997. *Differing Visions: Administering Indian Residential Schooling in Prince Albert 1867–1995*. Halifax: Fernwood.

Einhorn, L. 2000. *The Native American Oral Tradition*. Westport, Conn.: Praeger.

Emberley, J. 2001. 'The Bourgeois Family, Aboriginal Women, and Colonial Governance in Canada: A Study in Feminist Historical and Cultural Materialism', *Signs* 27: 59–85.

Environics. 2010. *Survey of Urban Aboriginal People*. Toronto.

Episkenew, J.-A. 2009. *Taking Back Our Spirits*. Winnipeg: University of Manitoba Press.

Erasmus, G. 2002. 'The Healing Has Begun'. Ottawa: Aboriginal Healing Foundation presentation.

Ermine, W. 1995. 'Aboriginal Epistemology', in M. Battiste and J. Barman, eds, *First Nations Education in Canada: The Circle Unfolds*. Vancouver: University of British Columbia Press, 101–12.

Feit, H. 2004. 'Hunting and the Quest for Power: The James Bay Cree and

Whiteman Development', in Morrison and Wilson (2004: 101–28).

Fenelon, J., and T. Hall. 2008. 'Revitalization and Indigenous Resistance to Globalization and Neoliberalism', *American Behavioral Scientist* 51: 1867–1901.

Fiske, J., and E. George. 2006. 'Bill C-31: A Study of Cultural Trauma', in J. White, E. Anderson, W. Comet, and D. Beavon, eds, *Aboriginal Policy Research: Moving Forward, Making a Difference*. Toronto: Thompson Educational Publishing, 99–120.

Flanagan, T. 2000. *First Nations? Second Thoughts*. Montreal and Kingston: McGill-Queen's University Press.

———, C. Alcantara, and A. Le Dressay. 2010. *Beyond the Indian Act: Restoring Aboriginal Property Rights*. Montreal and Kingston: McGill-Queen's University Press.

Flannigan, R. 2004. 'The Boundaries of Fiduciary Accountability', *Canadian Bar Review* 83: 30–55.

Flisfeder, M. 2010 'A Bridge to Reconciliation: A Critique of the Indian Residential School Truth Commission', *International Indigenous Policy Journal* (online) (Spring).

Florida, R. 2002. *The Rise of the Creative Class*. New York: Basic Books.

Francis, D. 1992. *The Imaginary Indian*. Vancouver: Arsenal Pulp Press.

Frideres, J. 2008. 'A Critical Analysis of the Royal Commission on Aboriginal Peoples Self-Government Model', in Belanger (2008).

———. 2009. 'Social Distance and Ethnicity: Changes over Time', paper presented at University of Calgary, Calgary, Alberta.

——— and R. Gadacz. 2008. *Aboriginal Peoples in Canada*. Toronto: Prentice-Hall/Pearson.

Furniss, E. 2000. *Victims of Benevolence*. Vancouver: Arsenal Pulp Press.

Galley, V. 2009. 'An Aboriginal Languages Act: Reconsidering Equality on the 40th Anniversary of Canada's Official Languages Act', *Canadian Diversity* 7: 35–41.

Gibney, M., and E. Roxstrom. 2001. 'The Status of State Apologies', *Human Rights Quarterly* 23: 911–39.

Gionet, L. 2009. 'First Nations People: Selected Findings of the 2006 Census', *Canadian Social Trends* (June, special edn).

Goldman, G., and S. Delic. 2008. 'Ethnic Mobility—An Historical and

Contemporary Outcome for Aboriginal Peoples in Canada: Evidence Drawn from Past Trends and Current Census Data', paper presented at Aboriginal Population in Transitions—Demographic, Sociological and Epidemiological Dimensions conference, University of Alberta, Edmonton, 17–18 Oct.

Graham, J. 2007. *Rethinking Self-Government: Developing a More Balanced, Evolutionary Approach*. Ottawa: Institute on Governance.

Graham, K., and E. Peters. 2003. *Aboriginal Communities and Urban Sustainability*. Ottawa: Canadian Policy Research Networks.

Green, L. 1973. 'North America's Indians and the Trusteeship Concepts', *Anglo-American Law Review* 137: 140–56.

———. 1976. 'Trusteeship and Canada's Indians', *Dalhousie Law Journal* 104: 110–45.

Grenier, L. 2010. *Working with Indigenous Knowledge*. Ottawa: IDRC.

Grenoble, L. 2008. 'Endangered Languages', in L. Grenoble, ed., *One Thousand Languages: Living, Endangered and Lost*. Berkeley: University of California Press, 214–35.

Grimaldi, C. 2008. 'First Nations Claims to Self-Determination', *Journal of Undergraduate International Studies* 4: 16–25.

Grimes, B. 2000. *Ethnologue*. Dallas: Summer Institute of Linguistics.

Guimond, E. 2003. 'Fuzzy Definitions and Population Explosion: Changing Identities of Aboriginal Groups in Canada', in D. Newhouse and E. Peters, eds, *Not Strangers in These Parts*. Ottawa: Policy Research Initiative.

———, R. Robitaille, and S. Senecal. 2009. 'Aboriginal Populations in Canadian Cities: Why Are They Growing So Fast?', *Canadian Issues* (June): 11–18.

Hagege, C. 2000. *Halte a la mort des langues*. Paris: Odile Jacob.

Haig-Brown, C. 1988. *Resistance and Renewal: Surviving the Indian Residential School*. Vancouver: Tillacum Library.

Hall, T., and J. Fenelon. 2009. *Indigenous Peoples and Globalization: Resistance and Revitalization*. Boulder, Colo.: Paradigm.

Hanselmann, C. 2001. *Urban Aboriginal People in Western Canada*. Calgary: Canada West Foundation.

Harden, A., and H. Levalliant. 2008. *Boiling Point!* Ottawa: Polaris Institute.

Harris, C. 1987. *From the Beginning to 1800*. Toronto: University of Toronto Press.

Hatcher, A. 2009. 'Two-Eyed Seeing in the Classroom Environment', *Canadian Journal of Science, Mathematics and Technology Education* 9: 141–53.

Health Canada. 1999. *A Second Diagnostic on the Health of First Nations and Inuit People*. Ottawa: Health Canada.

———. 2006. *A Statistical Profile on the Health of First Nations in Canada: Self-Rated Health and Selected Conditions 2002–2005*. Ottawa. At: www.hc-sc.gc.ca.

———. 2008. *Determinants of Health, 1999–2003*. Ottawa: Health Canada.

———. 2009. *Self-Rated Health and Selected Conditions, 2002–2005*. Ottawa: Health Canada.

Helin, C. 2006. *Dances with Dependency*. Vancouver: Orca Spirit.

——— and D. Snow. 2010. 'Free to Learn: Giving Aboriginal Youth Control over Their Post-Secondary Education', *True North* (Mar.): 3–26.

Herman, J. 1992. *Trauma and Recovery*. New York: Basic Books.

Herman, M., Y. Vizina, C. Augustus, and J. Sawyer. 2008. *Learning Indigenous Science from Place*. Saskatoon: Faculty of Education, University of Saskatchewan.

Herring, R. 1997. 'The Creative Arts: An Avenue to Wellness among Native American Indians', *Journal of Humanistic Education and Development* 36: 105–13.

Hier, S., and B. Bolaria. 2006. *Identity and Belonging*. Toronto: Canadian Scholars' Press.

Hughes, P., and M. Mossman. 2005. *Criminal Justice in Canada*. Ottawa: Department of Justice.

Hull, J. 2001. *Aboriginal Single Mothers in Canada, 1996, A Statistical Profile*. Ottawa: Indian and Northern Affairs Canada.

Hunter, A. 2006. 'The Politics of Aboriginal Self-Government', in J. Grace and B. Sheldrick, eds, *Canadian Politics: Critical Reflections*. Toronto: Pearson Education Canada, 24–39.

Hurley, M. 2009. *Aboriginal Self-Government*. Ottawa: Library of Parliament.

———. 2009. *The Indian Act*. Ottawa: Library of Parliament.

——— and J. Wherrett. 1999. *Aboriginal Self-Government*. Ottawa: Library of

Parliament, Parliamentary Information and Research Service.

Indian and Northern Affairs Canada (INAC). 1995. *Bluberry River Indian Band v. Canada.* S.C.R. 344.

———. 2004. *Basic Departmental Data.* Ottawa: Queen's Printer.

———. 2010. *Discussion Paper: Changes to the Indian Act affecting Indian Registration and Band Membership.* At: www.ainc-inac.gc.ca/br/is/mci-eng.pdf.

———. n.d. Discussion paper on changes to the Indian Act. At: www.ainc.inac.gc.ca.

Ing, R. 2000. 'Dealing with Shame and Unresolved Trauma: Residential School and Its Impact on the 2nd and 3rd Generation Adults', Ph.D. dissertation, University of British Columbia.

Iribacher-Fox, S. 2010. *Finding Dahshaa.* Vancouver: University of British Columbia Press.

Jedwab, J. 2007. 'Lessons of Recognition: What, If Anything, Did Canadians Learn from Debates over the Charlottetown Accord', *Essays on the Charlottetown Accord and Its Aftermath.* Montreal: Association for Canadian Studies, 95–110.

Johnston, B. 1988. *Indian School Days.* Toronto: Key Porter.

Jones, P. 1861. *History of the Ojebway Indians: With Especial Reference to Their Conversion to Christianity.* London: A.W. Bennett.

Jorgenson, M., ed., 2007. *Rebuilding Native Nations: Strategies for Governance and Development.* Tucson: University of Arizona Press.

Jung, C. 2009. *The Moral Force of Indigenous Politics.* New York: Cambridge University Press.

———. 2009. 'Race, Class and Ethnicity in the History of Mexican Indigenous Politics', paper presented at the American Political Science Association meeting, Toronto, 5 Sept.

Kane, R., J. Kasteler, and R. Gray. 1976. *The Health Gap: Medical Services and the Poor.* New York: Springer.

Kaufman, Thomas, & Associates. 2002. *Review of Indian Residential Schools Dispute Resolution Projects.* Ottawa: Office of Indian Residential Schools Resolution.

Kennedy, R., S. Kasi, and V. Vaccdarino. 2001. 'Repeated Hospitalizations and Self-rated Health among the Elderly', *American Journal of Epidemiology* 153: 232–41.

King, T. 2003. *The Truth about Stories: A Native Narrative.* Toronto: House of Anansi.

Kinkade, M. 1991. 'The Decline of Native Languages in Canada', in R. Robins and E. Uhlenbeck, eds, *Endangered Languages.* Oxford: Berg.

Kirmayer, L., G. Brass, T. Holton, K. Paul, C. Simpson, and C. Tait. 2007. *Suicide among Aboriginal People in Canada.* Ottawa: Aboriginal Healing Foundation.

Krauss, M. 1992. 'The World's Languages in Crisis', *Language* 68: 4–10.

Kroskrity, P., and M. Field. 2009. *Native American Language Ideologies.* Tucson: University of Arizona Press.

Kymlicka, W. 2007. *Multicultural Odysseys: Navigating the New International Politics of Diversity.* Oxford: Oxford University Press.

Ladislaus, M., and J. Kincheloe, eds. 1999. *What Is Indigenous Knowledge? Voices from the Academy.* New York: Falmer Press.

Laidlaw, D., and M. Passelac-Ross. 2010. *Water Rights and Water Stewardship: What about Aboriginal Peoples?* Calgary: Canadian Institute of Resources Law.

Laitin, D. 1998. *Identity in Formation: The Russian-Speaking Populations in the Near Abroad.* Ithaca, NY: Cornell University Press.

Lalonde, C. 2005. 'Creating an Index of Healthy Aboriginal Communities', *Developing a Healthy Communities Index.* Ottawa: Canadian Population Health Initiative, 21–5.

Laplante, L., and S. Spears. 2008. 'Out of the Conflict Zone: The Case for Community Consent Process', *Yale Human Rights and Development Law Journal* 11: 71–114.

Lehmann, R. 2009. *Summary of the McIvor Decisions.* Ottawa: Ratcliff and Company, National Centre for First Nations Governance.

Lehner, E. 2007. 'Describing Students of the African Diaspora', *Cultural Studies of Science Education* 2: 123.

Leigh, D. 2009. 'Colonialism, Gender and the Family in North America: For a Gendered Analysis of Indigenous Struggles', *Studies in Ethnicity and Nationalism* 9: 70–88.

Lenihan, D., and J. Kaufman. 2001. *Leveraging Our Diversity: Canada as a Learning Society.* Ottawa: Centre for Collaborative Government.

Leslie, J. 2004. 'The Policy Agenda for

Native Peoples from World War II to the 1969 White Paper', in J. White, P. Maxim, and D. Beavon, eds, *Aboriginal Policy Research: Setting the Agenda for a Change*. Toronto: Thompson Educational Publishing, 16–23.

Levitte, Y. 2004. 'Bonding Social Capital in Entrepreneurial Developing Communities—Survival Networks or Barriers?', *Journal of the Community Development Society* 35: 44–64.

Little Bear, L. 2000. 'Jagged Worldviews Colliding', in M. Battiste, ed., *Reclaiming Indigenous Voices and Vision*. Vancouver: University of British Columbia Press.

Liodakis, N. 2009. 'The Social Class and Gender Differences within Aboriginal Groups in Canada: 1995–2000', *Canadian Diversity* (Winter): 93–8.

Llewellyn, J. 2002. 'Dealing with the Legacy of Native Residential School Abuse in Canada: Litigation, ADR, and Restorative Justice', *University of Toronto Law Journal* 52: 253–300.

——— and R. Howse. 1998. *Restorative Justice: A Conceptual Framework*. Ottawa: Law Commission of Canada.

Loh, S., and M.V. George. 2003. 'Estimating the Fertility Level of Registered Indians in Canada: A Challenging Endeavour', *Canadian Studies in Population</IT>* 32: 117–34.

Lomawaima, K.T. 2004. 'American Indian Education: By Indians vs. For Indians', in P. Deloria and N. Salisbury, eds, *A Companion to American Indian History*. Malden, Mass.: Blackwell, 422–40.

McCarty, T. 2005. 'Revitalising Indigenous Languages in Homogenising Times', *Comparative Education* 39: 147–62.

McHardy, M., and E. O'Sullivan. 2004. *First Nations Community Well-Being in Canada*. Ottawa: Indian and Northern Affairs Canada, Strategic Research and Analysis Directorate.

McKinley, E. 2007. 'Post Colonialism, Indigenous Students, and Science Education', in S. Abell and N. Lederman, eds, *Handbook of Research on Science Education*. Mahwah, NJ: Lawrence Erlbaum.

Macleod, L.H. 2008. *A Time for Apologies: The Legal and Ethical Implications of Apologies in Civil Cases*, Cornwall Public Inquiry, Research and Policy Paper. Toronto, 12 Apr.

McNeil, K. 2001. 'Fiduciary Obligations and Federal Responsibility for the Aboriginal Peoples', in K. McNeil, ed., *Emerging Justice: Essays on Indigenous Rights in Canada and Australia*. Saskatoon: University of Saskatchewan Native Law Centre.

———. 2004a. *The Inherent Right of Self-Government: Emerging Directions of Legal Research*. Chilliwack, BC: First Nations Governance Centre.

———. 2004b. *The Inherent Right of Self Government*. Toronto: Osgood Hall Law School.

———. 2006. 'What Is the Inherent Right of Self-Government?', presentation at the Governance Development Forum, Parksville, BC, 3 Oct.

Manitoba Metis Federation v. Attorney General of Canada and Attorney General of Manitoba. 2008. At: www.mmf.mb.ca.

Mann, M. 2009. 'Disproportionate and Unjustifiable: Teen First Nation Mothers and Unstated Paternity', *Canadian Issues* (Winter) 31–6.

Marger, M. 2006. *Race and Ethnic Relations*. Toronto: Thomson-Wadsworth.

Marti, F., et al. 2005. *Words and Worlds: World Languages Report*. Clevedon, UK: Multilingual Matters.

Martin, C., and E. Guimond. 2009. 'Measuring Changing Human Development in First Nations Populations: Preliminary Results of the 1981–2006 Registered Indian Human Development Index', *Canadian Diversity* 7: 53–62.

Martin, T., A. Curran, and J. Lapierre. 2006. 'Banking in Winnipeg's Aboriginal and Impoverished Neighbourhood', *Canadian Journal of Native Studies* 26: 331–59.

Mathews, G.H. 2005. 'Apologies Can Make All the Difference in Dispute Resolution', *Legal Intelligencer*, 1 June, A6.

Mendelson, M. 2006. *Aboriginal Peoples and Postsecondary Education in Canada*. Toronto: Caledon Institute of Social Policy.

Mihesuah, D. 2003. *Indigenous American Women: Decolonization, Empowerment, Activism*. Lincoln: University of Nebraska Press.

Miller, J.R. 1990. *Skyscrapers Hide the Heavens: A History of Indian–White Relations in Canada*. Toronto: University of Toronto Press.

———. 2009. 'Which "Native" History?

By Whom? For Whom?', *Canadian Issues* (June): 33–6.

Morellato, M. 2003. *The Existence of Aboriginal Governance Rights within the Canadian Legal System*. Ottawa: Blake, Cassels & Graydon.

Morgan, A., and C. Swann. 2000. 'Social Capital for Health'. At: www.pulicnet.co.uk.

Morita, L. 2007. 'Discussing Assimilation and Language Shift among the Chinese in Thailand', *International Journal of Sociology of Language* 186: 43–58.

Morrison, R.B., and C.R. Wilson, eds. 2004. *Native Peoples: The Canadian Experience*, 3rd edn. Toronto: Oxford University Press.

Morse, B. 2008. 'Regaining Recognition of the Inherent Right of Aboriginal Governance', in Y. Belanger, ed., *Aboriginal Self-Government in Canada: Current Issues and Trends*. Saskatoon: Purich, 39–68.

Mountain Horse, M. 1979. *My People the Bloods*. Calgary/Standoff, Alta: Glenbow Museum/ Blood Tribal Council.

Mueller, R. 2004. 'The Relative Earnings Position of Canadian Aboriginals in the 1990's', *Canadian Journal of Native Studies* 24: 37–64.

Nagel, J. 1996. *American Indian Ethnic Renewal: Red Power and the Resurgence of Identity and Culture*. New York: Oxford University Press.

Native Women's Association of Canada. 1986. *An Explanation of the 1985 Amendments to the Indian Act*. Ottawa.

———. 1986. *Guide to Bill C-31*. Ottawa. At: action.web.ca/home/narcc/attach/guide tobillC31-%20amendment%20to20%.

Nettle, D., and S. Romaine. 2000. *Vanishing Voices: The Extinction of the World's Languages*. Oxford: Oxford University Press.

Newhouse, D. 2004. 'Indigenous Knowledge in a Multicultural World', *Native Studies Review* 15: 139–54.

———. 2009. *The Duty to Consult: New Relationships with Aboriginal People*. Saskatoon: Purich.

Nisga'a Final Agreement. 2001. *The Nisga'a Final Agreement*. Ottawa: Library of Parliament (PRB 99–2E).

Nobles, M. 2008. *The Politics of Official Apologies*. New York: Cambridge University Press.

Norris, M.J. 1996. 'Contemporary Demography of Aboriginal Peoples in Canada', in D. Long and O.P. Dickason, eds, *Visions of the Heart: An Introduction to Canadian Aboriginal Issues*. Toronto: Harcourt Brace Canada.

———. 2003. 'The Diversity and State of Aboriginal Languages in Canada', in *Canadian and French Perspectives on Diversity*. Ottawa: Canadian Heritage, 38–55.

———. 2006. 'Aboriginal Languages in Canada: Trends and Perspectives on Maintenance and Revitalization', in J. White, S. Wingert, D. Beavon, and P. Maxim, eds, *Aboriginal Policy Research: Moving Forward, Making a Difference*, vol. 3. Toronto: Thompson Educational Publishing, 197–227.

———. 2007. 'Aboriginal Languages in Canada: Emerging Trends and Perspectives on Second Language Acquisition', *Canadian Social Trends* 83: 20–8.

———. 2008. 'Voices of Aboriginal Youth Today: Keeping Aboriginal Languages Alive for Future Generations', *Horizons* 10, 1: 60–8.

———. 2009. 'Linguistic Classifications of Aboriginal Languages in Canada: Implications for Assessing Language Diversity, Endangerment and Revitalization', *Canadian Diversity* 7: 21–33.

——— and L. Jantzen. 2005. 'From Generation to Generation: Survival and Maintenance of Aboriginal Languages within Families, Communities and Cities', in *From Generation to Generation: Survival and Maintenance of Aboriginal Languages within Families, Communities and Cities*. Ottawa: Indian and Northern Affairs Canada.

——— and M. Snider. 2008. 'Endangered Aboriginal Languages in Canada: Trends, Patterns and Prospects in Language Learning, Personal Correspondence', in T. de Graaf, N. Ostler, and R. Salverda, eds, *Endangered Languages and Language Learning*, Proceedings of the 12th Foundation for Endangered Languages Conference. Bath, UK/Leeuwarden, The Netherlands: Foundation for Endangered Languages/Fryske Akademy.

Oakerson, R. 1999. *Governing Local Public Economies: Creating the Civic Metropolis*. Oakland, Calif.: ICS Press.

O'Donnell, V., and H. Tait. 2004. 'Well-being of the On-Reserve Population', *Canadian Social Trends* (Spring).

O'Sullivan, E. 2006. *The Community Well-Being (CWB) Index*. Ottawa: Indian and Northern Affairs Canada, Strategic Research and Analysis Directorate.

Pacini-Ketchabaw, V., and A. Armstrong de Almeida. 2006. 'Language Discourses and Ideologies as the Heart of Early Childhood Education', *International Journal of Bilingual Education and Bilingualism* 9: 310–41.

Patterson, E. Palmer. 1972. *The Canadian Indian: A History since 1500*. Don Mills, Ont.: Collier-Macmillan Canada.

Pendakur, K., and R. Pendakur. 2008. *Aboriginal Income Disparity in Canada*, No. 08–15. Vancouver: Metropolis British Columbia.

Peroff, N.C., and D.R. Wildcat. 2002. 'Who Is an American Indian?', *Social Science Journal* 39: 349–61.

Peters, E. 2002. 'Our City Indians: Negotiating the Meaning of First Nations Urbanization in Canada, 1945–1975', *Journal of Historical Geography* 30: 75–92.

Piquemal, N. 2004. 'Relation Ethics in Cross-Cultural Teaching', *Canadian Journal of Educational Administration and Policy* 32: 41–59.

Pitawanakwat, B. 2009. 'Anishinaabemodaa Pane Oodenang—A Qualitative Study of Anishinaabe Languge Revitalization as Self-Determination in Manitoba and Ontario', Ph.D. dissertation, University of Victoria.

Pitty, R. 2001. 'Indigenous Peoples, Self-Determination and International Law', *International Journal of Human Rights* 5, 4: 44–71.

Portney, C. 2003. 'Intergenerational Transmission of Trauma: An Introduction for the Clinician', *Psychiatric Times* 20: 58–72.

Proulx, C. 2006. 'Aboriginal Identification in North American Cities', *Canadian Journal of Native Studies* 26: 405–38.

Quigley, J., S. Raphael, and E. Smolensky. 2001. *Homelessness in California*. Los Angeles: Public Policy Institute of California.

Rafoss, B. 2005. 'The Application of the Canadian Charter of Rights and Freedoms to First Nations' Jurisdiction: An Analysis of the Debate', MA thesis, University of Saskatchewan.

Rahman, T. 2001. 'Language-Learning and Power: A Theoretical Approach', *International Journal of the Sociology of Language* 152: 53–74.

Ram, B. 2004. 'New Estimates of Aboriginal Fertility, 1966–1971 to 1996–2001', *Canadian Studies in Population* 31: 179–96.

Ray, A.J. 1974. *Indians in the Fur Trade*. Toronto: University of Toronto Press.

Regular, W.K. 2009 *Neighbors and Networks*. Calgary: University of Calgary Press.

Reid, J. 2008. *Louis Riel and the Creation of Modern Canada*. Albuquerque: University of New Mexico Press.

Retzlaff, S. 2005. 'What's in a Name? The Politics of Labeling and Native Identity Constructions', *Canadian Journal of Native Studies* 25, 2: 609–26.

Reynolds, J. 2005. *A Breach of Duty*. Saskatoon: Purich.

Richards, J. 2008. *Closing the Aboriginal/Non-Aboriginal Education Gaps*. Vancouver: C.D. Howe Institute, No. 116.

———. 2009. *Dropouts: the Achilles' Heel of Canada's High School System*. Vancouver: C.D. Howe Institute.

———, J. Hove, and K. Afolabi. 2008. *Understanding the Aboriginal/Non-Aboriginal Gap in Student Performance*. Vancouver: C.D. Howe Institute.

Richmond, C. 2009. 'Explaining the Paradox of Health and Social Support among Aboriginal Canadians', *Canadian Issues* (Winter): 65–71.

Romaniuc, A. 2003. 'Aboriginal Population of Canada: Growth Dynamics under Conditions of Encounter of Civilizations', *Canadian Studies in Population* 30: 75–113.

———. 2008. 'Canada's Aboriginal Population: From Encounter of Civilizations to Revival and Growth', presentation at Demographic Change and Development Conference, Edmonton, Oct.

Romero, M. 2004. 'Language Shift and the Socialization of Pueblo Children', Ph.D. dissertation, University of California, Berkeley.

Ross, R. 1996. *Returning to the Teachings: Exploring Aboriginal Justice*. Toronto: Penguin.

———. 2008. 'Telling Truths and Seeking Reconciliation: Exploring the Challenges', in Castellano et al. (2008: 145–59).

Royal Commission on Aboriginal Peoples. 1996. *Report*, 5 vols. Ottawa: Minister of Supply and Services.

Russell, D. 2000. *A People's Dream: Aboriginal Self-Government in Canada*. Vancouver: University of British Columbia Press.

Rustand, J. 2010. *Is Inherent Aboriginal Self-Government Constitutional?* Toronto: Canadian Constitution Foundation.

Salee, D. 2006. 'Quality of Life of Aboriginal People in Canada', *Choice* #12, Institute for Research on Public Policy.

Samek, H. 1987. *The Blackfoot Confederacy 1880–1920*. Albuquerque: University of New Mexico Press.

Sawchuk, G., and P. Christie. 2004. *Aboriginal Entrepreneurs in Canada*. Ottawa: Industry Canada, Micro-Economic Policy Analysis.

Scholtz, C. 2009. 'The Influence of Judicial Uncertainty on Executive Support for Negotiation in Canadian Land Claims Policy', *Canadian Journal of Political Science* 42: 417–42.

Scott, C. 2004. 'Conflicting Discourses of Property, Governance and Development in the Indigenous North', in R. Blaser, *The Way of Development: Indigenous Peoples, Life Projects and Globalization*. International Development Research Centre. London: Zed Books, 299–312.

Scott, J. 2006. 'Doing Business with the Devil: Land, Sovereignty, and Corporate Partnerships in Membertou, Inc', in T. Anderson, B. Benson, and T. Flanagan, eds, *Self-Determination*. Stanford, Calif.: Stanford University Press, 242–72.

Segall, A., and J. Goldstein. 1989. 'Exploring the Correlates of Self-Provided Health Care Behaviour', *Social Science and Medicine* 29: 153–62.

Semali, L., and J. Kincheloe. 1999. 'What Is Indigenous Knowledge and Why Should We Study It?', in M. Ladislaus, ed., *What Is Indigenous Knowledge? Voices from the Academy*. London: Garland Science.

Siggner, A. 2003. 'Impact of "Ethnic Mobility" on Socio-economic Conditions of Aboriginal Peoples', *Canadian Studies in Population* 31: 137–58.

Skutnabb-Kangas, T. 2004. *Linguistic Genocide in Education, or Worldwide Diversity and Human Rights?* Mahwah, NJ: Lawrence Erlbaum.

Slattery, B. 1987. 'Understanding Aboriginal Rights', *Canadian Bar Review* 66: 697–739.

Slavik, H. 2001. 'Language Maintenance and Language Shift among Maltese Migrants in Ontario and British Columbia', *International Journal of the Sociology of Language* 152: 131–52.

Sluman, N., and J. Goodwill. 1982. *John Tootoosis*. Ottawa: Golden Dog Press.

Sochting, I. 2007. 'Traumatic Pasts in Canadian Aboriginal People: Further Support for a Complex Trauma Conceptualization?', *BC Medical Journal* 49: 320–6.

Statistics Canada. 2006. 'Aboriginal People as Victims and Offenders', *The Daily*, 6 June.

———. 2006. *Aboriginal Peoples in Canada in 2006, Inuit, Métis, and First Nations*. Ottawa: Statistics Canada. At: www12.statcan.ca/census-recensement/2006/as-sa/97-558/pdf/97-558-XIE2006001.pdf.

———. At: www.statcan.ca/English/concepts/definitions/aboriginal.htm#1.

Steinhauer, E. 2002. 'Thoughts on an Indigenous Research Methodology', *Canadian Journal of Native Education* 26: 69–82.

Stevens, G., and R. Schoen. 1988. 'Linguistic Intermarriage in the United States', *Journal of Marriage and the Family* 50: 267–79.

Stewart-Harawira, M. 2005. 'Cultural Studies, Indigenous Knowledge and Pedagogies of Hope', *Policy Futures in Education* 3: 153–63.

Stonechild, B., and B. Waiser. 1997. *Loyal Till Death: Indians and the Northwest Rebellion*. Toronto: Fifth House.

Stutnabb-Kangas, T. 2004. Interview in *Berria* newspaper, Basque Country, 10 Nov.

Sullivan, P. 2007. *Indigenous Governance: The Harvard Project, Australia Aboriginal Organizations and Cultural Subsidarity*, Working Paper 4. Alice Springs, Australia: Desert Knowledge CRC.

Sunseri, L. 2010. *Being Again of One Mind*. Vancouver: University of British Columbia Press.

Suzack, C., S. Huhndorf, J. Perreault, and J. Barman. 2010. *Indigenous Women and Feminism*. Vancouver: University of British Columbia Press.

Switzer, M. 2000. 'Language Key Part of First Nations "Voice"', *First Nations Messenger* (Feb.). Ottawa: Assembly of First Nations.

Tavuchis, N. 1991. *Mea Culpa: A Sociology of Apology and Reconciliation*. Stanford, Calif.: Stanford University Press.

Taylor, J.L. 1983. *Canadian Indian Policy during the Interwar Years, 1918–1939*. Ottawa: Queen's Printer.

Taylor, J., and M. Bell, eds. 2004. *Population Mobility and Indigenous People in Australasia and North America*. London: Routledge.

Tennant, P. 1991. *Aboriginal Peoples and Politics*. Vancouver: University of British Columbia Press.

Thompson, J. 2001. 'Historical Injustice and Reparation: Justifying Claims of Descendants', *Ethnics* 112 (Oct.): 114–35.

Tiedemann, M. 2009. *Bill C-8: Family Homes on Reserves and Matrimonial Interests or Rights Act*. Ottawa: Library of Parliament, Parliamentary Information and Research Service.

Timpson, A. 2009. *First Nations, First Thoughts*. Vancouver: University of British Columbia Press.

Tofoya, T. 1995. 'Finding Harmony: Balancing Traditional Values with Western Science in Therapy', *Canadian Journal of Native Education* 21: 7–27.

Travato, F. 2008. 'Death and the Family: A Half Century of Mortality Change (1950–2000) in the Registered Indian Population of Canada as Reflected by Period Life Tables', paper presented at Aboriginal Population in Transitions—Demographic, Sociological and Epidemiological Dimensions conference, University of Alberta, Edmonton, 17–18 Oct.

Turcotte, M. 2006. 'Passing on the Ancestral Language', *Canadian Social Trends* 80: 20–6.

Ubelaker, D. 1988. 'North American Indian Population Size AD 1500–1985', *American Journal of Physical Anthropology* 77: 289–94.

United Nations. 2007. *United Nations Declaration on the Rights of Indigenous Peoples*. At: www.un.org/esa/socdev/unpfii/en/drip.html.

Van Ijzendoorn, M., M. Bakermans-Kranenburg, and A. Sagi-Schwartz. 2003. 'Are Children of Holocaust Survivors Less Well Adapted? A Meta Analytic Investigation of Secondary Traumatization', *Journal of Traumatic Stress* 16: 459–69.

Verma, R. 2008. 'Population Projections for the Aboriginal Population in Canada: A Review of Past, Present and Future Prospects, 1991–2017', paper presented at Aboriginal Population in Transitions—Demographic, Sociological and Epidemiological Dimensions conference, University of Alberta, Edmonton, 17–18 Oct.

——— and R. Gauvin. 2004. 'Abridged Life Tables for Registered Indians in Canada, 1976–1980 to 1996–2000', *Canadian Studies in Population* 32: 197–235.

Voyageur, C. 2007. *Firekeepers of the 21st Century: First Nations Women Chiefs</IT>*. Montreal and Kingston: McGill-Queen's University Press.

Waldram, J., D. Herring, and T. Young. 2006. *Aboriginal Health in Canada: Historical, Cultural and Epidemiological Perspectives*, 2nd edn. Toronto: University of Toronto Press.

Wallerstein, I. 1979. *The Capitalist World-Economy*. Cambridge: Cambridge University Press.

Warry, W. 2007. *Ending Denial: Understanding Aboriginal Issues*. Peterborough, Ont.: Broadview Press.

Waters, A., ed. 2004. *American Indian Thought*. Malden, Mass.: Blackwell.

Wesley-Esquimaux, C., and M. Smolewski. 2004. *Historic Trauma and Aboriginal Healing*. Ottawa: Aboriginal Healing Foundation.

West, J. 2003. 'Aboriginal Women at the Crossroads'. At: www.firstnationsdrum.com.

Wherrett, J. 1999. *Aboriginal Self-Government*. Ottawa: Library of Parliament, Parliamentary Information and Research Service.

White, J., and P. Maxim. 2007. *Community Well-Being: A Comparable Communities Analysis*. Ottawa: Indian and Northern Affairs Canada, Strategic Research and Analysis Directorate.

Wilkes, R. 2006. 'The Protest Actions of Indigenous Peoples', *American Behavioral Scientist* 50: 510–25.

Willis, D., A. Dobrfec, and D. Bigfoot Sipes. 1992. 'Treating American Indian Victims of Abuse and Neglect', in L. Varfgas and J. Koss-Chioino, eds, *Working with Culture*. San Francisco: Jossey-Bass.

Wilson, S. 2001. 'What Is an Indigenous Research Methodology?', *Canadian Journal of Native Education* 25: 175–9.

———. 2003. 'Progressing toward an Indigenous Research Paradigm in Canada and Australia', *Canadian Journal of Native Education* 27: 161–77.

———. 2008. *Research Is Ceremony: Indigenous Research Methods.* Halifax: Fernwood.

Wolfe, D., P. Jaffe, J. Jette, and E. Samantha. 2002. *Child Abuse in Community Institutions and Organizations: Improving Public and Professional Understanding.* Ottawa: Law Commission of Canada.

Wright, R. 2004. *A Short History of Progress.* Toronto: House of Anansi.

Wurm, S. 2001. *Atlas of the World's Languages in Danger of Disappearing.* Paris and Canberra, Australia: UNESCO and Pacific Linguistics.

Yael, D., ed. 1998. *International Handbook of Multigenerational Legacies of Trauma.* New York: Plenum Press.

Ybanez, V. 2008. 'Domestic Violence: An Introduction to the Social and Legal Issues for Native Women', in S. Deer, ed., *Sharing Our Stories of Survival.* Lanham, Md: Rowman & Littlefield, 245–67.

Yellow Horse Brave Heart, M. 2003. 'The Historical Trauma Response among Natives and Its Relationship to Substance Abuse: A Lakota Illustration', *Journal of Psychoactive Drugs* 35: 7–13.

——— and L. DeBruyn, 1998. 'The American Indian Holocaust: Healing Historical Unresolved Grief', *American Indian and Alaska Native Mental Health Research: The Journal of the National Center* (Denver) 8: 60–82.

Younging, G., J. Dewar, and M. DeGagne. 2009. *Response, Responsibility, and Renewal: Canada's Truth and Reconciliation Journey.* Ottawa: Aboriginal Healing Foundation.

Zietsma, D. 2010. *Aboriginal People Living Off-Reserve and the Labour Market: Estimates from the Labour Force Survey, 2008–2009.* Ottawa: Statistics Canada, Labour Statistics Division.

Index ....

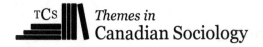

This series of concise texts, the work of Canadian scholars, reflects recent research and trends in sociology. Lorne Tepperman and the late James Curtis were founding editors of the series, which is now edited by Tepperman and Susan A. McDaniel.

Children in Canada Today

PATRIZIA ALBANESE

This engaging text explores the process through which children become members of our society—how, where, when, and with whom children grow up to be socially 'functioning' adults. The roles played by various 'agents of socialization' and the places and situations in which socialization takes place are also discussed. Ideal for sociology courses dealing with children, family, socialization, the life cycle, social policy, and social problems, *Children in Canada Today* provides an accessible, insightful look at childhood in this country.

CONTENTS: 1. Histories of Childhood. 2. Social Theories of Childhood. 3. Doing Research on and with Children. 4. Parent(s) and Child(ren)—Socialization in the Home. 5. Schooling and Peer Groups. 6. Children, the Mass Media, and Consumerism. 7. Early Childhood Education and Care in Canada. 8. Immigrant, Refugee, and Aboriginal Children in Canada. 9. Child Poverty in Canada. 10. Divorce, Custody, and Child Support in Canada. 11. Child Abuse and Child Protection in Canada. 12. The Disappearance of Childhood? Glossary.

Paper, 2009, 248 pp., ISBN 9780195428896

Deconstructing Men and Masculinities

MICHAEL ATKINSON

This comprehensive introduction to masculine identity politics in Canada offers a range of viewpoints, narratives, and evidence about the contested nature of masculinity. Drawing primarily on author Michael Atkinson's ethnographic research of Canadian men over the past decade, the text explores the idea of masculinity in crisis and the attempt by many men to move beyond this perceived crossroads. Atkinson reviews the historical links between masculinity and social power, the cultural associations between masculinity and violence, the role of masculinity in sports cultures, the problems of masculinity for young men, the mass mediation of masculinity and misandry, and the rise of alternative and 'feminine' masculinities. Never before have men's social roles, statuses, and identities been so open to cultural critique and redefinition; *Deconstructing Men and Masculinities* provides an engaging sociological narrative to guide readers through this ground-breaking area of study.

CONTENTS: Introduction: Masculinity in Crisis? 1. Men, Power, and Pastiche Hegemony. 2. Violence, Residue, and Pastiche Hegemony. 3. The Lost (and Found) Boys. 4. Male Femininities, Metrosexualities, and Liquid Ubersexualities. 5. Sporting Masculinities. 6. Mass-Mediating Risk Masculinities. 7: The Unbearable Whiteness of Being. Epilogue.

Paper, 2011, 248 pp., ISBN 9780195430769

This series of concise texts, the work of Canadian scholars, reflects recent research and trends in sociology. Lorne Tepperman and the late James Curtis were founding editors of the series, which is now edited by Tepperman and Susan A. McDaniel.

Choices and Constraints in Family Life, Second Edition

MAUREEN BAKER

Designed specifically for sociology of the family courses, this text examines the choices and constraints placed on individuals, relationships, and marriages in light of both family circumstances and societal expectations. Using an interdisciplinary approach that draws on the latest research in sociology, psychology, anthropology, and social history, the author explores emerging patterns in family life, including rising rates of cohabitation among both heterosexual and same-sex couples; trends in birth rates; and higher rates of separation, re-partnering, and stepfamilies. With the most up-to-date statistical data, new information on aging and on women in the workforce, and extensive coverage of historical and theoretical perspectives, this new edition is a concise yet comprehensive examination of family life in Western society.

CONTENTS: 1. Conceptualizing Families. 2. Forming Relationships. 3. Cohabitation and Marriage. 4. Child-bearing, Child-rearing, and Childhood. 5. Household Work and Money. 6. Separation, Divorce, and Re-partnering. 7. Midlife, Aging, and Retirement. 8. Constraints on Personal Choices. Glossary.

Paper, 2010, 264 pp., ISBN 9780195431599

Understanding Health, Health Care, and Health Policy in Canada: Sociological Perspectives

NEENA L. CHAPPELL • MARGARET J. PENNING

This brief introduction to the sociology of health and health care emphasizes health (promotion, maintenance, and prevention) as well as illness (treatment, cure, and care), offering a broad and balanced treatment of the sociological debates within the field. The first half of the text introduces three important themes in the study of the sociology of health: (1) the importance of approaching health issues from a lifespan perspective; (2) the need to attend to both the public and the private, the micro and the macro, and the individual and the structural; and (3) issues of inequality as they intersect with health, health care, and health policy. The second half of the text focuses on self care, formal care, and informal care, along with Canada's health care policy. Discussion on topical issues such as obesity, smoking, homelessness, AIDS, stress, and mental illness is incorporated throughout the book.

CONTENTS: 1. Health and Health Care: Sociological History and Perspectives. 2. Health and Illness. 3. Self- and Informal Care. 4. Formal Care. 5. Health-Care Policy. 6. Conclusions: The Sociology of Health and Health Care in the Future. Glossary.

Paper, 2009, 296 pp., ISBN 9780195424768

TCs ▙ *Themes in*
      Canadian Sociology

This series of concise texts, the work of Canadian scholars, reflects recent research and trends in sociology. Lorne Tepperman and the late James Curtis were founding editors of the series, which is now edited by Tepperman and Susan A. McDaniel.

The Schooled Society: An Introduction to the Sociology of Education, Second Edition

SCOTT DAVIES • NEIL GUPPY

The Schooled Society examines how education has come to occupy a central place in society and how its function and form continue to evolve. Structured around the three core roles of modern schooling—selection, social organization, and socialization—the text integrates classical and contemporary theoretical approaches to discuss schooling within a sociological framework. This new edition has been revised and updated to include the latest data, research, and statistics, and includes new and expanded coverage on critical pedagogy, contemporary theory, lifelong learning/early learning, technology in the classroom, curriculum changes and policy controversies, legitimacy and integrity in Canadian universities, and teacher education and preparation. A completely revised and expanded chapter on inequality (Chapter 6) exposes students to this important topic in the sociology of education.

CONTENTS: I. Introduction. 1. Thinking Sociologically about the Schooled Society. 2. Classical Sociological Approaches to Education. 3. Contemporary Sociological Approaches to Schooling. II. Selection: Inequality and Opportunity. 4. Education Revolutionized: The Growth of Modern Schooling. 5. The Structural Transformation of Schooling: Accommodation, Competition and Stratification. 6. Unequal Student Attainments: Class, Gender, and Race. III. Social Organization and Legitimation. 7. The Changing Organization of Schooling. 8. Curriculum: The Content of Schooling. 9. The Sociology of Teaching. IV. Socialization. 10. Socialization: The Changing Influence of Schools on Students. 11. The Limits of School Socialization: Competing Influences on Students. V. Conclusion. 12. Future Directions for Canadian Education. Glossary.

Paper, 2010, 344 pp., ISBN 9780195431742

First Nations in the Twenty-First Century

JAMES S. FRIDERES

Focussing exclusively on First Nations peoples, this innovative new text addresses crucial issues such as the legacy of residential schools; intergenerational trauma; Aboriginal languages and culture; health and well-being on reserves; self-government and federal responsibility; the political economy of First Nations; and the federal Indian Affairs bureaucracy. Through an in-depth treatment of historical and contemporary topics, including recent court decisions and government legislations, students will learn about the experiences of First Nations peoples and their complex, evolving relationship with the rest of Canada.

CONTENTS: 1. Knowing Your History. 2. Who Are You? 3. Indigenous Ways of Knowing. 4. Aboriginal Residential Schools: Compensation, Apologies, and Truth and Reconciliation. 5. Intergenerational Trauma. 6. 'Hear' Today, Gone Tomorrow: Aboriginal Languages. 7. Well-Being and Health. 8. The Duty of Government and Fiduciary Responsibility. 9. Self-Government, Aboriginal Rights, and the Inherent Right of First Nations Peoples. 10. The Political Economy of First Nations. 11. The Bureaucracy: Indian and Northern Affairs Canada. 12. Surviving in the Contemporary World: The Future of First Nations Peoples in Canada. Conclusion. Glossary.

Paper, 2011, 272 pp., ISBN 9780195441437

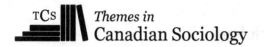

This series of concise texts, the work of Canadian scholars, reflects recent research and trends in sociology. Lorne Tepperman and the late James Curtis were founding editors of the series, which is now edited by Tepperman and Susan A. McDaniel.

Mediated Society: A Critical Sociology of Media

JOHN D. JACKSON • GREG M. NIELSEN • YON HSU

Taking a sociological approach to the study of mass media, *Mediated Society* explores how the media affects individuals and society. Within this unique framework, the authors analyze media and mass communication as a social rather than as a technological construct while addressing issues such as democracy, citizenship, class, gender, and cultural diversity. Drawing attention to the way in which media frames everyday experiences and events, the text examines media and communication in urban, national, and global settings, as well as the power and structure of dominant mass media. With a wide range of Canadian and international examples, along with two real-life case studies and a wealth of pedagogical features throughout, this innovative, engaging text encourages students to consider how social identities, norms, and values are mediated by various forms of mass communication.

CONTENTS. I. Sociology, Media, and Citizenship. 1. Sources for a Critical Sociology of Mediated Society. 2. The Public Sphere. 3. Citizenship and Audiences. 4. Consumption and Advertising. 5. New Media, New World? II. Media Events and the Sociological Imagination. 6. Global Media Events. 7. National Media Events. 8. Urban Media Events: Toronto and Montreal Case Studies. III. Social Problems through Journalism and Media. 9. Reporting on Social Problems. 10. Journalism and Seriocomedy: Framing Poverty in Montreal Media. 11. Framing Immigration as a Social Problem in *The New York Times*. Glossary.

Paper, 2011, 296 pp., ISBN 9780195431407

Violence Against Women in Canada: Research and Policy Perspectives

HOLLY JOHNSON • MYRNA DAWSON

Examining a wide range of theoretical perspectives, empirical research, and policy responses, *Violence Against Women in Canada* emphasizes connections among different forms of violence—connections that have too often been ignored or downplayed. Taking a gendered sociological approach, the text reveals how violence against women stems from unequal access to power and resources. While gender is the central focus, the authors also show how intersections of race, ethnicity, class, and sexuality serve to deepen inequalities for particular groups. Comprehensive and concise, this text explores the evolution of methods to measure violence, the impact of these methods on the social framing of violence issues, the impact on victims, and current policy responses and their effectiveness.

CONTENTS: 1. Introduction. 2. Theoretical Debates. 3. Methods of Measuring Violence Against Women. 4. Intimate Partner Violence. 5. Sexual Assault. 6. Femicide. 7. Policy Outcomes and Impacts. Glossary.

Paper, 2011, 240 pp., ISBN 9780195429817

This series of concise texts, the work of Canadian scholars, reflects recent research and trends in sociology. Lorne Tepperman and the late James Curtis were founding editors of the series, which is now edited by Tepperman and Susan A. McDaniel.

Crime in Canadian Context: Debates and Controversies, Second Edition

WILLIAM O'GRADY

This concise, accessible introduction to criminology explores how crime is defined, measured, and controlled within a Canadian context. In-depth and well-balanced, the text covers the fundamentals of the discipline before exploring non-sociological explanations of crime, criminological theory, social inequality and crime, organizational crime, and intersections between the law and the criminal justice system. Drawing on the latest Canadian statistics and research, the text examines a range of contemporary topics from hate crime to homeless youth in an engaging and succinct style. Thoroughly updated with expanded discussions on policy, youth justice, and criminal law, along with boxed coverage of global and media issues, this second edition is essential reading for students studying criminology in Canada.

CONTENTS: 1. Crime, Fear, and Risk. 2. Measuring Crime. 3. Non-Sociological Explanations of Crime. 4. Classical Sociological Explanations of Crime. 5. Recent Sociological Approaches to Crime. 6. Crime and Social Exclusion. 7. Crime in the Context of Organizations and Institutions. 8. Responding to Crime. 9. Summary and Conclusions.

Paper, 2011, 296 pp., ISBN 9780195433784

Law and Society Redefined

GEORGE PAVLICH

Written by one of Canada's most prominent socio-legal scholars, *Law and Society Redefined* is a comprehensive introduction to law and society. Drawing on the foundational contributions of such prominent social theorists as Émile Durkheim, Max Weber, and Michel Foucault, author George Pavlich uses social theory to explore the relationship between law and society. With extensive coverage of many of the most important topics in socio-legal studies, including morality, race, gender, and violence, the text questions the traditional definition of the 'sociology of law' to determine how the field has developed, while also examining the ideas and critiques that might redefine it in the future.

CONTENTS: Introduction. I. Law *Sui Generis*. 1. Classical Natural Law. 2. Natural Law Theory: Morality and Law. 3. Positing Law. 4. Realizing Sociological Jurisprudence. II. Society *Sui Generis*. 5. Durkheim Socializes the Law. 6. Law, Ideology, and Revolutionary Social Change. 7. Max Weber, Modern Disenchantment, and the Rationalization of Law. 8. Critical Confrontations: Law, Race, Gender, and Class. III. Promising Justice: The *Becoming* of Law and Society. 9. Michel Foucault: The Power of Law and Society. 10. Contested Sovereignties, Violence, and Law. 11. Just Events: Law and Society. Conclusion: After Law and Society?

Paper, 2011, 248 pp., ISBN 9780195429800

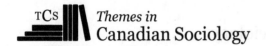

TCs Themes in Canadian Sociology

This series of concise texts, the work of Canadian scholars, reflects recent research and trends in sociology. Lorne Tepperman and the late James Curtis were founding editors of the series, which is now edited by Tepperman and Susan A. McDaniel.

'Race' and Ethnicity in Canada: A Critical Introduction, Second Edition

VIC SATZEWICH • NIKOLAOS LIODAKIS

'Race' and Ethnicity in Canada: A Critical Introduction provides students with a comprehensive look at the major approaches and explanations to the key concepts in this field of study. Through their exploration of the central issues that affect Canadians today—immigration, multiculturalism, assimilation, racism, and Aboriginal and non-Aboriginal relations—the authors argue that race is not a biologically real category, but rather, a socially constructed label used to describe and explain certain kinds of human difference. The text questions whether there are patterns of race and ethnic relations that are truly unique to Canada and puts Canada into a wider global context. Fully updated and revised, 'Race' and Ethnicity in Canada, second edition, includes new discussions of the economy, education, and policing and their impact on race and ethnic relations, as well as new coverage of French–English relations, racism, globalization, and ethnic and religious fundamentalism.

CONTENTS: 1. Theories of Ethnicity and 'Race'. 2. The Dynamics of Nation-Building: French/English Relations, Aboriginal/Non-Aboriginal Relations, and Immigration in Historical Perspective. 3. Immigration and the Canadian Mosaic. 4. Understanding Social Inequality: The Intersections of Ethnicity, Gender, and Class. 5. Identity and Multiculturalism. 6. Racism. 7. Aboriginal and Non-Aboriginal Relations. 8. Transnationals or Diasporas? Ethnicity and Identity in a Globalized Context.

Paper, 2010, 344 pp., ISBN 9780195432299

Gender Relations in Canada: Intersectionality and Beyond

JANET SILTANEN • ANDREA DOUCET

Today it is widely recognized that the experience of inequality depends on the intersections of gender, race, and class in each individual life. This text traces the way the implications of gender play out for women and men throughout the life course, from the formation of gender identity in childhood through the identity struggles of adolescence to adulthood, where gender continues to play a major role in the structure of work and family life alike. At the same time the authors underline the importance of moving beyond intersectionality as a framework for research in this area.

CONTENTS: 1. Sociology and the Analysis of Gender Relations. 2. The Multiple Genders of Childhood. 3. Gender Intensification: Adolescence and the Transition to Adulthood. 4. Diverse Paths: Gender, Work, and Family. 5. Making Change: Gender, Careers, and Citizenship (by Mary Ellen Donnan). 6. Analyzing the Complexity of Gender: Intersectionality and Beyond. Glossary.

Paper, 2008, 204 pp., ISBN 9780195423204

About Oxford University Press Canada

The Canadian branch of Oxford University Press was established in 1904. It was the first overseas branch to be set up after an office was established in New York in 1896. Although the branch did not open until 1904, the first book published for the Canadian market actually appeared eight years earlier—a hymnal for the Presbyterian Church of Canada.

Before the twentieth century, the main suppliers of books to the trade in Canada were the Copp Clark Company, the W.J. Gage Company, and the Methodist Bookroom (in 1919 renamed The Ryerson Press after its founder, Egerton Ryerson). These three firms acted as 'jobbers' for other lines that were later to be represented either directly by branches of their parent houses or by exclusive Canadian agents. Prior to 1904, Oxford books had been sold in Canada by S.G. Wilkinson, who, based in London, England, travelled across Canada as far west as Winnipeg. Wilkinson did a large trade with S.B. (Sam) Gundy, the wholesale and trade manager of the Methodist Book-room. When Oxford University Press opened

OUP Canada's first home, at 25 Richmond Street West in Toronto.

its own branch in Canada, Gundy, already familiar with Oxford books, was invited to become its first manager. The premises were at 25 Richmond Street West and, lacking an elevator of any kind, were hardly ideal for a publishing house.

An etching of Amen House on University Avenue, created by Stanley Turner.

The original reception area and library at 70 Wynford Drive. The library was later removed to make room for offices.

In 1929, the branch moved to Amen House, located at 480 University Avenue, and in 1936, after Gundy's death, the branch became closely allied with Clarke, Irwin and Company under W.C. Clarke. This association continued until 1949 when Clarke, Irwin moved to a separate location on St Clair Avenue West. In 1963, the Press moved to a new building at 70 Wynford Drive in Don Mills, which served it well for the next 46 years. By 2009, however, the branch had outgrown the 70 Wynford site. An extensive search process culminated in the move that November to a split-site configuration. The offices relocated to new premises at the Shops at Don Mills, an innovative retail/office/residential development, while the warehouse moved to a site in Brampton that not only offered more affordable rent and carrying charges but also provided a modern high-bay space much closer to major customers and Pearson International Airport.

Today OUP Canada is a major publisher of higher education, school, and English-as-a-second-language textbooks, as well as a significant trade and reference publisher. The Higher Education Division publishes both introductory and upper-level texts in such disciplines as sociology, anthropology, social work, English literature and composition, geography, history, political science, religious studies, and engineering. The division publishes more than 60 new Canadian texts and 150 student and instructor supplements each year, and derives about 60 per cent of its total sales from books and other learning materials written, edited, and published in Canada.

Some of the many books recently published by Oxford University Press Canada.